PARANORM 2.0

THE NEW REALITY

JAMES T ABBOTT

Copyright © 2023; James T Abbott.

Paperback ISBN: 978-1-80443-058-3
Ebook ISBN: 978-1-80443-059-0

All rights reserved, including the right to reproduce this book, or portions thereof in any form. No part of this text may be reproduced, transmitted, downloaded, decompiled, reverse engineered, or stored, in any form or introduced into any information storage and retrieval system, in any form or by any means, whether electronic or mechanical without the express written permission of the author.

Attributions

Horned-God-Symbol by Otourly Wikimedia Commons; CC BY-SA 3.0, https://commons.wikimedia.org/w/index.php?curid=4082544

Ankh by Alexi Helligar – Wikimedia Commons; CC BY-SA 3.0, https://commons.wikimedia.org/w/index.php?curid=29094008

Yin-Yang symbol by Alexandramander – Wikimedia Commons; CC BY-SA 4.0, https://commons.wikimedia.org/w/index.php?curid=113565129

CONTENTS

Preface	vii
1. RATIONALITY FAILS	1
Rational Limits	3
History and Statistics	7
2. THE FIRST GHOST HUNTER	13
Rosalie – Touching a Ghost	15
Borley Rectory	20
3. PARANORMAL PLACES	31
RAF Bircham Newton	32
Other Airfields	38
Haunted Aircraft	39
4. PHOTOGRAPHS 1	47
The Brown Lady	49
The Queen's House Ghost	52
Mabel's Mum	54
Viscount Combermere	56
5. PHOTOGRAPHS 2	63
Bobby Capel's Ghost	63
The Double Exposure Possibility	73
Can ghosts be photographed?	82
6. GHOSTS IN FLIGHT	83
Flight across the Atlantic	84
The Last Flight of the R-101	89
Eastern Airlines' Flight 401	98
American Flight 191	101
7. A VERY VARIED PHENOMENON	103
A Policeman's Solace	104
The Haunted Cottage	107
Great-Grandmother in the Pantry	109
Ghost or Time Window?	110
What are they?	114

8. REINCARNATION	123
Evidence	125
Dorothy Eady	127
Dr Ian Stevenson	130
The Tucker Files	133
Cameron Macaulay	135
James Leininger	137
Ryan Hammons	139
9. DEATH – THE FINAL FRONTIER?	147
Out of Body Experiences (OBEs)	147
Near Death Experiences (NDE)	152
End of Life Experiences (ELE)	156
10. PAST AND FUTURE	161
Versailles	162
Nebraskan Library	165
Pictish Battle	166
The Drem Incident	169
The Dakota Crash	171
The Criteria for Premonitions	174
11. DREAMS	177
The Titanic	177
The World Trade Centre	184
Flight 191	185
Winning the Lottery	187
The Power of Dreams	188
12. THE POWER OF THE MIND	193
Mind over body	194
The Power of Belief	202
Telekinesis	204
Telepathy	209
Remote Viewing/Clairvoyance	213
13. IMPOSSIBLE EXPERIMENTS	217
The Experimental Conundrum	222
Emotion is King	230
The Universe That Should Not Be	234

14. TIME & CONSCIOUSNESS	237
The Fourth Musketeer	237
Filters & Flickers	243
15. THE BOTTOM LINE	255
The Secret Bookshelves	255
One Paranormal to Rule them All	256
Notes	259
Glossary	267
Bibliography	275
Index	281

PREFACE

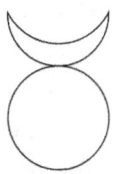

 ... the serious study of the impossible has frequently opened up rich and unexpected domains of science.

— PROFESSOR MICHIO KAKU *THE PHYSICS OF THE IMPOSSIBLE*

The 'paranormal' is defined as anything above and beyond what we call 'normal'. But neither of those terms can ever be precisely defined, because 'normal' and 'paranormal' are relative – they change as human knowledge and understanding grows. In early Victorian times any claim that people could communicate at a distance would be regarded as paranormal. Less than a century ago, anything that could be in two places at once or that only resolved when it was measured, or that could communicate almost instantaneously over galactic distances would have been called unbelievably paranormal. Today, distant communication is possible using radio waves, and the second group of phenomena are accepted, proven outcomes of quantum physics.

There are thousands of books about paranormal topics. The shelves of large bookstores are crammed with them. Books on the ghosts of New York or the hauntings of British castles stand alongside learned tomes on magic and alchemy, and huge volumes focused on the intricacies of astrology. If you want to dabble in the history of fairies or the ways of witches, there are books on those too. The shelves are usually hidden away in the darkest, farthest reaches of bookstores, generally under the curious overall title of 'Spiritualism'. They cover an incredible range of topics. Books on religion are, of course, kept well separated. Even the implication that religion is part of the paranormal is a step too far. Yet, lurking below the surface of all those topics and those yards and yards of bookshelves lie three very important questions.

They are the fundamental questions that this book asks: What is the paranormal? How do the scores of topics hinted at above relate to each other? And how, if at all, does the human mind fit in to the grand scheme of things? The answers are very simple but incredibly powerful. Where life, the universe and everything is concerned, the great Douglas Adams came up with the answer '42' and, depending on how you define the concept of '42', he could well be correct. But, in order to approach the answers to our three questions we have to undertake a long journey. It begins with negotiating the impossible mess that is our early relationship with the paranormal – what I call Paranorm 1.0. Only then can we begin to look at the profound question as to whether humans possess paranormal powers and the even greater mystery of where those powers might originate.

We have been trying to find answers ever since humans could think about such things – probably a lot longer than we currently believe. We've come up with thousands of them. Many of the answers have led to considerable bloodshed as one group of humans has disagreed with another and attempted to impose its own views on everyone else. The battles have extended over hundreds, sometimes thousands, of years and cost many millions of lives.

The tragedy of current human existence is that we are thinking about the paranormal in the wrong way – as a series of distinct topics gathered together under the heading 'paranormal' simply because none of them are normal. Anything we decide is not normal gets relegated to the huge bin in the corner marked 'paranormal' but essentially each is considered to be a very separate topic. In some ways that's understandable – UFOs and ghosts seem to have very little in common, witches are rarely thought to have any links to reincarnation, and precognition seems a million miles from the issue of out-of-body experiences.

Yet they are not separate issues. There is a single, fundamental thread that connects them all. Once we accept that truth, the paranormal becomes a single field of study. Its components can only be studied in isolation if we first accept the immense importance of the interconnections. A biologist might study the human liver as a single organ but they would never forget when doing so that it is an integral part of a very complex organism and that nothing that happens in the liver is ever going to be totally free of the influence of the rest of the body – or, indeed, of the mind.

This book is a plea for the paranormal to be dragged into the twenty-first century, for it to be divested of its ancient, medieval, Victorian, and New Age baggage, for it to be treated as a field of serious scientific and metaphysical study in the way that many top scientists – medics, physicists, biologists, etc. – have already explored.

A single book will not solve our problems, but it might just help us to work our way through the questions by changing the paradigm. Transitioning from Paranorm 1.0 to Paranorm 2.0 sounds very simple. All I am proposing is that we abandon the fragmented, fantasy-world of the old paranormal and replace it with a unified study based on logic and evidence.

That might seem an easy transition but, in common with all the greatest challenges facing the human race, it will be existentially difficult. Paradigm change is never a walk in the park but, like all long journeys, the secret is to take things one step at a time.

JTA; August 2023

CHAPTER 1
RATIONALITY FAILS

> *A scientist would have to be either massively ignorant or a confirmed bigot to deny the evidence that the human mind can make connection with space, time, and matter in ways which have nothing to do with the ordinary senses. Further, he cannot deny that these connections are compatible with current thinking in physics and may in the future become accepted as a part of an extended science in which the description 'paranormal' no longer applies and can be replaced by 'normal'.*
>
> — DR. KIT PEDLER

There cannot be a single person on this planet from the age of five upwards who has not heard of ghosts – those supposedly insubstantial apparitions that float around and scare people. They are the subject of both humour and terror. We laugh at cartoon and comedy ghosts from *Blythe Spirit* and *Topper* to *Caspar* and *Ghostbusters* but audiences have always loved a good ghost story whether comedic or spine-chilling.

Ghost films with a solid core of blood-curdling terror have

included *The Exorcist*, *The Shining*, and *Poltergeist*. All are modern takes on the creepier, hair-raising aspects of the subject, but tales of hauntings go back to the most ancient of times. The spirits of the dead are described and illustrated in Sumerian texts and on the walls of ancient Egyptian tombs. They are reported in ancient Greece and from the Roman Empire in factual and fictional form. Shakespeare uses them to great effect in his dramas, and Charles Dickens invented three of the most famous spirit ghosts of all time. In more recent years Henry James, Oscar Wilde, and J K Rowling used the theme to create memorable characters.

The subject of ghosts is extremely crowded. Almost every town in the world has its own stock of ghost tales. Indeed, almost every *family* in the world has its own stock of ghostly stories. Commercial enterprises thrive by selling ghost tours and guided trips through haunted castles, stately homes, and spooky neighbourhoods. And that immense commercial effort hangs on the single word 'ghost'. The topic is treated as a unique phenomenon which, to my mind, is a bit like forgetting the names of every creature in the world and then trying to study them under the single category of 'animals'.

To put it mildly, the subject is nowhere near as simple as the overarching term 'ghosts' would imply. You may disagree but I hope to show you that ghosts are *not* a single phenomenon even though they are linked by a fundamental force.

The topic of ghosts links Paranorm 1.0 with Paranorm 2.0 by providing a field of study that, at first sight, seems thoroughly embedded in ancient lore and medieval superstition but that, with study, is supported by very modern, empirically-testable evidence. It is surprisingly easy to demonstrate that ghosts are real. Although ridiculed since at least the times of ancient Greece, we have mounting modern evidence that they exist and that they link our view of the paranormal to other powerful phenomena like communication with the dead, end-of-life events, and near-death experiences.

Rational Limits

The subject carries into the twenty-first century a huge amount of somewhat confusing baggage from the past. There are millions of ghost reports and probably tens of thousands of photos out there which show what appear to be ghostly activities. The vast majority 'could be' double exposures, tricks of the light, software manipulation, and other photographic tricks. Everyone claims that their own photos are not falsified but the neutral observer has no way of knowing for sure. This means that, real or fake, no ghost photos are ever taken seriously. I once attended a dinner party at which some highly intelligent people discussed whether they had ever seen a ghost. At first there was scornful laughter, but it was clear that the smirks and giggles disguised serious amounts of nervous tension. The group consisted of old friends and, after one person had taken the risk of admitting to having had a ghost-related experience, they eventually trusted each other enough to begin revealing other personal experiences and to tell of the things that had happened to close relatives or friends. Many readers will have exchanged similar sensitive anecdotes with family, close friends and even work colleagues. My group sat for two or three hours, telling of inexplicable ghostly encounters, and trying not to meet the eyes of other guests too often. It was a marvellous evening which was, to everyone's surprise, made wonderful by the exchange of such confidences.

Thousands of ordinary people – many of them supremely sceptical – see and report ghosts every year. Many do so in exactly the same way as a high proportion of witnesses report UFOs – with a self-deprecating smile and a claim that they don't 'believe' but want an explanation. Most are frightened by the anomalous event and want only to be reassured that what they experienced was something perfectly normal seen in an unusual way. The combination of regular and numerous ghost sightings by ordinary people, the almost inevitable bafflement that follows them, and the rigid avoidance of publicity or even telling other friends or relations are all extremely powerful indications that there is a genuine phenomenon to be addressed.

Scientists can often prove that a photo is fake, and they can come up with a string of *possible* causes of sightings for which there are no photos, but in two centuries of serious, if carefully distant, scientific investigation they have yet to conclusively explain why people see ghosts and, perhaps more to the point, they never ever say that a photo might be the real thing (not even to the point of giving a probability rating). Instead, there are lots of 'could be' ideas about ghost sightings. Leaving aside the frauds and hoaxers, the reason people see ghosts 'could be' as a result of a whole range of stimuli including:

- drugs and hallucinogens which affect perceptions
- carbon monoxide poisoning from indoor heaters
- lights from a passing car reflected through a window or blinds at night
- pareidolia (a human tendency to see patterns in random shapes)
- waking dreams
- electromagnetic fields
- ball lightning
- infrasound (low frequency noise)
- geomagnetic fields
- early onset dementia
- suggestibility/peer pressure while in the company of other people
- tiredness
- and so on.

Looked at rationally almost all ghost reports *could be* due to one or more of these causes. But, to throw the scientists back on their own tests, no one has yet *proved* that they can replicate the effects and results. After the event, scientists might propose that the 'ghost' was a reflection of street lights on a net curtain being blown around in a draught, but they have never yet been able to duplicate the event persuasively. If, for example, waking dreams are a possible explanation, why do so few people who experience waking dreams report them as ghosts? All the things listed above *might* cause people to see and report ghosts – indeed it is entirely likely that one or more of them explain some of the sightings but that does not mean that they explain all of them.

Ghosts that make noise and seem to move inanimate objects are probably a different matter. There are many reports of poltergeists that are faked but there are a few that carry considerable credibility – especially when the ghost is experienced by more than one person unconnected to the people who are being persecuted by it. Some poltergeist activity is not even reported as being the work of a ghost. The lady whose family had so much trouble at the Skinwalker Ranch in Utah[1] in the 1990s reported that the shopping she had put carefully away after returning home, sometimes, while she was out of the room, got removed from the cupboards and put back on the kitchen counters. On other occasions things – even heavy equipment – went missing and turned up in the strangest places (like halfway up a tree).

However, this is where we need to be careful. Just because poltergeists are *called* ghosts and have been reported as such throughout the period covered by Paranorm 1.0 does not mean that they *are* ghosts. They are most certainly a paranormal phenomenon, but modern researchers feel there may be strong reason to consider poltergeist activity in a separate box to ghosts. Many suspect that the cause of poltergeist activity is actually telekinetic – that living humans, especially young ones and without them necessarily being aware of it may be the culprits.

Science says that ghosts cannot be falsified and that, therefore, science cannot prove that they do not exist. It's the same argument that makes scientists avoid the subject of religion – if it cannot be falsified then drop the subject like a hot potato. The argument is sound, but all it really shows is that there are clearly limits to what science can know and, more to the point, of what the empirical method is capable.

The overwhelming consensus of science is that there is no proof that ghosts exist. Their existence is impossible to falsify, and ghost hunting has been classified as pseudoscience. Despite centuries of investigation, there is no scientific evidence that any location is inhabited by spirits of the dead.

— WIKIPEDIA

Isn't that a lovely position for the scientists? The best of both worlds. Scientists have a 'consensus' that ghosts do not exist. 'Consensus' is a good word. It is academically weighty and superficially impressive to the layperson, but virtually never supported by evidence as to who, exactly, is included in the alleged consensus and what the weight of agreement really is. The other slight problem is that, although there may be a consensus, the opposing minority may still be right. So, scientists cannot prove the existence or non-existence of ghosts and, also, cannot explain why people see ghosts. Instead, they have only a set of fairly vague and all-inclusive theories on the matter and those wonderful words: the incredibly vague twins – 'pseudoscience' and 'consensus'.

As we explore the subject in this book we will encounter a wide range of experiences which cannot be explained by the scientists. Not, you will note, things that scientists cannot prove or disprove but a whole mass of events for which science cannot even get close to a possible reason. In the discussion above we have skirted the edges of the conflict between science and the paranormal. What we have not addressed, however, is the possibility that science can *never* explain aspects of the paranormal – that materialist, so-called rational explanations can never be used to understand what is happening in paranormal realms.

History and Statistics

A ghost/spook/shade/spirit/spectre/wraith/phantom is usually regarded as the soul or spirit of a dead person that, for some reason, cannot rest or depart to another place but is forced to remain close to the physical realm and, usually, close to the physical location in which they died. This, it must be stressed, is only one possible explanation for what people report – there are many others. Sometimes the ghost is not that of a dead person but of a living one. There is also at least one more paranormal explanation for ghostly sightings. A good many people (and a few scientists) have wondered whether there might not be occasions when the division between dimensions or even time itself 'slips'. The theory is a bit like the way a gramophone needle can sometimes skip over the grooves of a vinyl record. A vibration in the room, heavy footsteps, or perhaps a loud noise causes the needle to jump tracks. The 'time or dimension slip' hypothesis is very similar in that students argue an instability in other realms can 'reveal' part of reality that existed before or later, or that might exist in another dimension. With 'time-slips' witnesses get a vision because, somehow, the fabric of space-time unravels a little to allow us a glimpse of something that happened in the past or something that will happen in the future. Sounds way-out doesn't it? But don't reject the ideas simply because they sound strange. There is strong empirical evidence to suggest that such time-slips occur.

Reports of ghostly activity can be traced back to Mesopotamia and Assyria and are part of the history and culture of virtually every society on the planet to this day. In Sumer they were called 'gidim' and they came from the Underworld (Iraklia). The belief was that ghosts that became visible were unsettled or tormented because the living had not provided sufficient food and gifts as offerings. Three and a half thousand years ago the young Pharoah Tutankhamun was buried in a small tomb that was stuffed to the rafters with food, furniture, weapons, gold, and images of servants and warriors. His culture believed that only someone who was provided with these things to take to the afterlife would have a smooth and successful transition.

Only in this way would the boy-king not come back to haunt and torment his people.

These beliefs about ghosts go back to the beginnings of writing and are essentially exactly the same as those held by modern humans: that ghosts are the essence of deceased people, that they live in another dimension, and that, if they are seen by living humans, it is because they are unsettled or tormented in some way. Some cultures to this day give offerings to deceased ancestors to minimise the possibility of them coming back to haunt. In parts of south-east Asia and South America there are societies, today, that go to extreme lengths to revere and support their deceased ancestors.

In 2021 the British Museum announced a fascinating find on an old Babylonian clay tablet dating back 4,000 years. The tablet shows a relief of a ghost or spirit being led into the underworld. The tablet evidently advises anyone who has problems with a spirit to get rid of it by finding it a lover. Sounds like good advice to me! The oral traditions of the Australasian aborigines include fear of the ghosts of the recently deceased (Migaloo) and of the ancient spirits who control all creation. As mentioned above, these fears are echoed in the modern world in the cultures of the indigenous tribes of New Guinea and, more generally, in the far east. In the imagination of Charles Dickens it was the lack of charity and human compassion that burdened the spirit of Jacob Marley with the torment of chains and weights and with the task of somehow redeeming himself through good deeds like the saving of Scrooge. Dickens may or may not have known but he was mirroring the belief in 'karma' of the Buddhists and others.

There is also a good deal of evidence for amazing continuity. The idea of a ghost has not changed much in more than seven thousand years. The Sumerians had a theory of ghosts, where they lived, and why they visited living humans. Ancient Egyptian hieroglyphs describe malevolent ghosts and, in Homer's *Odyssey*, written around 2,750 years ago, a ghost is described as vanishing like a vapour. The concept of a ghost as the spirit of the departed is the solid core of all beliefs to this day. Fear of what the dead wanted and what they could do to the living naturally led to the idea of placating ghosts, giving them food and objects, and sometimes holding festivals in their honour. Ancestor reverence is not mere politeness.

In the 1st century CE, Plutarch described the haunting of the baths at Chaeronea by the ghost of a man who had been murdered there. The ghost's loud and frightful groans caused the people of the town to seal up the doors of the building. Plutarch does not say whether that solved the problem but the inference is that it did – perhaps because it turned the baths into a personal crypt. Another celebrated account of a haunted house from the ancient classical world is given by Pliny the Younger (ca. 50 CE). Pliny describes the haunting of a house in Athens which had been bought by the Stoic philosopher Athenodorus (who lived about a century before Pliny). Knowing that the house was supposedly haunted, Athenodorus intentionally set up his writing desk in the room where the apparition was said to appear most often. He sat there writing until late at night when he was disturbed by a ghost bound in chains. He was built of stern stuff, this Athenodorus, because he calmly followed the ghost outside where it somehow showed him a particular a spot on the ground. The apparition then disappeared. When Athenodorus had the indicated ground excavated, a shackled skeleton was unearthed. The haunting ceased when the skeleton was given a 'proper' reburial[2].

In Europe the spirits of the dead and other inhabitants of the underworld are supposed to be able to visit the physical world at the time of Samhain - traditionally celebrated for up to three days around the end of October and early November. In Mexico and much of Latin America the same time of the year (November 1st and 2nd) is their time for honouring the dead and bringing them gifts of food[3].

The sceptics may be right about the marketing power of a famous ghost, but the truth is that ninety-nine percent of all ghost tales do not involve eminent personages or grisly executions and, most definitely, do not make anyone any money. The other thing we need to note is that a large proportion of people believe in ghosts. According to a 2009 study by the Pew Research Center in the United States, 18% of Americans say they have seen a ghost (around one in five people).

That's over 60 million people in the US who admit to having seen or experienced what they thought of as a ghost. YouGov polls in 2014 and 2019 revealed that about 34% of Brits[4] and 45% of Americans believe in ghosts. A British online survey in 2017 revealed that around 40% of young people believe in ghosts compared to 26% of the over 50s.

In cold hard figures these statistics mean that roughly 20 million Britons and 160 million Americans believe in ghosts. If those statistics are even roughly representative of the whole world[5] then somewhere between two and three billion people believe that ghosts are a genuine phenomenon. So, either between a quarter and a half of the world's population are credulous fools, or the scientists and sceptics might be wrong.

The question for any author attempting to describe and analyse the ghost is the sheer over-abundance of evidence. Underlying the whole issue is the problem of monocausality. Humans like to keep things simple and we are therefore fond of attributing any given phenomenon to a single cause. But the unfortunate fact is that the universe seldom works in simple ways. More often than not things can be caused by several different factors and this principle could well apply to ghosts. Any particular theory may be entirely valid but, equally, it would be foolish to exclude other theories.

It's an impossible task to evaluate and categorise millions of experiences with ghosts over a period of around 7,000 years, but it is certainly possible to identify some common threads. There are far more complex categorisations of ghosts, but this is a simple list of the main types:

1. **Passive spirits of the dead** – usually insubstantial. They do not seem to create any danger or even physical disruption.

2. **Active spirits of the dead** – poltergeists. There may however be other causes of this phenomenon.
3. **Revenants** – solid-seeming ghosts of dead people. They can seem to be very real and have been known to speak to living people.
4. **Fetches** – a solid-seeming ghost of a living person, effectively a sort of hologram of the real person who is in a different geographic location.
5. **Lights, mists, and orbs** – more common than you would think. No-one really knows what these apparitions are, but they have been seen for thousands of years.

The first group contains all the passive manifestations; the misty forms that walk the corridors of stately homes, pubs, and hotels, that appear to walk through brick walls, that are seen wistfully gazing out of windows, and that stroll along castle walls, through gardens, and down roadways. Some have active elements; they might emit a perfume or smell of leather or tobacco. A few smell of less attractive things – like burning or jet fuel or even of decayed flesh.

The second broad type includes the more disturbing instances of ghosts that not only make noise but sometimes also manage to levitate, and destroy, items of property. Some cause floorboards to creak or footsteps to sound, others might make wailing noises and even speak to people.

Revenants are apparently-solid ghosts appearing to be the real person. Even today a few authorities believe that revenants are the *actual* dead person returned to a semblance of life – similar to a vampire. Some, but not all, are reputed to be violent and focused on revenge for perceived wrongs. The famous Eastern Airlines case, which we will look into later, provides not one but two examples of revenant ghosts whose main motivation appeared to be guilt.

A 'fetch' is an apparition of a person who is still alive. The occurrences tend to follow a traumatic experience in the life of the 'ghost' and their appearance can frighten their loved ones. Fetches may actually be a form of emotionally-enhanced telepathic communication – a sort of video call as compared to a simple phone call.

These four ghost categories are extremely simplistic and do not include a wide variety of strange ghostly phenomena which may or may not have something to do with dead people. The ghost phenomenon is generally taken to include such things as bright, floating orbs of light (sometimes wispy and sometimes quite solid), vortexes of light and air that appear and cause havoc for a while, and the inanimate ghosts of objects like trains and ships and phantom stagecoaches all of which have been reported across the world and on many, many occasions.

CHAPTER 2
THE FIRST GHOST HUNTER

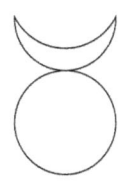

> *98% of reported hauntings have a natural and mundane explanation ... it is the other 2% that have interested me for over 40 years.*
>
> — PETER UNDERWOOD

He was probably not the very first ghost hunter – Athenodorus arguably has a prior claim although he only hunted one ghost – but a chap named Harry Price was one of the first successful debunkers of fake mediums, and he carried out some of the best (and the most controversial) investigations into paranormal events and alleged ghosts during the 1920s and 1930s.

Harry Price doing a radio broadcast. The Harry Price Website, Public Domain, Author unknown. https://commons.wikimedia.org/w/index.php?curid=20404611

Price was a skilled amateur magician and he may have perpetrated a few paranormal scams himself in the early days. By the late 1920s and early 1930s, however, he was a valuable addition to the Society for Psychical Research (SPR), identifying and testing mediums and examining a steady stream of supernatural occurrences. He debunked a lot of mediums but he also found a small number of genuine ones. Harry Price was giving the medium Eileen Garrett an initial test at the SPR when she suddenly started to get messages from the officers who had been in the ill-fated R-101 airship disaster. He was as surprised as the medium but soon became as convinced of her capability as Major Villiers (and as had Mrs Emilie Hinchliffe before them). We'll look at the Hinchliffe and R-101 affairs in due course. Price wrote that he discovered very few genuine mediums in his life but that a handful were the real deal. He was convinced that they possessed legitimate paranormal powers.

Two of his later escapades are also worth exploring. In one, sceptical as he always was, he was astounded to be involved in a séance in which the ghost was so real that he could feel a heartbeat. In the other, a much more confused and controversial set of events, he probably blotted his copybook a little, but it still remains a credible and fascinating set of ghost events.

Rosalie – Touching a Ghost

In the era of Paranorm 1.0 ghosts were seen and recorded but the task of communicating with the dead was left to what we now call mediums. The Victorians treated the whole subject very seriously and they ignited for the modern world a chain-reaction of interest in séances, mediums, trances, and seers. The sheer abundance of such people in the US, the UK, and Europe from about the middle of the nineteenth century presents us with a serious dilemma. The vast majority of them were fakes and we know this because Harry Price did a great deal of research on this issue. He not only unmasked a goodly number of fraudsters but was also able to show how they had perpetrated their tricks. In the early twentieth century he was responsible for debunking hordes of mediums and not a few alleged ghost tales. Price was an intelligent man whose interest in the paranormal was lifelong, but he was also one who did not suffer fools gladly. He was the Honorary Secretary for the University of London's Council for Psychical Investigation and he often worked with the Society for Psychical Research. His research is summarised in his 1939 book[1].

Like all of us, Harry Price was not perfect. In his younger years he may have created a few fraudulent paranormal events himself. Some of his critics use these alleged indiscretions to negate all later work but my own feeling is that those youthful extravagances probably made him better at spotting the frauds committed by others. He did not shy away from controversy and, at times, he may even have strayed across the line into being too gullible or insufficiently critical. But read his book and see what you think.

Price discusses and describes the strangely Skinwalker-like events of the 'Ringcroft Disturbances' (1696) and explains the so-called 'Stockwell Ghost' of 1777. This event centred on poltergeist activity which today we suspect is most probably the result of telekinetic disturbances. In this case it seems to have been caused by a young maid named Ann Robinson. The Stockwell Ghost is interesting because several independent witnesses, as well as the maid's employer, saw such things as plates falling unprompted from shelves, a clock falling off the wall (again without a human near it), random noises, and objects being thrown around rooms. All the violent and weird events ceased as soon as the maid had been dismissed and had left the house. It says a lot that some modern scientists are beginning to accept that poltergeist activity is sometimes the result of telekinetic forces (thereby accepting to a large extent that such a phenomenon exists). Scientists now call it Recurrent Spontaneous Psycho-Kinesis - RSPK[2]).

Price believed that there is a genuine phenomenon called the paranormal but he also complained that *'real phenomena are obscured by quackery and charlatans'*. He managed to debunk almost every case he was presented with, but, after diligent investigations, he accepted that certain mediums and certain events were genuine. He therefore had great respect for the mediums he identified as the genuine article. Among these was the famous Victorian medium, Daniel Douglas Home (pronounced 'Hume'; 1833-1886), Home was examined by a string of eminent scientists of the day and was always found to have been exhibiting genuine powers. Indeed, he was partly behind the establishment of the Society for Psychical Research in 1882 by Professor William Barrett (later Sir William Barrett). The SPR is still in existence.

Price highlights in his book a few of the telekinetic mediums he'd tested and had decided were genuine. He also praised certain diviners and dowsers. Among the former was Major C A Pogson who was evidently an extremely good proponent of the art of divination. The latter included Captain W H Trinder who was remarkably successful in dowsing with a wooden bobbin over maps. Dowsing has a large number of practitioners these days[3]. It is an art which is hard to explain but even gas and water companies use dowsers on occasion in order to locate lost underground mains. The art of dowsing seems to require a human mind to exercise subconscious control over the muscles while somehow communing with external powers. A water or gas pipe buried three feet or so under the ground can be sensed by the dowser. How it works is totally unknown but work it certainly does as long as the dowser is sufficiently gifted. The 'skill' seems to have a strong resonance with paranormal abilities like remote viewing in that it appears to link something in the human mind with a geographic component. Dowsers can spot underground cavities and trenches and, according to some European researchers, they can sometimes locate and even return lost or stolen property.

Where debunking is concerned, Price was extremely tough and his long experience with fraudsters taught him virtually all the tricks. Occasionally, however, he came across an incident which all his sceptical experience could not break. The Rosalie case demonstrates his scepticism but, above all, the scrupulous care he took when testing an alleged paranormal case. It centred on a couple who had called him in to witness the incredible manifestation of a young girl whose death had left a huge hole in her mother's life. That lady – who was a close friend of the couple in question – told them that her deceased daughter appeared to her regularly. At first her friends believed that grief had caused her to imagine things but they, themselves, saw the girl appear and felt that Harry Price should also experience the strange manifestation. They prevailed upon the lady to allow him to attend a special evening but stressed to Price that their friend would only allow a single experience, for fear of destroying the precious link between her and her daughter.

So, one evening, Harry Price turned up at the suburban home of the couple. He examined the exterior of the building first to make sure that he understood how many windows and doors led into and out of the house. Once inside he examined and sealed each and every door and window leading into the house and every internal door that was not connected to the séance room. Prior to the séance Price removed any superfluous ornaments and furniture from the room in which it was to take place. After everyone concerned had entered the séance room, he sealed and taped the only door to the room, sealed the (unlit) fireplace in the room with newspaper (which could not be broken without noise or leaving evidence), thoroughly searched all the male attendees and had the females also searched, checked under all tables and in all drawers and cupboards (sealing them afterwards), sealed all the windows and ensured they were completely secured shut, checked the curtains and raised them from the floor so that no-one could hide behind them, spread flour on the floor in front of the doors, windows, the fireplace, and any other area which led towards and away from the séance table. It was a typically meticulous set of precautions born of long experience of how fraudsters could trick audiences.

What happened that evening has become famous as the 'Rosalie Manifestation'. The mother never publicised her psychic meetings with her daughter, the case only came to Price's attention through the mother's friends, and, as I have said, he was permitted only a single séance.

Price was initially extremely sceptical and thought that perhaps any manifestation was merely a psychological result of the mother's intense grief. His scepticism did not survive the evening, however. He was deeply impressed by what occurred. The ghost seemed to be so solid that Price was able to sense the warmth of the girl's body and her heart beating. He even measured her pulse rate at ninety. This took place in a sealed room and Price was no-one's fool. Neither the friends, nor the mother – nor indeed Harry Price - was making any money or gaining any publicity out of any of it[4]. Rosalie's mother was extremely private and did not permit any further séances. She wrote no books, published no articles, attracted no newspaper coverage, and Price was never able to question her again. It was a one-off opportunity for a paranormal investigator to experience a profound supernatural link between a mother and daughter.

Among a number of 'exemplary' mediums including Mrs Crandon, whose tests by the Scientific American magazine were inconclusive but impressive, and a lady named 'Stella C' (Dorothy Stella Cranshaw[5]), was, of course, Eileen Garrett whose abilities were astounding but who, nevertheless, received much of what we would today term 'abuse'. It is worth noting that an unknown number of mediums keep their heads well below the media radar. Good mediums tend to be extremely wary of publicity and it is for this reason that they are rarely subjected to any independent testing. Stella C was an example of this type of medium. She was very capable and, as far as Price could test her, incredibly successful, but she never courted publicity and, in fact, did not even practise the art except in tests.

Price met her by chance on his train home to Pulborough in West Sussex. In conversation the then hospital nurse told Price that she often heard inexplicable noises and suffered from unexplained chills from her surroundings and of occasions on which objects flew around without human intervention. Price used the facilities of the London Spiritualist Alliance to test Stella[6]. Because she had to take unpaid time off work, Price or the LSA paid her a small stipend for attending the tests. The full story of Price's testing of Stella C is extremely compelling because the woman not only never practised as a medium, professionally or otherwise, but dropped out of the tests on at least two occasions. Harry Price put her through controlled séances the results of which were astounding. He was able to measure temperature fluctuations and record objects – even very heavy objects – being moved.

Every séance that Price held with Stella C – and she participated in around forty in all – was attended by witnesses other than Price himself. On one, now famous, occasion a table was elevated into the air and then completely destroyed without the human participants doing more than lay their hands lightly upon it. As arguably the world's first ghost hunter, Price invented a number of technical mechanisms for tracking paranormal activity. He developed something he called the 'telekinetoscope' which was basically a telegraph key linked to a red light. When the key was pressed home the light would come on. Price placed the key under a glass dome so that no human participant could press it. The red light came on many times during Stella C's séances. As I say, she was a truly remarkable talent but even less prepared to have that talent publicised or used for commercial purposes than many other mediums.

Harry Price was very open about the fact that he had not been able to get the Rosalie experience corroborated in any way. He admitted too that his experience – impressive as it was – was probably nowhere near as profound as the extended experiences of Sir William Crookes with the Katie King manifestations in the 1870s[7]. Crookes was a scientist first and foremost and was initially very sceptical of the claims of the highly active spiritualist movement of the 1850s and 1860s. He decided to test those claims and set stringent conditions including:

> *It must be at my own house, and my own selection of friends and spectators, under my own conditions, and I may do whatever I like as regards apparatus* [8]

Over the course of his experiments Crookes and his family and friends saw the manifestations of Katie King many times and took a number of now famous photos. The scientific consensus in 1874, when Crookes was unwise enough to publish a report on his findings, was that he had been duped and, today, one has to be a little suspicious of a spirit that allowed itself to be measured, touched, weighed, and photographed. Notwithstanding our scepticism, however, it is also important to remember that Sir William Crookes was one of the finest scientists of his day. He never wavered from his assertions that the Katie King manifestations were genuine.

Borley Rectory

> *Borley Rectory stands by itself in the literature of psychical manifestation. The large numbers of the public who are*

interested in these things are under a debt of gratitude to Mr. Harry Price, for without his untiring energy and skilled experience as an investigator, the story of Borley Rectory would have remained unrevealed. The manifestations are proved by the evidence, to the point of moral certainty.

— SIR ALBION RICHARDSON, RECORDER OF NOTTINGHAM

No self-respecting treatment of the topic of the paranormal could possibly ignore the Borley Rectory story. Situated in north Essex almost on the Suffolk border, the hamlet of Borley has been able to boast of an impressive church from ancient times. Its rectory, having been destroyed by fire, was rebuilt in the 1860s. The evidence points strongly to local opposition to its location due to the fact that the previous Hall on the site was reputed to be haunted. But the Church went ahead anyway and, in its new form, the house immediately gained a reputation for being haunted. Borley village and its Hall had a reputation for being haunted long before the nineteenth century but we do not have any (plausible) recorded accounts of hauntings in the pre-1860 era. After about sixty years and many accounts of hauntings, the alleged events at the 'new' rectory came to the notice of Harry Price, fresh from his investigations into famous cases like the Hinchliffe death, the medium Stella C, the Rosalie case, and the ghosts of the officers of the R-101. Borley Rectory eventually became one of his main interests.

It is a complex story involving a lengthy period during which ghosts were experienced, a number of different types of ghosts, horse-drawn carriages and headless drivers, a ghost nun, random writings on walls, and a BBC photographer who caught a shot of what looked like a floating brick. As usual, the entire story is coloured by the characters of the people reporting and investigating the events and there is considerable controversy surrounding the whole matter. Nevertheless, it is arguably one of the most complete and compelling accounts of an extended period of paranormal activity anywhere in the world.

In 1841 the old rectory in the hamlet of Borley was destroyed. Twenty years later the building was replaced, in a different location, by a splendid Victorian house and in 1862 its first family moved in. The Reverend Henry Bull, his wife, and a host of young Bulls took occupation of the magnificent new home. It boasted no less than thirty-two rooms, which included eleven bedrooms and stood in eleven acres of grounds. These days not so much manse as mansion.

Reports of strange ghostly activity began to circulate almost as soon as the Bull family had moved in. There were noises and footsteps and even a report of a phantom coach with headless drivers. In the locality, the new rectory quickly got a reputation for being haunted – as had the church itself and some surrounding farms. But the Bull family remained there quite happily in spite of the children reporting the ghost of a nun being seen near the house in 1890. Nothing was reported to the press, so the stories were confined to local gossip and mainly to the vicar's family. When his father died, one of his sons, the Reverend Henry (Harry) Bull, took over the living in 1892 and he, too, remained in the property until he died. In some ways this is an important part of the story. Two generations of vicars and their families lived happily at the rectory for over sixty years. The house was well known for being haunted but no-one appears to have been in the least hysterical about it and no-one attempted to sensationalise the tales in the press.

After Harry Bull died, the next occupant was the Reverend Guy Smith and wife, who moved into the dwelling in 1928. They appear to have immediately run into paranormal trouble and were definitely a lot less cool about it. They reported the ringing of long-disconnected servants' bells, seeing lights from windows whose rooms were not being used, strange footsteps, and even the appearance of a horse-drawn carriage late at night. Most of what they reported was not new, even the horse-drawn carriage was a relatively well-known phenomenon in the local community. The house was never fitted for any major utility – there was no electricity, gas, or piped water throughout its existence as a dwelling.

There had now been paranormal events at the Rectory for around seventy years. All were well known to locals but not to a wider audience. They'd mainly been experienced by Church of England vicars and their families. Such men had an aversion – especially in Victorian and early twentieth century times – to becoming involved in supernatural scandals or, indeed, to telling untruths. This background is of crucial importance because, in spite of the excitements following the arrival of Harry Price, the events had already had a long history. Two generations of the Bull family had lived reasonably happily amid the paranormal goings-on.

The Smiths, for some reason known only to themselves, did not wish to coexist peacefully with ghosts. They took the unusual step of writing to the Daily Mirror, explaining the situation and asking to be put in contact with the Society for Psychical Research. The involvement of the Daily Mirror meant two things – firstly that the whole affair became a national cause célèbre, and secondly that Harry Price got involved. The Society for Psychical Research asked him to look into the Smiths' story. While he was at the house a remarkable number of paranormal activities and events took place and, even though he was only there because the Smiths had complained of being beset by ghosts, Mrs Smith told the press that, in her opinion, most of the events were faked by her husband and Harry Price.

The result, at least partly due to the publicity, was that the Smiths left the Rectory in July of 1929. In just a year of occupancy they'd created a national sensation which resounds even to this day. One can only imagine the excitement and gossip in the local community resulting from the Smith's domestic infighting and the descent of newspaper reporters and photographers.

Borley Rectory, 1892. Author unknown, Wikimedia Commons; Public Domain.
https://commons.wikimedia.org/w/index.php?curid=8113080

A little more than a year later the Reverend Lionel Foyster and his wife Marianne took up residence along with their daughter Adelaide[9]. Once more there followed a steady stream of paranormal events and incidents including bell-ringing (as for the Smiths), windows shattering, stones and bottles being hurled around the place, writing appearing on walls and, on one occasion, the daughter being locked in a room.

The SPR was once more involved but, this time, its researchers tended to regard most of what had happened as being of human origin. They reported back their suspicions that most of it was due to the wife Marianne who evidently later admitted using the alleged events for her own purposes. After the Foysters left the vicarage in 1935 the house remained empty until, in May 1937, Harry Price began a one-year tenancy. He had maintained a close watch on events in and around Borley Rectory and had negotiated a short lease with the

Church of England while they were finding a new tenant. Anticipating a continuation of paranormal incidents and the need to have a credible source of supervision, Price advertised for a group of independent observers. The ad, in The Times, read as follows:

 HAUNTED HOUSE: *Responsible persons of leisure and intelligence, intrepid, critical, and unbiased, are invited to join a rota of observers in a year's night and day investigation of an alleged haunted house in the Home counties. Printed Instructions supplied. Scientific training or ability to operate simple instruments an advantage. House situated in lonely hamlet, so own car is essential. Write Box H.989, The Times, E.C.4*

For the purposes of the experiment Price developed the world's first 'ghost hunting handbook'. Called the Blue Book it contained advice and instruction on what to do and how to set up and use various pieces of equipment. The group of forty people that he appointed (and personally paid for) included a chap named Sydney Glanville, whose detailed notes and drawings on the experiences of the observers during that year were handed over to Price and became what is now known as the Locked Book (sometimes misleadingly called the Locked Box). Its contents are available online and most of them appear in Price's own book[10]. The group of observers was given almost completely free rein by Price. They were chosen as a mix of believers and sceptics who Price largely left to investigate how and when they wished. If you read the various books – especially the Locked Book – you will find that people's experiences at the Rectory spanned the whole range from absolutely nothing happening to pretty spectacular manifestations. The fascinating thing is that most occurrences were observed by more than one person.

During the Foysters' occupation, one of the strangest manifestations was the appearance of writing on the walls. All of them seemed to be directed at 'Marianne', all asked for help, and some gave clear indications that the writer was a Catholic. No-one understood what these represented but Price suggested that they might be connected with the visions of a nun that had been regularly reported. During one of their visits, the Glanvilles held a séance, in which they had apparently been contacted by a spirit named 'Marie Lairre'. She told the Glanvilles that she had been a nun in France but had abandoned her calling to marry Henry Waldegrave, whose manor house had once stood where the rectory now stood. According to Glanville the séance revealed that the ex-nun had been strangled by her husband who had buried the body in the cellar.

Once Harry Price's tenancy ended, the house once again lay empty until a new tenant, Captain W H Gregson, moved in in February 1939. Unfortunately, while he was unpacking, an oil-lamp was knocked over and the Rectory burned to a shell. There is still considerable uncertainty as to what happened and whether the lamp was knocked over by Captain Gregson or whether it somehow overturned when no-one was present. The rectory was never reconstructed and the sad ruin was completely demolished in 1944.

Thus ended the tale of the Rectory at Borley. The only surviving bit of the property is a separate building, the old 'cottage' into which you could probably fit three modern shoe-box houses. Ghostly stories still emerge from the area but the key issue is whether there was anything to the whole eighty-year-long episode at the Rectory or whether it was all made up. Perhaps the most insightful assessment was made by a senior clergyman with the somewhat unlikely name of the Reverend W J Phythian-Adams who was, at the time a Canon of Carlisle. He read Price's book and, on that basis, began a very lengthy and detailed examination of the whole affair. One of the most interesting outcomes was that the Canon told Harry Price where to dig to find the remains of the nun. Price arranged a dig during August of 1943 at which there were a number of reputable witnesses including the Rev. A.C. Henning; Dr Eric H. Bailey (Senior Assistant Pathologist at Ashford County Hospital); his brother Roland F. Bailey; Flying Officer A. A. Creamer; and Captain W.H. Gregson and his two nieces,

Georgina Dawson and Mrs. Alex English. They found a number of items including a brass preserving pan, a silver cream jug, and – most importantly a jawbone with five teeth still attached, and part of a skull. The doctor's conclusion was that the jawbone was human and female and that the partial skull was also human. All of the remains were given a Christian burial in May 1945 and the ghost of the nun has never been seen again. Harry Price died in March 1948 at the age of just 67 in the middle of creating a third book on the subject of Borley Rectory.

The evaluations of the affair by sceptics are pretty damning. One of them, Louis Mayerling (if that was indeed his name), claimed that the whole thing was deliberately faked. He published a book – 'We Faked the Ghosts of Borley Rectory' back in 2000[11]. Mayerling, however, turned out to be a somewhat dubious character in his own right and Peter Underwood, one of the most assiduous of modern ghost hunters, who interviewed many of the central characters in the Borley affair, argued that Mayerling's book was more fiction than fact. Other sceptics have put a number of 'could be' arguments on the table – such as that the Foysters were in financial difficulties and therefore had a solid motive for encouraging 'ghost-tourists'. The notion of ghost tourism is not new and is definitely a modern phenomenon but I fail to see how the Foysters could have made any money out of people travelling to Borley to see the rectory (there's no evidence that they ever attempted to charge an entrance fee for people to be given guided tours, for example). Other sceptics have questioned just about every element of the story.

Yet, as someone who has read widely on the topic including investigating newspaper articles both local and national, there remains for me an extremely strong sense of credibility to many of the paranormal events at Borley Rectory. The various suspicious happenings at the Rectory were extensive well before the matter became public knowledge in 1928-29. Two generations of Church of England vicars and their families had experienced the strange occurrences but had not attempted to gain benefit from them. Neither father nor son of the Bull family tried to publish a book on the subject in spite of the fact that headless coachmen, ghost nuns, and all the rappings, noises and lights could be seen as a licence to print money in Victorian and Edwardian years. At least one of them attempted a Christian exorcism. The Smiths were also a credible pair of witnesses. They experienced paranormal events before calling the newspaper and permitting the involvement of Harry Price. The issue with the Smiths was their decision to involve the Daily Mail. National publicity was not necessary for them to find help and it was not as though Mrs Smith avoided publicity thereafter with her accusations against Harry Price and her husband. Marianne Foyster was another matter entirely and it is all-too-easy to see her as the instigator of the paranormal events at the rectory while she and her husband were in residence. But the fascinating thing is that the wall-writings carried on after the Foysters left. Observers during Price's tenancy reported quite a few writings of a similar character.

The hamlet of Borley had had lengthy experience of weird goings-on for around seventy years before the story received wide publicity and began to get complicated by newspapers and visits by Harry Price. Price may have been a bit of a showman but, by that time in his career, he was developing a very significant vested interest in making his investigations as bullet-proof as possible. He was fast developing a reputation as an assiduous investigator and one has to recognise that he'd probably have made even more money publishing a couple of sensational exposé books entitled something like 'A Psychist's Revelations of the Borley Rectory Ghost Fraud' or 'The Gullible Vicars' as he did by the ones he actually published. The investigator Peter Underwood had a strong and highly credible track record and interviewed most of the main players in the saga. He was convinced that at least a high proportion of the events at Borley Rectory actually happened[12].

The case may often be portrayed as a veritable feast of sensational fakery but the core of the story is highly credible – that of a hub of *recorded* paranormal activity for around eighty years. The fact that credible reports continue to emerge from the geographic area – especially the church – underpins a high degree of certainty that something genuine occurred at many points over that period of time (albeit possibly amid other faked events). Locations with strong associations with the paranormal are not uncommon. Perhaps the hamlet of Borley is one of those.

CHAPTER 3
PARANORMAL PLACES

> *A lot of things happened in that house, a lot of flying objects and voices and strange, strange things happened ... When you live in old houses, you get this energy there.*
>
> — STING (ORIGINALLY A SCEPTIC, HE ALSO EVIDENTLY WITNESSED A DOPPELGANGER OF HIS WIFE AND CHILD IN THEIR BEDROOM) BBC RADIO 2 INTERVIEW; 2009)

I have mentioned the famous Skinwalker Ranch in Utah and we could talk about the ghosts of Washington DC, Paris, Prague, Tokyo, and San Francisco for an entire book. In the UK we are absolutely submerged in paranormal locations – places where there are enough spooky tales to keep Albert Hall-sized audiences enthralled for days on end. So, you will understand if I say that I have had to be extremely brutal in culling the places and stories down to a number small enough to fit into a single chapter.

For very good reasons, I've opted to major on the best Royal Air Force (RAF) examples. Mainly because they avoid the key issue raised by most sceptics: that stories of the paranormal variety attract tourists, publicity, and paying guests, and are therefore to be ignored. The argument has some weight of course. Money talks. So, best to focus on examples that do not make money for, or bring fame to, those whose property is alleged to be haunted.

We will begin with the story of RAF Bircham Newton. Its value lies in the fact that it is more than a ghost story. Although there are undoubted ghosts on the premises it has immense weight in that it offers examples of many other paranormal events and a very wide variety of witnesses over a long period of time.

RAF Bircham Newton

Located in the north of the county of Norfolk in the UK, RAF Bircham Newton was established for the Royal Flying Corps in 1916 and was finally closed down by the RAF in late 1962. The land and buildings were then bought by the Construction Industry Training Board (CITB) for use as a national construction college which opened for business in 1964. Today, much of the old airfield has been demolished for use in training activities but many of the original buildings are still in use and its heritage as an RAF base is very evident in the style of the old officers' mess, the Station Commander's house, the gatehouse, and some of the admin buildings that remain in use as offices alongside modern additions. One original building that has been left in place is that containing the squash courts.

RAF Bircham Newton never possessed paved runways – which was one reason it became a training base in the 1950s and was closed down in the early-60s. It did, however, have a long history as an active airfield. During World War One and for many years thereafter it hosted squadrons of heavy bombers (the Handley Page V/1500), and it was a Coastal Command airfield – complete with two satellite airfields – during the Second World War. Around 530 men lost their lives flying from Bircham Newton in the two world wars.

In 1918, the RAF constructed two squash courts on the base. They have now been in use for over a century. Although by no means the only haunted areas on the base the courts are probably the best known and most studied. There are too many accounts to mention all of them but trainees at what is now the CITB college have reported weird things: sheets being ripped off beds during the night, items being moved, and inexplicable physical restraint of people while sleeping. Two trainees at the college – on separate occasions – said that they were pushed back onto their beds when they woke up during the night. In one case the chap said that he was sleeping on his stomach and was pushed firmly and with some strength back onto the bed. The room was empty apart from himself. Another reported that he woke up to a noise in his room and had his head pushed back down. Again, there was no-one else in the bedroom. These examples of physical effects are baffling but they are difficult to dismiss because they have been experienced by a number of individuals over a span of time. Their numbers include a female journalist.

Emily Wright a young reporter from 'Building' magazine spent two nights at the training centre in 2008 and said that, on the first night, she awoke to find something, or somebody, tracing her eyebrows and eyes with what she perceived as a finger. She was terrified but was clear-minded enough to suspect that she had done it herself. A quick mental review of her situation, however, showed that the room was empty and that it was not possible that she'd done it herself. Her arms were down by her side beneath the sheets and she knew that she had not moved them in the seconds after the experience[1]. If you read her story you will find that, on that particular night, she did not know of Bircham Newton's reputation for paranormal activity. She was informed of it the day after her experience.

There are unconfirmed reports of a CITB staffer quitting their job after being tapped on the shoulder in an otherwise deserted room. Another trainee is reported to have left his course early after seeing what appeared to be an RAF officer in one of the training rooms. Before he could say anything to the apparently solid apparition, the RAF man turned and walked through a solid partition. The partition was post-war, erected to segment a much larger room into several offices.

The 1918-built Squash Courts at ex-RAF Bircham Newton (photo by Evelyn Simak)

But, as intimated earlier, a key story at Bircham Newton concerns the 1918 squash courts. As seen in the photo above, the squash court building – albeit having been re-roofed and with modern windows – is the one constructed by the newly-formed RAF in 1918. To the unwitting visitor, and the author has been in the building several times, it looks exactly like any other set of modern squash courts built into an older building. But to those who know their history, merely entering it is a trip through time. It has been used by generations of service personnel over the past century and, with some modern repairs and amendments, the interior is exactly as it was when the first RAF officers played in it a hundred or so years ago – changing rooms, toilets, courts, and gallery, all would be instantly recognisable to one of the base's twenty-year-old Pilot Officers from 1919.

The building's tiny changing rooms, two side-by-side squash courts, and narrow viewing gallery are all pretty standard stuff. On my first visit I was told of the paranormal history of the courts by a senior manager at CITB and, at first, I thought he was pulling my leg. He took me into the right-hand court and it did, indeed, feel unusually cold. I remarked on this, but he laughed, saying that this was the normal temperature. He went on to say that this particular court became absolutely freezing-cold whenever there was any paranormal activity. He had experienced this himself when at the courts for a game.

As I left the building to be shown some of the bedrooms and other locations where paranormal events had occurred, I remarked to my guide that the squash courts were well-fitted and that they seemed very normal and typical. He chuckled as he replied that those squash courts were anything but normal. A few of his present and past colleagues had vowed never to use them again.

Paranormal events at Bircham Newton may have affected its inhabitants for a very long time but the modern story begins about fifty years ago - in the 1970s. A few years after CITB took over the old airbase the powers-that-be decided to make a management training film. They commissioned a script and hired a film company to come and do some filming for a week or so. This would probably have been in the summer of 1969 or 1970. The story of what happened to a couple of members of the film crew was briefly aired by the local newspaper – the Lynn News & Advertiser – on December 12th 1971. In brief, one of what were probably two soundmen on the project decided one night to get some serious exercise. Kevin Garry asked a colleague whether he would like a game of squash and, when the colleague declined, he went to the court by himself for a good workout.

He had the entire building to himself that evening and first played against himself in the left-hand court. After a while, and probably just because he could, he decided to try out the other court too and moved to the right hand one. As soon as he entered that court he noticed a very decided drop in temperature but carried on working up a sweat. After a while he heard footsteps up on the gallery behind him and assumed that his colleague had decided to come after all to watch him – or even to join him in a game. He did not look up but continued to play against himself. Then, while he was retrieving the ball between serves, he heard a loud sigh and turned around. He did not, as he expected, see his colleague. There in the gallery, apparently watching him, was a chap in RAF uniform. Almost immediately the apparition disappeared. A very frightened Kevin Garry left the courts in a hurry and found his colleague, Peter Clark, to whom he related his unusual experience.

The two men talked it over and, being sound technicians, decided to try to get whatever it was – the footsteps and sighs – on tape. They returned to the courts at about 11.30 that night expecting to sit quietly for a while with the tape recorder running until they got sufficient noises. But first, they searched the building to make sure they were alone – not a long job in such a small structure – and decided to set up the recorder in the right-hand court, the one from which Kevin had witnessed the apparition. Peter Clark later described the atmosphere in the right-hand court as cold and frightening. Some have described the feeling in the right-hand court as being oppressive. One person told me it was 'threatening'. The two debated whether to stay and, wise men that they were, decided to leave the recorder running, lock the outside door, and go and sit outside in the warm night air in a location from which they could monitor the entrance.

They waited comfortably about twenty-five minutes, until the tape would have run out, and then returned. Even as they walked across the court to switch-off the machine they heard footsteps on the gallery behind them. No-one was there. They scooped up the recorder and left very quickly. Now this is the great thing about this particular story – what those two chaps recorded is available online for all to hear. I have listened to it many times and it never ceases to intrigue. You can hear the sounds of them leaving the court after setting-up the recorder, the sounds of strange metallic bangs and what seem to be muffled voices. There are no buildings near or attached to the squash building and, on that night there were no other people either in or near the courts – it was, after all, after one in the morning when they finished.

When they left the base, the two men sent the tape to what was then a very popular BBC radio programme called the Jack De Manio Show. BBC sound technicians vetted the tape and the tape recorder. They were baffled. They ruled out internal problems with the tape machinery by comparing that tape to others recorded during the filming sessions, and they decided that the sounds must have been inside the building rather than outside. The Jack de Manio programme played the recording for the benefit of its large audience complete with its unbelievably strange sounds. The show received a lot of feedback from listeners but the most unexpected thing was that many listeners reported that their pets had been driven mad when the recording was aired. Animals that were normally completely quiet and docile while their owners were listening to the radio suddenly began barking or hissing, became restless, and many left the room or even the house. In some way the animals seemed to be picking up sound or messages that humans could not hear even though the radio – in theory - only transmits sound within the range of human hearing (i.e. it does not transmit ultra- or infra-sound). So, how did the animals (and there is a huge number of similar reports available) pick up the sounds or feelings that disturbed them? We will be addressing the sound issue a bit later but it could be that the sounds recorded by the tape recorder were not 'normal' and that animals are better equipped to distinguish abnormal sounds than humans.

After a reporter had been dispatched to Bircham Newton from the Jack de Manio Show, the broadcasts created so much interest that the BBC decided that the next stage of the saga would be a séance. This was arranged to include two highly respected mediums. It was carried out in the right-hand squash court one evening. Both mediums agreed there was an extremely strange atmosphere and one began to pick up voices which were recorded during the séance (these can be found online). At one point a voice is heard saying the name of an airman who allegedly committed suicide at the base. But the most interesting element of the recording was the section in which the medium is supposed to have drawn out the voice of one of three dead airmen. The hissing voice asks for help, asks 'what can we do', and repeats the names of three men – Dusty Miller, Gerry Arnold, and Pat Sullivan.

Of all the tales told about Bircham Newton the noises, muffled voices, the RAF officer walking through a partition, people being forced down in their beds, and the apparition of the RAF person on the gallery of the squash court are all unspectacular and, for that very reason, carry considerable weight. The séance and second recording – of the hissing voice and the reference to Wiley – is not at all convincing. I can find no evidence of the airmen mentioned on the recording from the over 80,000 names listed in the official RAF losses database for World War Two. While this is not necessarily unusual and there may well have been such people who were killed at or near Bircham Newton it is equally the case that the medium could have known of the losses before the séance took place. As Harry Price would say – the most convincing evidence from a psychic is the evidence they could not possibly have known or been able to find out prior to the séance. None of what is contained on that second tape recording meets those criteria. But listen to both and decide for yourself[2].

Whatever you may think about the mediums who examined the squash courts, there remains a huge amount of testimony on the table which seems to validate the claim that Bircham Newton is haunted – that is, that it is subject to paranormal activity. No-one seems to have made any money out of the situation with the exception of the BBC. There are no books and not only does the CITB not arrange guided tours, it has discouraged all paranormal investigations since those of the Jack De Manio Show.

Other Airfields

Reports of similar paranormal activity on existing and former RAF bases are legion. Almost all of them mirror – to one extent or another – the events at Bircham Newton. At the former RAF Metheringham in Lincolnshire there are many accounts of a female ghost which is said to be that of Catherine Bystock who, aged 19, was due to be married to a Flight Sergeant at the base. Metheringham was only active for a little over three years from about 1943 to 1946. The story goes that Catherine and her fiancée were returning on his motorcycle from a dance when the bike skidded on the rainy road surface and they crashed. Tragically she was killed, having sustained terrible head injuries. Her apparition, still wearing WAAF (Women's Auxiliary Air Force) uniform, is said to flag down passing cars at about 9.30 pm on some rainy summer nights and then disappear. In some cases, the ghost is reported as asking the drivers to help her boyfriend who is injured. The spectre disappears quite quickly. The main common feature of reports being that the events begin with s strong smell of lavender and end, once the ghost disappears, with a terrible smell of putrid flesh.

At RAF Grove in Oxfordshire a ghostly figure wearing flying gear and an oxygen mask is sometimes seen, while at other airfields, locals report hearing singing and laughter emanating from buildings long since disused and abandoned. Another ex-RAF airbase – Thurleigh in Bedfordshire – is also haunted, possibly by Americans who died there[3].

Travel to almost any country in the world and you will be able to collect notebooks full of ghost tales from military and civilian airfields. In Australia the airfield at Archerfield claims the ghost of an airman who may have died in a bad accident to a military C-47 transport aircraft which killed twenty-three Australian and American service personnel in 1943. The USS Hornet, an ex-USN aircraft carrier, is berthed as a museum at Pier 3 at the former Naval Air Station of Alameda, California. The ship boasts a number of ghosts some of which have been reported well into the twenty-first century. And finally, one has to mention the island of Okinawa. This fifty-mile long Pacific island was fiercely defended by Imperial Japan during the allied invasion of 1945 – an invasion which involved over half a million personnel on the allied side alone – mainly US Army and Marine Corps – supported by naval forces from the UK, Australia, New Zealand, and Canada. In total around 160,000 people lost their lives in the fighting so it is no surprise that Okinawa is known today as one of the most haunted locations in the world.

Haunted Aircraft

The story of RAF Cosford's Avro Lincoln bomber is another of those paranormal stories that has almost everything. It has an admitted hoax, an alleged hoax, noises recorded on tape recorders, lights seen in the night, apparitions experienced in and around the aircraft, and even a very weird account of an accident being prevented by paranormal means. And all this is associated with an aircraft that saw very little in the way of combat operations and then only in the 1950s.

The four-engined Avro Lincoln in question - an upgrade of the famous Avro Lancaster of World War Two fame –was only produced towards the end of the war. The type was designed specifically for long-range bombing missions against Japan from Far East bases. The Lincoln was bigger, had more range, could fly higher, carried more load than the Lancaster, and possessed a more formidable defensive armament. But, by the time the Lincoln was in full production the war was almost over and this particular example – registration RF398 – did not even see squadron service until 1952.

Avro Lincoln RF398 at RAF Cosford. Wikimedia Commons; by Ducatipierre. https://commons.wikimedia.org/w/index.php?curid=126628030

It did, however, have an active service life and was not retired until the early 1960s when it was flown for the last time to RAF Cosford and placed into 'store' (a euphemism meaning 'left to deteriorate for a long time'). By the time of its final flight in April 1963 the bomber had completed 1,043 flying hours and 792 take-offs and landings.

The old aircraft mouldered for years but eventually a bunch of enthusiasts got permission to renovate it. They worked on it for even more years and, sometime around 1980, were informed that the Lincoln was going to be moved to a museum in Manchester. You can imagine how the group of restorers felt about having their beloved Lincoln taken away. They did not like the plan one little bit and, therefore, decided to invent a ghost. The objective of 'Pete the Poltergeist' was to keep the plane at Cosford and prevent its transfer to Manchester. The idea was that, if the Lincoln began to attract lots of visitors to Cosford, those in charge would not allow it to be moved. The hoaxers contacted the local press and told tales of parts being moved by themselves, of tools going missing and turning up in strange places, and of 'strange feelings'. In a way the hoax worked too well. The prank got out of hand as outsiders began to take it all very seriously. The newspapers loved the 'haunted' story and a local vicar even offered to exorcise the ghost. Nevertheless, the aircraft remained at Cosford and, eventually, a paranormal investigator from Chesterfield – a chap named Ivan Spenceley – began a longer-term investigation of the bomber. Officially he was part of a team from the Chesterfield paranormal society but he clearly took a leading role and was dedicated enough to visit the aircraft around two-dozen times over a four or five year period. He first set up a tape recorder in the wireless operator's position of the aircraft and then had the hangar evacuated. In Harry Price[4] style, he sealed all the external doors with signed strips of paper to prevent hoaxers from entering while the recorder was running. The next day the tape revealed strange banging and clicking noises. Spenceley spent many years investigating the paranormal qualities of Lincoln RF398. He evidently made several more recordings and made all the usual checks on ambient noise in the hanger and particularly of the hangar and the aircraft cooling down during the night.

Ongoing attempts to record ghostly activity were accompanied by sightings and feelings not only from staff of the museum but from members of the public. Airmen in old-fashioned service uniform were seen in the hangar, faces appeared in the (empty) observation dome and cockpit of the Lincoln, and feelings of 'unnatural' chill in the aircraft itself were reported. In the mid-1980s a TV cameraman who was working on a general entertainment programme called 'Wish You Were Here', featuring the museum and its attractions, said that he saw a 'pilot' in the cockpit when no-one was in the aircraft.

Media interest in the story continued and BBC Radio 4 produced a documentary called *'Strange Stories: The Haunting of RF398'* which they aired on February 16th 1991. It used many of the recordings made by Spenceley but the sound engineers for the BBC also separately recorded some weird sounds in the aircraft. The museum probably felt that it was gaining a degree of unwanted notoriety from all the ghost stories and, after the BBC programme, in a similar way to the CITB at Bircham Newton, it withdrew permission for outsiders to investigate the aircraft. There are odd stories from recent years, however, that seem to indicate that the paranormal activity has not ceased.

Quite a few accounts online refer to someone called 'Master Pilot Hiller' who is supposed to have been killed near Cosford in an air crash sometime after the Lincoln was stored there (i.e. after 1963). The tale hangs on his 'love' for the Lincoln and an allegedly stated wish to haunt the aircraft. On lists of RAF crashes there is no record of one occurring near Cosford in the mid- to late-1960s but, as is typical with such claims, there is also no detail as to Hiller's full name, the date of his death, or any corroboration of his alleged desire to haunt the Avro Lincoln. The only aspect of the story which lends it a degree of credibility is the 'Master Pilot' rank. If someone today were to make up a story about a dead pilot they would almost certainly give an RAF officer's rank – Pilot Officer, Flying Officer, Flight Lieutenant, and so on – because all RAF pilots today are commissioned officers. Most people know that there were Sergeant Pilots during the last war but very, very few would know that the RAF also had a rank of 'Master Pilot'. This was warrant officer level –

between the Sergeants and the Officers. This lends the account a small degree of credibility.

Perhaps the most compelling evidence for paranormal effects in RF398 comes from a BBC radio producer, Gwyn Richards, who sat with Spenceley in RF-398 two nights in a row during the 1991 investigation. He says that he personally heard strange sounds and that, during one long night, he also saw a light coming towards the pair from the rear-gunner's position. The light wavered from side to side as it apparently approached the pair and then it disappeared. It was only much later that they were told by ex-Lincoln crew that it was the crew's habit to reverse the light reflector in their torches so that it sat in front of the bulb and not behind it. This meant that only a small pinprick of light emerged to help them find their way along the fuselage. The object was to create as little light as possible in order to maintain the pilots' night vision (a bright torch being shone in the rear of the aircraft would reflect off the windscreens and effectively blind the two pilots for a few minutes). Richards said that the light they saw was exactly like one of these doctored torches coming towards them from the rear of the aircraft. The swaying from side to side, he said, was just as though it was being carried by a person walking towards the cockpit.

Following this experience, Richards invited a group of ex-Lincoln aircrew to visit the museum, to listen to the recorded sounds, and try to identify them. There were the bangs and clicks that had been recorded by Spenceley in his very first and subsequent recording sessions, as well as the separately obtained BBC recordings. On the latter, in addition to bangs and clicks, there was also a strange whining sound that did not appear on any of Spenceley's tapes. Phil Pritchett, Gareth Lewis, and Peter Palma – the ex-Lincoln pilots and aircrew – identified the clicks and bangs as being uncannily like the sounds made by a crew as they readied the aircraft for flight. Switching on electrical gear, clicking rotary switches, and the bangs of mechanical linkages to things like flaps being opened. The whining sound – one that the BBC had confidently expected to be entirely discounted as a spurious external noise – shocked the three ex-aircrew. They recognised it at once as being a 'Consol' navigation system. One of the older navigation systems on RAF aircraft, Consol was based on the wartime German system 'Sonne'. It went out of use by the RAF after the mid-1950s. If anyone had wanted to fake a sound from the Avro Lincoln in the early 1990s how would they have gotten hold of a recording of the Consol operating sounds and why fake just that instrument – why not much easier sounds to obtain like the sound of engines starting up, or the muffled intercom chatter between the crew?

Another, uncorroborated but interesting, story concerns an electrician who was working on the outside of the aircraft some fifteen feet above the floor of the hangar. The man had already hurt his back quite badly in a previous fall from height, and on this particular day he fell again. As he lost his footing and began to fall he remembered thinking 'This is it' – meaning that he had already damaged his back and that this fall would probably kill him. Instead, he claims that he just floated to a gentle stop on the concrete floor as if some invisible force had prevented the accident from being fatal.

There has been some doubt cast on Spenceley's recordings over the four years he spent investigating the aircraft but there are two reasons for dismissing such doubts. Firstly, his results have been duplicated on several occasions by BBC radio and film crews, and secondly, the case for paranormal activity in and around that aircraft does not rely solely on what Spenceley recorded. The YouTube video is definitely worth watching[5].

Paranormal activity at RAF airfields and aircraft has to be subject to the same scrutiny and scepticism as similar stories from hotels, pubs, castles, and such like but the lack of commercial motives should give us all pause for thought. At Bircham Newton construction trainees and a journalist testify to the weird experience of being physically restrained in their beds. At Cosford an electrician's fall was mitigated by physical force. In both locations apparitions of apparently historic

RAF personnel have been reported and, in both, BBC sound crews recorded strange noises. At Borley Rectory doors were locked and bells were rung without human involvement. At the Skinwalker Ranch in Utah groceries were removed from cupboards and equipment was lost and subsequently found halfway up trees. The ability of paranormal forces to move objects and to physically affect them is well recorded but these few examples really bring home their credibility.

These forces can influence the physical realm in weird ways and hundreds of people in all the locations can testify to having seen things that were not there. Those human trainees, sound technicians, visitors, and museum staff say they saw people and faces that could not have been where they appeared. A few walked through walls or disappeared while the witnesses were watching them. The human ability to feel and perceive the paranormal is heavily supported by these instances.

Humans can not only see ghosts, they can sense their presence and feel them, too. The next question, I guess, is: can cameras record 'ghosts'?

CHAPTER 4
PHOTOGRAPHS 1

> *Extraordinary claims require extraordinary evidence.*
>
> — CARL SAGAN

Thousands of photos of alleged ghosts now adorn hundreds of websites on the Internet. Based on a simple search you can find all sorts of visual evidence ranging from what appears to be wispy smoke and pictures of globes of light which could be anything, to more or less faint images of human beings and some intriguing snaps of apparently human forms which look reasonably solid. A few are of anomalies in photos which are unlikely to be mistakes or double exposures. The famous 1900 portrait of 'Irish Linen Girls' is a case in point. It is now a Getty Image which can be found on the Internet very easily. The century-old photo reveals a hand resting on the shoulder of a girl to the right of the photo. The hand cannot belong to anyone in the group.

A century later there is the famous and highly mysterious 2003 security camera photo from Hampton Court Palace near London. The picture seems to show a robed person looking out of an open fire exit. The security staff – who recorded the anomalous activity on three consecutive days in 2003, gave it the nickname 'the Skeleton'. It appeared for only one of those days, but the door was mysterious flung open on the day before and the day after. Incredibly, the physical activity of the doors being flung open and the appearance of the mysterious figure were never experienced again. On the first day, palace security staff were ordered to close one particular fire door near the palace's 'Introductory Exhibition' because CCTV footage had shown the doors flying open with great force. But they saw and found nothing to reveal why this had happened. On the second day, the door did the same thing and the cameras recorded a strange figure in a long cloak standing in the open doorway. The figure closed the doors. On the third day the doors opened again but this time there was no ghostly apparition and they stayed open until the security people closed them. The story is particularly intriguing because the events were so weird and so short-lived. A prankster might have opened the door, but one has to doubt that they would have been able to resist the temptation of revealing their ghostly apparition on each of the three days. Instead, we have the door being flung open on three days but only on one of them did a 'ghost' show itself (and then it politely closed the door).

Here, I want to present five highly credible photos from the early to the late twentieth century. All are compelling and all have been accused of being double exposures. It is a very easy allegation but it can sometimes succumb to logic and science. Photographic hoaxes have been around ever since the camera was invented but just because things *can* be faked does not mean that all unexplained photographic incidents are fake. In 1917 two young ladies faked pictures of themselves with 'fairies'. The apparitions were cardboard cut-outs but they fooled a lot of people for getting on for sixty years.

If you want to check out some of the more interesting ghost photos from the USA and the UK visit the 'Ghosts n' Ghouls' website[1]. Some of the pictures are not credible but others certainly are. One should not automatically dismiss ghost photos from locations and institutions that will benefit financially by having a ghost associated with them, but it is probably wise to examine them more critically. Having said that, a lot of the photos are not from such institutions and one struggles to fathom why the photographers would fake them. What follow are five very credible ghost photos.

The Brown Lady

One of the most famous passive ghosts in the UK is called the Brown Lady. In September of 1936, at Raynham Hall in England, Captain Hubert C. Provand and his colleague Indra Shira took a photo of a stairway. The pair had been commissioned by Country Life magazine to compile a visual audit of the best features of the house. Shira said later:

> *Captain Provand took one photograph while I flashed the light. He was focusing for another exposure; I was standing by his side just behind the camera with the flashlight pistol in my hand, looking directly up the staircase. All at once I detected an ethereal veiled form coming slowly down the stairs. Rather excitedly, I called out sharply: 'Quick, quick, there's something.' I pressed the trigger of the flashlight pistol. After the flash and on closing the shutter, Captain Provand removed the focusing cloth from his head and turning to me said: 'What's all the excitement about?'*

Looking through the lens, Captain Provand had not noticed anything amiss on the stairway, but that innocent photograph of an architectural feature somehow captured the indistinct image of a female form apparently descending the stairs. It was published in the December 16th, 1936 issue of Country Life magazine.

That was when the mass-excitement about the ghost began, but the so-called Brown Lady had been seen many times before Provand took his photograph. Nevertheless, sceptics still claim that the photo was faked. The ghost had been seen and reported by household staff and guests during the early nineteenth century – well before Captain Provand's encounter. It is alleged that the then Prince Regent who was to become George IV saw the ghost in his bedroom while staying at the Hall. The tale is that he left the next day and refused ever to return to the house. In spite of these alleged sightings, the fact that the house acquired a 'haunted' reputation was directly due to the Brown Lady being seen by another highly credible witness.

A century before Provand's photograph, in 1836, a regular house guest was Captain Frederick Marryat (RN), the famous Royal Navy officer and author[2]. He had a violent encounter with the ghost. Being a very practical and intelligent person, Marryat was highly sceptical about ghosts and he readily agreed to sleep in a room which was reputed to be the most haunted bedroom in the house. Nothing happened for the first two nights of his stay but on the third night, he was returning towards the bedrooms with two fellow guests.

The famous photo of the Brown Lady at Raynham Hall; LIFE Magazine. 4 January, 1937. Public Domain, Wikimedia Commons. https://commons.wikimedia.org/w/index.php?curid=57863579

On reaching the upstairs corridor they encountered the ghost of the Brown Lady coming towards them. Marryat was so amazed and affronted that he reacted by firing his pistol at her. He was adamant that he shot her in the face, whereupon she vanished. That was in 1836 and Provand took his photograph almost exactly one hundred years later in 1936. As with all such old-time photos the evidence trail has long since been irremediably damaged. The negative is of uncertain provenance and the original examinations of the original negative have been questioned (probably unfairly) by modern sceptics. The result is that we'll never know for sure whether it was a fake or not. But we must remember that accusing something of being fake is very easy. Proof is rarely as simple. The evidence of Provand's character, the existence of another witness who, unlike Provand, actually saw something on the stairs, and his and Shira's detailed story seem highly credible. On top of that there are many previous witnesses of the ghost of the Brown Lady, she had been sighted on many occasions by staff, one of the witnesses may have been the Prince Regent and another was the eminent, and highly sceptical Captain Marryat, RN.

The ghost of the Brown Lady has been seen by many people over the past two centuries and by at least two supremely credible witnesses (plus the Prince Regent). Marryat was so shocked that he actually fired his pistol at the ghost. The Prince Regent could be perhaps seen as a questionable witness but a man with Marryat's fighting background – he'd been in action many times – could not have been easy to spook or panic. There is little doubt that he must have seen something very much out of the ordinary for him to discharge a pistol inside a house in which he was a guest.

The other credible witnesses – Provand and Shira – took a photo of the Brown Lady when they were really trying to get a shot of the stairway for a commercial assignment – an object that was thought of by Country Life as a notable example of the architect's work. Can we really throw all this circumstantial evidence out just because a few sceptics think that ghosts are impossible and that any and all evidence of them is faked?

The Queen's House Ghost

In 1966 a retired Canadian clergyman, the Reverend Ralph Hardy, was on a tour of England and, like millions before and after him, he visited what is now the National Maritime Museum at Greenwich. The site has a lengthy history. The first stately house was built there in the fifteenth century. Eventually a grand royal residence called the Palace of Placentia was erected. The first Queen Mary and the first Queen Elizabeth were born there. Over the years Greenwich has seen a palace built and demolished, a tower or fort built and demolished, and several magnificent buildings constructed and thankfully not demolished. Among these are the Royal Observatory, the old Royal Naval College, and the so-called Queen's House. Built in the early seventeenth century, originally for Anne of Denmark, James I's queen, it was designed by Inigo Jones. The building was completed many years later for Charles I's wife - Queen Henrietta Maria – so it should really be called the Queens' House.

The 'Tulip Staircase' at the Queen's House, Greenwich by Poliphilo. https://commons.wikimedia.org/w/index.php?curid=53159556

The Queen's House is nothing short of magnificent – a classical masterpiece with an unrivalled vista down to the River Thames. But one of the most stunning elements in the house is a helical staircase called the Tulip Stairs. Jones designed a circular staircase with totally unsupported (cantilevered) treads spiralling upwards to a beautiful circular lantern roof at the top. Any lover of architecture, indeed, any lover of intrinsically beautiful things, would travel a long way to see it. You can get a good idea of it from the picture displayed on the Royal Museums website[3].

And that is exactly what the good Reverend wanted to see in that year of the Beatles *Revolver* album and of England's only success in the World Cup. There is no record of what else Hardy did during his visit to Greenwich, but he certainly took several snaps of the Tulip Staircase. When those photos were developed one of them was found to show an apparently hooded figure (or perhaps two figures) climbing the stairs with what look to be both hands holding onto the rail. The photo was examined by photographic experts from Kodak who concluded that it had not been faked in any way.

The Reverend Hardy's photo is now available to examine online on many websites[4]. If you check it out I think you will agree that the second hand which seems to grip the wrought-iron railing highest up may actually be too far forward to be one of those belonging to the main figure. There is also the strong possibility that it is of a left hand (note the apparent thumb position). This is a highly credible photograph. It was taken by a clergyman who was on holiday with his wife, who did not see anything at all until the photo was developed and returned to him. His wife was present at the time and swore that there was no-one on the stairs. In fact, there could not have been any people on those steps because they had been closed off to visitors. Rev. Hardy had been a bit put-out because he had wanted to get a shot from the top of the stairs but could not because of the closure.

The figures look very much like monks but the Queen's House was not completed until well into the seventeenth century, after the last Franciscan friars had been cast out by Queen Elizabeth I. There is the possibility that the hooded figures might be the 'ghosts' of Catholic priests smuggled into the house during the latter years of the reign of Charles I. It was widely rumoured during those years that the King, his Queen, and many of their courtiers, clung onto their Catholic faith and, although illegal, it was very common for Catholic households to hold private and very secret Masses.

Mabel's Mum

The story of Mabel's mother is another of those 'high strangeness' events that happen to ordinary people on perfectly ordinary occasions. At the beginning of Spring 1959 – on March 22nd to be precise – a married couple, Mr. and Mrs Chinnery, travelled to a cemetery in Ipswich, England to visit the grave of the wife's mother – Mrs Ellen Hammell. The couple went in their car and the husband waited in the driving seat while his wife, Mabel, paid her respects and placed flowers on the grave. Mabel wanted some photos of the grave so she snapped a few shots and was returning to the car when she took an impromptu photograph of her husband patiently waiting in the vehicle.

As with many such photos it wasn't until the roll returned from the chemists after being developed and printed that Mrs Chinnery noticed something weird. In the back seat of the car was a figure that looked exactly like her mother. The apparition was sitting in the place Mrs Hammell normally occupied when they took her for a drive, dressed in a dark coat with a white scarf and wearing spectacles identical to those her mother wore when alive. The April 19th 1959 edition of the Sunday Pictorial published the mysterious photo and one has to imagine that they paid the Chinnerys for the privilege. I have checked the relevant edition and the photo is certainly there, along with a short article asking readers to try to explain things. The American media also picked up the story in the weeks that followed.

Today, the photo appears in a number of places but the reader might care to look at the one on the Getty Images site when thinking about the theories discussed below[5]. In 1985 the BBC ran an edition of *Arthur C Clarke's World of Strange Powers* in which the photo was presented to two photographic experts. They both came to the conclusion that it was probably an accidental double exposure. They pointed to what they argued was a slight overlap between the apparition's white scarf and the frame of the driver's window and the presence of a strange board or item sticking up to the left of the doorframe as one looks at the picture. Several people have since suggested that this could have been the chair in which the lady was sitting when the original photo was taken.

The negatives were examined by the Sunday Pictorial's photographers and also by a local Ipswich photographer. Both said that it showed no signs of double-exposure or having been tampered-with. While the scarf does appear to overlap very slightly with the frame one has to bear in mind that there was obviously more of that scarf around the apparition's neck and that the additional white scarf did *not* overlap the frame. The door frame is dark enough at that point for all of the light-coloured scarf to overlap the door if someone had tried a double exposure.

The other problem with the double-exposure theory is the sheer difficulty of getting the positioning right. Remember, this was a 1950s hand-held consumer camera. The roll probably had eight or twelve shots at most. Even if a way could be found around the doorframe problem it would have been virtually impossible to get the apparition sitting in precisely the right place and distance, and at the right angle, and with the glasses correctly lit, and with the daylight illuminating the correct side of the face for the first shot without getting any other light-coloured items in the way. Just assuming for the moment that the original photo had been of Mrs Hammell sitting in a chair and that, miraculously, the photographer was at precisely the right distance and angle and height from the subject, why was she sitting in the dark? The lady would have had to be in complete darkness apart from her upper torso, otherwise other lighter items in that accidental first shot would have appeared through the darker parts of the later one. I have to say that it would be a little unusual to take a photo of someone sitting in a chair from twenty feet away.

If it had been faked, the original shot would have had to be masked very carefully to exclude any such lighter items that might overwrite the darker elements of the car. And finally, the second shot – of her husband – would have required *pinpoint* positioning in terms of angles and heights so that it precisely overwrote the first photo and positioned the lady in exactly the right position. I'm guessing that even top professionals with the correct studio set ups and very accurately levelling and positioning instruments would have found it extremely difficult to pull this off. Mrs Chinnery probably had a handheld Brownie camera.

Finally, there is also the fact that the shot in question was the last on the reel of film. Mrs Chinnery had taken almost the whole reel of her mother's grave (most amateur films in those days were either eight or twelve shots only). So how did that final frame on the reel get overwritten with a previous photo without exposing any of the other earlier frames? Why would Mrs Chinnery wind the roll forwards all the way to the last shot to attempt the double exposure? Why wouldn't she have made the first shot on the reel the double exposure? Making it the last one risked all sorts of dangers from subsequently having to rewind unexposed film.

If like the author you have ever had to cope with an old roll-film camera you will know that attempting to take a shot on a later part of the roll and then trying to rewind the film to then take the earlier shots was next to impossible. Those cameras simply did not mechanically allow one to rewind until the last shot had been taken. The problem was not really the rewinding, it was trying to rewind to exactly the right place so that all the shots were in precisely the right place for the final shot. Sorry, but I do not accept the double exposure explanation. And that leaves us with a serious anomaly.

Viscount Combermere

Did the ghost of Lord Combermere (pronounced Cumbermeer) appear briefly in a comfortable chair in the library of his family home on the day of his funeral one hundred and thirty odd years ago? There is a photograph which suggests that he did. The photo, which is easily located on about a million websites (including the modern website of Combermere Abbey)[6], was taken on the day of his funeral by an amateur photographer – a lady named Sybell Corbet.

Combermere (whose full title was Colonel Wellington Henry Stapleton-Cotton, 2nd Viscount Combermere - 24 Nov 1818 – 1 Dec 1891) was an experienced soldier and politician who had had a successful career and who was still active. He spent most of his time in London and it was there that he suffered a tragic accident. Stepping out into the roadway one morning he was badly injured in a nasty encounter with a carriage or cab. In the course of his misadventure, Combermere's legs were badly crushed but not so badly that they needed to be amputated. The accident must have occurred sometime in October or early November 1891 judging by the timeframe. He was clearly a strong septuagenarian because he was cared for at his London home and was recuperating nicely from his painful injuries. The doctors were evidently very pleased with his progress.

Sybell Corbet's famous photo of the apparition in the chair at Combermere Abbey in December 1891. https://www. combermereabbey.co.uk/history-restoration/ghosts-the-paranormal/ Public Domain, https://commons.wikimedia.org/w/index.php?curid=56141058

The Viscount gave every appearance of being well on the road to recovery when, on December 1st, he suddenly died. It seemed that a clot had formed in his injured legs. It had taken a while, as these things do, but the clot had eventually broken loose into the bloodstream and caused a fatal coronary thrombosis. He died from a massive heart attack brought about by that relatively small clump of clotted blood. Today, doctors know the dangers of such processes and give blood-thinning drugs to patients recovering from accidents. A regular, small dose of aspirin would possibly have saved his life – but that wonder drug did not hit the market until 1899.

Combermere's body was subsequently carried by rail back to Cheshire where he was buried on December 5th 1891 at his family's traditional church of St Margaret's in Wrenbury. At that time Wrenbury was a stop on the Crewe to Whitchurch branch of the London and North-West Railway (it is still a station on the same line except that it has lost its twin sidings). His coffin probably travelled from Euston Station in London via Birmingham and Crewe and from thence to the Victorian station at Wrenbury. Once unloaded at the little station the coffin would have been taken by horse-drawn hearse on the one-mile journey to the church.

At this point it is worth stating that Combermere rarely lived at his home at the Abbey. He spent most of his time in London. Combermere Abbey was rented out in relatively short-term contracts. I will return to this issue shortly. On that particular day Ms Corbet took her expensive camera and tripod and set them up for a long-exposure shot of the library. Why she did this is unclear but it was probably because it represented a photographic challenge and because the room was a very attractive one. She checked the equipment, framed and established the shot, opened the camera's shutter and then went for a short walk with some of her fellow guests. It was a long exposure!

When she got back she developed the plate, and immediately saw a diaphanous figure apparently sitting in a chair opposite the camera. Ms Corbett printed a positive photo and showed it around. Some of the Abbey's staff said that it was the Viscount but that fact is not certain. To the neutral observer though it does look very like the elderly gentlemen. The sceptics argue that the photo was simply an accidental incursion on the lengthy exposure by one of the three men who were then present in the house. The Society for Psychical Research did some investigating and none other than Professor Sir William Barrett attempted to recreate the shot as a double exposure. By asking a volunteer to sit in a chair and to keep shifting his legs Barrett produced a shot that was very similar to Sybell Corbet's one. It was therefore agreed that someone could have entered the room during the long exposure, sat themselves briefly in that chair, and then left – perhaps as soon as they realised the camera was facing them.

It's an entirely plausible scenario but there are a couple of problems. The 'ghost' appears to be a balding, bearded man wearing a white shirt. Sybell Corbet was not an idiot – she checked, and none of the men in the house at the time came even close to being able to match that description. Some websites claim that there was no-one in the house when the photo was taken but that is not the case. Many of the same websites also ask, their eyebrows raised in mock horror, why the lady in question was not at the funeral. After all, the Wikipedia article on the affair says that she was the sister of Viscount Combermere's wife. So why was she not at the funeral?[7].

It is a perfectly reasonable question. If Sybell really was Lady Combermere's sister she would certainly have been at her sister's side at the funeral instead of taking photographs and going for casual walks four miles away. The answer is that the Wikipedia article is wrong (everything needs to be checked even if – especially if – it appears on Wikipedia). Sybell Corbet certainly knew the Combermeres but she was not related to them. She was definitely not the sister of Viscount Combermere's wife. She was half her age and, anyway, was not related to her - even distantly.

Sybell was the sister of the lady whose husband had rented the estate for the hunting season in 1891. Lady Constance Sutton (neé Corbet) was eight years younger than her sister Sybell but was then already a widow. She'd married one of the richest men in England only three years previously and had delivered him of a son – also named Richard – seven months previously. But in February of 1891 Sir Richard Sutton died tragically of peritonitis. Lady Constance decided to honour her husband's lease on Combermere Abbey. She did not want to hunt but felt that the peace and quiet of the country would help her grieve. That was why her elder sister was there and why none of them had attended the funeral of Viscount Combermere. They knew the Viscount, of course, but were not close enough in family or friendship terms to be invited to the funeral. None of the Combermere family was in residence at the Abbey, either.

Sybell Corbet was a keen photographer and she had good equipment but, with 1890s cameras and photographic plates, the exposure, in a relatively dark room, could be between thirty minutes and an hour long. So, it was normal practice with such lengthy exposures for the photographer to leave the camera and do something else. In this case, the lady along with others, went out for a walk while the camera did its stuff. They left in the house two young men and the butler. Sybell Corbet was adamant that none of them looked in the least like the deceased Combermere or the 'ghost' in the shot. Incidentally, before you ask, the butler was not at the funeral because he was employed by Lady Constance not by the Viscount. It was the accepted practice for the people who rented the estate to bring their own senior servants.

Personally, I lean heavily towards the photo being genuine. In principle it could easily be some sort of accidental incursion on the exposure but, quite apart from the fact that there was no-one in the house at that time who looked like the apparition in the chair, there are a few other notable points to consider. Take a look, for example, at the right arm. It is extremely clear, with very little blurring, and is as solid and well-lit as the furniture in the room. It must have been held very still for a long period of time in that exposure. However, if it had been an incursion, the rest of the body must have been moving constantly and was certainly not in the same place for long. But I ask you to try keeping one's head, one shoulder, and one's right arm perfectly still for perhaps ten or fifteen minutes (to achieve a relatively solid appearance) while, at the same time, moving the rest of your body around – particularly your legs and the other shoulder and arm. Furthermore, the critics propose that the reason the legs do not appear is that *'they were moving constantly and that the very light coloured seat wiped them out in the longer exposure that must have followed the person leaving the chair'*. Okay, but in that case why wasn't the right arm made considerably less 'solid' against the arm of the chair which was in bright sunlight? Once the person moved away from that brightly lit chair-arm the sun would have over-written the apparition's right arm.

The critics cannot have it both ways. If one part of the body is going to be 'wiped' by bright areas recorded by the camera over a period after the mysterious third-party moved on, why did that right arm not fade also? Why do dark areas on the floor and at the bottom of the chair not retain blurs of lighter-coloured legs and shoes?

If you examine the figure carefully you can see that it looks as though it is sitting more *within* the back of the chair than on the seat. Part of the body is in the right place, but the figure's left-hand side appears to be actually part of the back of the chair. It just does not look far enough forward to be a person caught for a few minutes sitting in the chair. Why, also do we not see a blurry white left-hand and shirt cuff against the darker arm of the chair? Where are they?

Miss Corbet was adamant that none of the men who were in the house at the time looked anything like the figure that appeared in her photograph. She made no financial gain from the photo and – in those days – no payment was forthcoming from any newspaper for such a story. As a well-off young lady, she did not need any additional income anyway and there's also the morality aspect. Her critics effectively propose that she perpetrated a fraudulent photograph at a time when the deceased was not yet in his grave, when the family were still in the earliest stages of mourning, and when her own sister was grieving for a lost young husband. I simply cannot imagine that someone in Sybell Corbet's position would have played such a nasty trick.

The photos of the Brown Lady and Lord Combermere were taken under circumstances which virtually negate any chance of fraud. They were taken by people with no motive for fakery and each picture had its own set of highly compelling reasons for believing it to be authentic. In the case of the Brown Lady it was the span of time over which the ghost had been reported, the number of times a similar apparition had been reported by unconnected people, the unquestionable character of Captain Marryat, and a total lack of motivation on the part of the photographer. Where Viscount Combermere is concerned we have circumstantial evidence of the photo's legitimacy together with sincere reasons for believing that Ms Corbett was completely honest[8]. What are we left with but two pictures whose content we simply cannot explain in conventional terms; two images that lead us nowhere but to paranormal realms[9].

CHAPTER 5
PHOTOGRAPHS 2

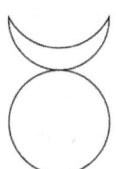

 ... the serious study of the impossible has frequently opened up rich and unexpected domains of science.

— MICHIO KAKU; THE PHYSICS OF THE
IMPOSSIBLE; DOUBLEDAY; 2008

Bobby Capel's Ghost

The pictures of the Brown Lady and of Lord Combermere are both highly persuasive as to the existence of anomalous phenomena that appear as insubstantial human beings, but there are many more such examples. It only takes a single one of these photos to be totally inexplicable by the known laws of optics, physics, and psychology for the reality of the paranormal to be proven.

The saying is that the 'camera cannot lie' but we all know that it most certainly can. There are many ghost photos but most are faked, or tricks of the light, or of vision. But, as I have said many times with respect to the UFO/UAP phenomenon, even if 99.9% are false, that still leaves one in every thousand that is not. And if that one incident actually happened or if one can be sure of it within the bounds of reasonable doubt, it proves that there is a paranormal phenomenon that can be perceived by humans and recorded by a camera (or, in more modern terms, a sensor).

The pictures taken of the Brown Lady and the apparition which might be Lord Combermere are certainly among the top candidates qualifying for the 'one in a thousand' group. Another is a very strange photograph from the year 1919. The case is known, erroneously, on the Internet and in many books as 'Goddard's Squadron'. There are accounts on scores of websites and in most of them the details are wrong[1].

The name Goddard refers to an RAF officer who was closely associated with the case – Air Marshall Sir Robert Victor Goddard. But there are a number of issues with the facts of the case as they are currently portrayed on the web and in many books and articles. Not only was Sir Victor Goddard not involved in the photo, it was not his squadron, and he was not there when it was taken. It is, also, not a photo of a squadron but of part of a squadron, and it was certainly not his squadron. The owner of the picture, who appears on the photo and who was the person who did their best to solve its mystery was a lady named Roberta ('Bobby') Capel.

On the surface it is the fairly standard story of a tragic death and the deceased supposedly appearing in a later photograph – similar to Lord Combermere. The tale is one of the internet's favourites but few of the people who copy photos and text from other sites and retail them on their own have ever really looked into the matter (with the exception of a few sceptics who have done a bit of homework).

And it is a case that definitely demands homework because it happened more than a century ago and many inaccuracies and misunderstandings have crept into the narrative over the years. These concern such important things as who was there at the time of the photo, where it was taken, what group of people were being photographed, and whether the alleged ghost ever existed as a person.

The setting for the famous photo was an RAF air base which, until the Spring of 1918, had been a Royal Naval Air Service (RNAS) airfield. The job of the squadron that was based there was training – mainly for airships but also some fixed wing training. Like all such squadrons it had a maintenance group whose role was to keep the airships and aircraft maintained, repaired, fuelled, and flying. The maintenance group in question tended to the engines, repaired the fabric of airships and aircraft, looked after the hydrogen gas that was stored to fill the envelopes of the airships, stored the petroleum to power the airships and fixed-wing aircraft, and performed the myriad other tasks that were necessary to keep those fragile early aircraft in the air.

Where the photo was taken is also a subject of confusion on the websites that repeat this tale. Many still claim the photo was taken somewhere on the south coast of England (due to a connection with the Royal Naval Air Service and a ship called HMS Daedalus which we will come to in a minute). The actual site of the photograph however was RAF Cranwell in Lincolnshire. Cranwell remains an RAF officer training base to this day. In 1918 it was in the process of switching from the control of the RNAS to the Royal Air Force (which had been formed in April 1918 by combining the Royal Flying Corps – RFC – and the Royal Naval Air Service). The First World War officially ended in November 1918 and the British government lost no time in demobilising almost all its large and incredibly expensive armed forces. Subsequently, the Cranwell base restructured and, in the process, demobilised a high proportion of its people. Getting conscripted personnel off the payroll as fast as possible was an urgent task.

A few in the Maintenance Group were offered positions in the new RAF or continued with roles in their own services – the Army or the Navy – but the majority were on their way back to civvy street. In early 1919, therefore, the Maintenance Group arranged, through a famous London photographic agency, to take a group-photo of its members before almost all of them scattered to different parts of the armed services or to civilian life.

On the appointed day the photographers, having arranged some staging and set up their heavy camera, dutifully took the group photo

– in all probability several of them just in case. Within a week or so the best of the prints had been sent back to Cranwell where it was displayed on the noticeboard. Under it was pinned a piece of paper for people to sign their names if they wanted to buy a copy for themselves. When people began to take a good look at the print, however, they noticed a ghostly face staring out from behind one member of the maintenance group who was standing in the upper back row. According to a later written account, the ghostly image belonged to a chap called Freddie Jackson who had recently been killed in an accident on the tarmac at Cranwell. He is said to have suffered an all-too-common fate in those days – that of mistakenly walking into a spinning propellor.

And that's it. A multitude of websites reprint the photo as it appears below and they variously place the incident at Lee-on-Solent in Hampshire, or Cranwell in Lincolnshire. To make matters even more confusing some even say that the group was actually the crew of a ship named HMS Daedalus.

The version of the photo that was probably created by the Navy News. It shows part of the full photo with the relevant section enlarged. Bobby Capel is second row up on the far left. Wikimedia Commons. https://commons.wikimedia.org/w/index.php?curid=28433287

So, first of all, let's put the background record as straight as possible. During World War I the names of bases changed frequently and, to complicate matters, the Royal Navy also had a policy of using old static hulks as the formal homes of servicemen and women who were not serving on Royal Navy vessels but were based elsewhere on land. It was, and is, a convenient method of 'grouping' personnel for payroll and admin purposes who were not directly attached to one of the RN's active ships. You might be a Sub-Lieutenant assigned to work in the Admiralty in London but for pay and rostering purposes you were actually a member of the ship's company of 'HMS Pinafore' (or whatever).

At that time HMS Daedalus was a very old warship seeing out the last of her days moored in the River Medway in Kent. The hulk was the nominal headquarters for training elements of the Royal Navy. Personnel were on the books of HMS Daedalus for pay and other purposes but they could be working in very different places around the country (or abroad) most of which were not ships. Many of the personnel in the photo were on the books of HMS Daedalus even though they were working on an airfield in the middle of Lincolnshire, and that fact has led many to believe that the photo is of that ship's company. But it is not. As the photo shows, Cranwell's maintenance group contained people from virtually every service of the UK armed forces: Royal Navy, Royal Naval Air Service (RNAS), Army, Women's Royal Navy Service (WRNS), Women's Auxiliary Air Force (WAAF), some wearing older Royal Flying Corps uniform, and a few wearing what was probably the new RAF uniform with the new insignia of rank.

When Cranwell was established as an RNAS training school in 1915 it was used mainly for airship training. It had two large airship sheds, a hydrogen plant, and several gas tanks to store the hydrogen before it was used to fill the envelopes of the base's airships. It is impossible to say when it started to also train fixed-wing pilots but that was possibly around 1917 or 1918. In the latter year the whole station was renamed the Central Training School for the newly-formed Royal Air Force, which it remains to this day as RAF College Cranwell[2]. The last airship departed the base in 1921.

In 1918 Cranwell was the Headquarters for No.12 Group and on November 1st 1919 it became the RAF (Cadet) College, the dream-child of Air Marshal Sir Hugh Trenchard. The period during which the photo was taken was, therefore, a triple interregnum – firstly between war and peace, secondly between temporary wartime-only personnel and permanent staff, and thirdly between the RNAS and the RAF.

The people shown in the photo were '12 Squadron Maintenance Group', working out their last few weeks in the forces on an RAF airbase. Some of them may already have been transferred to the RAF but most of the people in the photo appear to be Royal Navy, Army, or Royal Naval Air Service staff. The vast majority were going to be demobilised whether they wanted to stay or not. Until demobilisation, therefore, most of the characters looking out so thoughtfully at the massive camera apparatus were still people on Army, RAF, or Royal Navy books. For modern readers it is more accurate to call it the Cranwell Maintenance Group Photo, 1919.

The case centres on that single, intriguing photographic print which lay unknown and unremarked (at least in public) for getting on for half a century between the 1920s and the 1970s. The print of the photo may have been purchased by upwards of a hundred people but only one copy ever became famous - the copy first introduced to the public in 1975 by Air Marshall Sir Robert Victor Goddard, then retired after an illustrious and very eventful career in the RAF. He described the event in his book *'Flight Towards Reality'* (published 1975) which recounted his long-held views on, and experiences in, the field of the paranormal[3]. He was a distinguished Air Marshall in the RAF (three-star rank) but was also a lifelong researcher into paranormal activity and was possibly personally attuned to such activity for he had had several encounters with the paranormal during his life. As one would expect of such a senior military officer, Goddard was an astute and logical thinker. His considered views and conclusions on the paranormal and UFOs might be debatable, but they were based on a lifetime of scholarly research. His thinking was clear, and his honesty unquestionable.

Goddard's career began in the Royal Navy before World War One. He served in several battleships and specialised in the use of airships at sea. In those years he was a major player in the UK's development of airships (which was far behind that of Germany). We are incredibly fortunate that the historians of the Imperial War Museum have amassed an audio archive of detailed interviews with a great many serving members of the armed forces. Those interviews are now available online for almost anyone to access. In Goddard's 1970s interview with the Imperial War Museum he said that he had been invited to become the Captain of the famous R-101 airship but that he turned down the offer to focus on his service career and especially on fixed wing aircraft[4]. Goddard's role in the UK military airship programme means that he was almost certainly an occasional visitor during the 1914-18 war to the then new RNAS airship training base at Cranwell. On those visits he would have come into contact with many of the characters in this little drama.

Goddard's 1975 book contained the following, now famous, passage:

> *I have a photograph in front of me, taken at Cranwell officially by Bassano's at the time of Armistice after the First World War. It shows a group of airmen, airwomen and officers, some hundreds of them, in various uniforms, RNAS and Army, RFC and RAF, ATS and Women's Naval Service, all my contemporaries and one my friend (*). The photograph is typical of all the chaos of transition from the two old separate Services, into the Royal Air Force, which then was still quite new and unfamiliar. The RAF had not by then been lifted up into its corporate consciousness of entity and destiny.*
>
> *The Squadron, of which the photograph was taken, had no future; it was to be disbanded and almost everyone then photographed was also in transition back to that less authoritarian life which they called 'Civvy Street.'*
>
> *But one was otherwise.*
>
> *When the group photograph was put up on the noticeboard so that those who wanted copies could write their names below, those who scanned the photograph identifying*

friends then saw—or they were prompted then to see—the face of Freddy Jackson, air mechanic, in the topmost row. Capless and smiling, his face being partly hidden by another, his expression seemed to say, 'My goodness me—I nearly failed to make it! ... They didn't wait, or leave a place for me, the blighters!'

Well, there he was, and no mistake, although a little fainter than the rest. Indeed he looked as though he was not altogether there; not really with the group, for he alone was capless, smiling, all the rest were serious and set and wearing service caps. Most had not long returned from Church Parade and marching in a military funeral. For Freddy Jackson had, upon that very spot—the Squadron tarmac—three days before, walked heedlessly into the whirling propeller of an aeroplane. He had been killed stone dead instantly. He, evidently, was still quite unaware of it.

No, that is not a very rare event. There have been several of such unsought records brought into my experience. What is somewhat unusual, to say the least, is the official photograph, and some two hundred witnesses who knew; also the certainty that there had been no hanky-panky in the dark room. Not only would Bassano's not have dared to fake it; the negative was scrutinized for faking and was found to be untouched.

(*) here he is almost certainly referring to Bobby Capel.

— SIR ROBERT VICTOR GODDARD KCB, CBE; *FLIGHT TOWARDS REALITY*; 1975

Goddard does not say that it was his own copy of the photograph or that he was there at Cranwell at the time. It is always the case that, when investigating reported events, one must see them through the eyes of the time and place. In this case we are speaking of a time – certainly in the UK – when telling the truth was one of the most important rules of life. I am not saying that everyone always told the truth all the time, but honesty and integrity were highly prized attributes and, should a person be publicly found out in telling an untruth, particularly when it misled others, their reputation would suffer. The rules were, if anything, even stricter for officers in the armed forces. We also have to remember that, while young officers played pranks on their peers – usually in the privacy of the Officers' Mess – such japes were considered beyond the pale in wider society even in the 'modern' times of George V. They were regarded as childish and beneath the dignity of gentlemen and ladies. One might joke with and play pranks on one's friends but to do so when it affected other people was considered silly and dishonourable.

For that reason, fakery or fraud, if perpetrated maliciously on a wider group, branded a person for life and could certainly bring a premature end to an officer's service career. It is sadly humorous these days but men could be thrown out of their Clubs for such deeds. For someone like Sir Victor (he preferred his second name) telling a lie was to bring his name into dishonour and risk social exclusion and disgrace. Furthermore, the photograph was taken by the famous London-based photographic agency, Bassano's Ltd. This long-established company had an incredible reputation and was used by just about anyone who was anyone. In 1919 alone it boasted a clientele which included famous actresses, military officers of the highest ranks, the nobility, princes and princesses, the Kings of Iraq and of Denmark, and the future King George VI himself.

As Sir Victor quite rightly says, Bassano's would never have dared to put that custom in jeopardy by defrauding the public in such a tasteless and childish way. Faking a photograph would have been considered far worse than a schoolboy prank and faking a photograph so that it included the image of a man horrifically killed in very recent memory would have been insensitive in the extreme and totally unforgivable. Many of those who saw the photo on that noticeboard had been his friends and colleagues and his death was all-too-fresh in the minds of others.

Goddard said that the photograph had not been tampered-with, and no-one has yet found evidence of deliberate double exposure.

There is, of course, always the possibility of an innocent cause. The exposures for such photos were reasonably long, a matter of several seconds, and sometimes longer depending on the available light (which was clearly not good on that day). Therefore, while the lens cap was removed from the lens, anyone moving would have been blurred and their image rendered only indistinctly. The photographers would have told everyone to stand very still for the few seconds of the exposure. Several sceptics have mulled over the possibility that one of those in shot moved temporarily, but that cannot be. If a person in shot were to move there would have been two indistinct faces – a blurred face of the person as they moved and another blurred face of the person when they came to rest in the new position.

It is also not likely that a completely different person entered the shot and stood behind the person on the back row. If the faint image was of a person who appeared in the shot and then quickly ducked out of sight, the image would have been blurred by the motion required to first come into shot and then leave it again. On the other hand, if the trickster popped up and stayed in the shot his face would have been as solid and distinct as the rest. Our ghost, although diaphanous, is quite clear and shows no motion blur at all.

The original photo has been posted on his sceptical website by Blake Smith who has done some excellent investigative work and who writes intelligently and carefully about this topic[5]. His version of the photo includes virtually all of those who would have been in the original shot – some 79 people. He calls it the Daedalus Maintenance Group. It wasn't, but that is a minor error. Other sceptics have asked whether it is not possible that someone showed up without a hat and took up a position on the very back row – there is clearly room to do this because there are certainly more than a few spaces on that row. The theory is that this person squeezed onto the back row, then realised that they were incorrectly dressed, and promptly scooted off. Yes, it's possible. But either the miscreant braved it out and stayed put sans hat, in which case their face would have been clearly and solidly rendered, or they became embarrassed and quickly shot off to find their hat – in which case the face would be blurred not merely indistinct. So why is the image so clear yet so transparent for just that person and why no motion blur?

There is also the additional consideration that, whoever it was that appeared without a hat by mistake, was clearly on the top row of the bleachers when the lens-cap was removed, or the shutter was opened. Getting onto that row would have been no easy or silent task. There may have been a step-ladder placed behind the bleachers but getting up and down from the top row would have been awkward, disruptive, and probably noisy. But the main fact is that even a non-techie in 1919 would have realised they had no time to go and get their hat and be back before the shutter had closed.

In a sense, all this talk of double exposures and people skipping into and out of shot is totally redundant. That strange face behind the back row was not just anyone, not even another member of the maintenance group, it was recognised as the face of a man who had, very recently, been chopped to a very grisly death on the nearby tarmac.

People in those days (in spite of what you see in poorly-made modern films about the era) did not go hatless except at home or at their actual job (and most of the time not even then). Men wore their hats when out of the house at all times and women even wore them while dining and meeting people indoors. Members of the armed forces could be disciplined for appearing improperly dressed without their hats or caps.

The Double Exposure Possibility

It was a double exposure! That's the first line of attack by many sceptics. The honest answer to that charge is that, disregarding the actual face being that of a deceased airman, yes, it could have been. Photography and cameras were quite sophisticated by the end of World War I. The era had roll film, small cameras, even 35mm film and cameras, but all required manual focus and manual setting of lens speed and exposure. The science behind double exposures – whether accidental or deliberate – was well understood at the time and had been for decades.

In order to achieve a good double exposure, the shot has to be very carefully planned. As the name implies, it's done is by taking two photographs of the same scene on the same film frame or plate but with different people or objects in each. By exposing the same piece of film/plate to the light on two occasions, the danger is over-exposure. So, the first shot has to be very dark for everything but the element that one wants to appear as 'extra' to the second exposure. In this case the face on the first exposure would have had to be well-lit while the whole of the rest of the frame was kept very dark. The second photo would then be meticulously composed and given a close to normal exposure time but preferably with the area behind the face completely black. If you were careful, the image from the first shot would then appear as a faint one on the second exposure. The lighting and placement of the 'ghost' face were critical. The camera had to be in precisely the same place (for distance, focus, and the correct positioning), the face had to be well lit, but the rest of the first shot had to be in complete darkness, and people in the second shot would have needed to be very precisely positioned so that just the face – or some of it – appeared in the final photo.

This particular photo was taken on a large, old-style bellows plate camera. These cameras look very old fashioned today but actually they are still in use because they have advantages for certain types of shot. It would probably have been taken on a chemical plate with manual focusing and exposure. Assuming for the moment that the photographer decided to deliberately create the effect in Bobby Capel's photo, he would have taken a partial exposure first of the face and shoulders of one man standing on the top of the bleachers, ensuring that the whole of the rest of the shot was masked and in darkness. Then, when the second exposure was taken, the man's face would appear as being in focus but ghostly.

This is entirely possible as a deliberate act. It implies a night shot, only partially exposed, with just the photographer and the trickster on the 'set'. Sounds do-able but the lighting of the face would have been a really difficult given the technology of the time and the height of the bleachers. More to the point. If you were going to go to all that trouble, why take the risk that the trick 'ghost' would be almost entirely obscured by someone in the real shot? Wouldn't you want more of the face or even all of it to appear? It has to be said that choosing the top of the bleachers was not the most sensible choice. Lower down and to one side – where the image could be guaranteed to be free of other people – might have been more effective. The ideal would have been to locate the 'ghost' on the fourth row up and then organise the group so that the guys next to the chap with the overcoat were conveniently spaced so that the ghost appeared between them.

But there is a huge fly in the ointment. The face is that of a dead person who could not possibly have been physically there on the night before the group photo. In order to pull off the trick you would need to have an enlarged full-face photo of the dead man – extremely difficult in those days. And Bassano's would not have dared to perpetrate such a trick. For it to have been an *accidental* double exposure is even less likely. Taking a double exposure by accident is something many people in the age of chemical film experienced. I have myself ruined expensive bits of film stock by failing to wind a film on. Accidental double exposure requires a certain degree of incompetence. In this case it would have required a professional photographer to physically work the shutter mechanism for a shorter exposure time just when a single face (which happened to be the dead airman) was visible on the bleachers, correctly lit, and with the rest of the scene completely dark. This is theoretically possible. However, to believe that an accidental double exposure only captured a single person standing on top of the bleachers without a hat and with an enigmatic smile on his face, who looked exactly like the deceased mechanic Freddie Jackson, without any other people in shot, and with the rest of the bleachers in close to complete darkness is so unlikely on a busy airbase just before a major camera shoot as to be discounted.

A deliberate attempt to create a ghostly double exposure is also extremely unlikely given the sheer technical difficulty of achieving a double exposure in such circumstances, the reputation of Bassano's, the lack of any other evidence of double-exposure on the photo (washed out dark colours and faces, etc), the somewhat sick need for a large photographic copy of the dead man's face, and the fact that no-one ever claimed that it was a prank. The people who examined the photo on the notice board remarked that the faint image was exactly that of the dead air mechanic.

But, in order to understand the full story, we need to know who Bobby Capel was. In the photo above, she is the lady sitting second row up, extreme left just below the enlarged area. Technically, the name is correct because that was her name when she revealed the puzzle of the photo to Goddard (who then revealed it to the world) in 1975. But it was not her name at the time of the photo. She was mentioned in Sir Victor's 1975 book and was almost certainly a friend of his through her husband. Being a Women's Royal Naval Service (WRNS) Driver at Cranfield means that she may even have driven Goddard around during his visits. She is important to this story because the photo itself (the 1975 book told the story but did not include the photo) might never have seen the modern light of day had she not, at the age of 97, in 1996, mentioned the incident to a neighbour called John Roberts and showed him her copy of the photo. He kindly, but unsuccessfully, attempted to find out some of the truth for her by writing to the Editor of the Navy News. The magazine published the photo in 1997, with the additional enlarged element, and asked for information. As far as I have been able to ascertain, and probably unsurprisingly at that late date, no-one was able to throw any light on the matter.

One could date the photograph with confidence to sometime between November 1918 (the official end of the war) and the spring of 1919, by which time most of those on the photo would have returned to civvy-street. It is unlikely that the Maintenance Group would have been able to arrange a photo immediately after the Armistice was signed. The government did not begin to demobilise the forces for a while and most demobilisations are recorded as having been implemented at the end of April 1919. So, the Group would have waited until their fate was sealed and dates confirmed. I would imagine a date perhaps in early 1919 – say February or early March in view of the obviously cold, wet weather. It was to be a final memento for the Group of their war-time service and their comrades.

Victor Goddard's account was based on his knowing Bobby from those days and then being friends with the Capels. The story was provided to him by Bobby Capel whose first husband had served at the base and whose second husband, Arthur Capel, also served at Cranwell from about the end of 1919 for three years. Bobby Horn (for that was her maiden name) married a famous air ace, Flight Lieutenant Henry Moody, in 1922. Moody was killed in a tragic air accident in April 1931 when he was ferrying a senior officer (Air Vice Marshal Holt) to another airfield. As the pair took off from Cranwell and climbed to cruising altitude (quite low in those days), a squadron of the brand-new 'Siskin' fighters flew towards them. The Armstrong Whitworth Siskin was the UK's first all-metal fighter. The pilots of that squadron decided to 'salute' the senior officer, and this led to a slight coming together of wings. Moody's aircraft (mere fabric and wood) received the worst of the collision (the other aircraft landed safely with minimal damage). Flt Lt Moody was an incredible flyer. He managed to correct a spin even with a large chunk of a wing missing but had lost too much height. Both he and the senior officer were killed when the aircraft hit the ground.

His widow, Bobby Moody, eventually re-married. As with armed services the world over, the RAF has always been a small world – especially for the senior ranks. Everyone knew everyone else, and it is probable that Arthur Capel, who had almost certainly known Henry Moody, heard of Moody's death and contacted Bobby Moody at some point if only, at first, to offer his sincere condolences. The two must have gotten on together because they were married three years later, in 1934. The final piece of the jigsaw is that, as a senior officer, Capel also knew Goddard and it is not stretching the imagination too far to propose that Goddard and his wife were in a social situation with the Capel's at some point in the 1960s or 70s and that, with his enduring interest in the paranormal, Air Marshall Goddard was told (or remembered and discussed with Bobby Capel) the story of 'Freddie Jackson'.

At that time Goddard would have been finishing his book and would have asked Bobby for details and a copy of the photo. The story became part of his 1975 book, but it belonged to Bobby Horn/Moody/Capel and it is there that we need to look for the truth behind this whole affair. It is not unusual for people to keep photos for long periods of time. I still have photos taken by my father during World War Two. What is perhaps more unusual is that Bobby Capel never stopped trying to solve the mystery. She had protected the photo for half a century before she told the story to Goddard in the 1970s (at the latest). At that time she was a sprightly 70-year-old, so her memory is not likely to have been too faulty at that stage. But could she have got dates and names wrong?

As far as dates are concerned probably not too much. The photo was certainly taken by the London studio of Bassano's between December 1918 and March 1919. However, the other facts she told Goddard could have been mistaken to some extent. Did she remember correctly how soon before the photo 'Freddie Jackson' had been killed? After all those years did she remember Freddie's name correctly? Was the squadron recently returned from a funeral and church parade as Goddard reported? They all look smart enough – boots polished and shirts neat and clean but that could equally have been for the photo and not for a funeral. But there is no reason at all to doubt the core of the story that Mrs Capel told Air Marshall Goddard.

Goddard as an Air Commodore in 1942 by Thomas Cantrell Dugdale; Imperial War Museums. Public Domain. https://commons.wikimedia.org/w/index.php?curid=63289411

As to the name, a lot of people have searched for 'Freddie Jackson'. Like them, I have been unable to find any details of a Freddy/Freddie/Frederick Jackson with the correct credentials. The awkward fact is that Freddie or Frederick Jackson or even 'another first name' plus Frederick Jackson has proved elusive and none has yet surfaced with the correct circumstances. In principle, the failure to identify a 'Freddie Jackson' who died on the tarmac at Cranwell looks like a killer-blow to the 'ghost' theory. But military records of the two World Wars are notoriously incomplete. A huge number of records have been destroyed or lost – some by the British Government, some by German bombing, and some due to the passage of time. Bobby Horn cannot be found (under any of her first names or initials), even the available records for Victor Goddard are vague or incomplete for the period in question. So, while it may never be possible to prove that Freddie Jackson existed, the case remains extremely compelling for the following reasons:

a) the photo is almost certainly not faked,

b) the faint image of the dead airman was recognised by many of his colleagues at the time and this was attested to by Bobby Capel. She said that the photo contained an image of a dead airman – whatever his name might be. Mrs Capel, bless her soul, was puzzled by the mystery to the end of her life and had mentioned it to outsiders – at the very least to her friend Sir Victor Goddard and to her neighbour, John Roberts, and,

c) Mrs Capel's lifelong desire for answers is not the attitude one might expect of someone who knew – or even suspected – that it was all a prank. In spite of the conversations she must have had over the years with her husband and with Goddard she still felt it necessary to agree to Mr Johnson seeking more information through the Navy News in the late 1990s.

So, what do we actually know of the purported ghost in the photo? We know that …

1. The photo exists and has that strange image in it.
2. The image defies scientific photographic explanation because it is virtually certain that it is not a double exposure or other type of fake.
3. It was taken by a prestigious London photographic agency that would have had nothing to do with forgery or fakery and that would most certainly not have acted as a willing collaborator.
4. If faked in some way, the act was tasteless and cruel. A depiction of a dead man on a photo his friends and comrades were going to buy would be beneath contempt even against today's low standards but would have been unthinkable back in 1919.
5. On the photo there is a strange, diaphanous face in almost perfect focus which is clear enough for people to recognise its owner.
6. There is no motion blur and no overlap of the image into the lighter areas on the adjacent man's hat and face (as would almost certainly have happened in a double exposure).

7. The face was recognised by his colleagues at the time.
8. The effect of it being on the photo was profound enough to concern Bobby Capel (and possibly many others) for the rest of her life.
9. Mrs Capel remembered the name as being Freddie Jackson – but that may not have been the airman's real name. His service records – along with tens of thousands of others – may have been destroyed by German bombs or British bureaucracy.
10. Sir Victor Goddard probably had almost nothing to do with the affair except to be told the story and to include it in his 1975 book, which fact has led to the whole affair being named after him rather than the true owner.

My own feeling – but it cannot be proved in any sense – is that the story is genuine, that the photo was a puzzle in 1919 and remains so a century later, that it was not faked by Bassano's, and that the faint but recognisable image of a dead airman does, indeed, appear on it. The ghost on the photo may not have been that of a man named Freddie Jackson but the sceptics still have to convincingly explain how that face is in almost perfect focus, with no movement blur and yet indistinct, how just that single face came to be on that photograph (i.e. no other faint double-exposure images), how his colleagues recognised the face as belonging to 'Freddie Jackson' a man who had been killed on the very tarmac a week or so beforehand , and why perhaps the last survivor of that group – Bobby Capel – mentioned the event to Victor Goddard in the 1970s and tried to find out the truth to the very end of her life.

The somewhat puzzled face of that dead airman stares ruefully out at us to this day. One can almost feel the sadness in him and the anger he must have felt towards himself for being so careless as to turn around and walk into a spinning propellor. One can see a stubborn cast to his eye. He seems to be saying 'there's no way I was going to miss this'. Whoever that man was he left a mystery which reverberates across the Internet to this day. But at least he turned up for the photo, so that his friends and colleagues would not forget him. For our own part we are left with the uncomfortable probability that the image on Mrs Capel's photo was not of human origin.

Can ghosts be photographed?

The answer is most definitely yes. We not only have scores of credible images but a few highly probable ones such as those I laid out above. The photos of the Brown Lady, Lord Combermere, the figures at the Queen's House, Mrs Chinnery's mother, and 'Freddie Jackson' are well up there in the ninety-nineth percentile for credibility. I could probably list a dozen more at the same level of authenticity.

So, we can be virtually certain that anomalous images which we call ghosts can appear on both chemical and digital photographs. The real question is: how do those images get recorded if, according to conventional science, the things they are recording do not exist? The answer has to lie in some form of energy which can be manipulated and controlled in ways that we do not yet understand. In this book I describe a multitude of cases in which human beings (and animals) 'see' the same sorts of anomalies. At Bircham Newton people have reported seeing chaps in RAF uniform who disappear or walk through walls, a British TV star has watched solid-seeming apparitions of children playing in her home, taxi drivers in Japan tell of picking up drenched people near the area which suffered the tsunami who then disappear in the backs of their cars. These and many other similar tales which I will describe in the pages that follow all testify to the ability of humans to see or experience anomalistic apparitions. It cannot be surprising therefore that, if human eyes can receive and process the photons, so can cameras.

CHAPTER 6
GHOSTS IN FLIGHT

> *The R101's trials had not met expectations. Its lift was nearly 3.5 tons lighter than anticipated, and its weight was over 8.5 tons heavier.*
>
> — ADAM SMITH INSTITUTE

The accounts in this chapter are linked by the fact that they all centre on heart-breaking aviation accidents. They focus on the loss of a British aircraft attempting an almost impossible east-to-west crossing of the Atlantic, the infamous loss of the largest aircraft in the world at that time, and the losses of two American aircraft - Flights 401 and 191.

The accounts differ in many ways but share an important common factor – very high levels of emotion – something which is common to a high proportion of so-called ghost sightings and paranormal activity. It does not take much for us to imagine the feelings of people who suddenly (or not so suddenly) realise they are about to die in an accident. There would be an incredible explosion of terror, of raw, scintillating fear. This would be mixed with an immense outpouring of frustration and anger at having lives cut short, at never seeing their loved ones again, at not being able to fulfil their dreams. And finally, there would no doubt be an iron core of denial. This cannot be happening ... this is not happening to me.

If you stop to think about it, emotion is at the base of almost every paranormal tale in this book, and the higher the levels of emotional energy, the more profound the paranormal experience. The sources of energy in these accounts are quite different but the paranormal effects are very real.

Flight across the Atlantic

How a ghost image gets onto a photograph is a puzzler, but then so is the way a person can actually see a ghost. One is tempted to believe that many supposed ghosts are not really there, that they appear only in the minds of the beholders. But a camera does not have a mind into which a ghostly image can be projected. A camera sees only light – the photons or light waves that are reflected from the subjects in the frame. In view of the numbers of ghosts seen by living people it is logical that ghosts can and do reflect light, but the mechanism is more than just mysterious. In theory it could be a function of the quantum level – some interaction of pure energy with light but that, as with most other theories, is pure speculation.

In most cases a camera sees light that is reflected or emitted by an object but what if a focus of energy could actually *project* light in a similar way to a nuclear explosion sending out massive amounts of light? Such a mechanism could explain how ghosts appear in photos, it might explain why many ghosts are reported as 'glowing' and why they are seen in the dark, and it could also underpin the apparent ability of ghosts to convey sounds. This may have been the case in at least one sighting of the ghost of the first airman to attempt an east to west air crossing of the Atlantic.

In March 1928 a brave and highly skilled pilot named Captain W G R Hinchliffe, DFC, attempted to be the first pilot to conquer that most difficult of trans-Atlantic flights – an east to west flight, against the prevailing winds. He and a companion made the attempt in a

Stinson Detroiter single engine monoplane – a relatively new design. First flown in January 1926, it was a high wing six-seater with a 220hp Wright radial engine[1]. By comparison a modern car averages about 200hp and most SUVs are around 300hp. By taking just two people and using every bit of the remaining space for as much fuel as could possibly be carried, Hinchliffe aimed to be the first pilot to fly eastwards across the Atlantic.

'Hinch' as he was known to his friends was an experienced and skilled aviator who had lost an eye during a dogfight during the First World War. The eyepatch he wore made him look a little like a pirate. But 'mad, bad, and dangerous' he was certainly not. He was a meticulous planner, an excellent pilot, and a caring and considerate husband and father.

Not exactly the type of aircraft you'd choose to cross the Atlantic against the prevailing winds. Wikimedia Commons; by San Diego Air & Space Museum Archives - Public Domain. https://commons.wikimedia.org/w/index.php?curid=41508540

With him on that fateful flight travelled the sponsor of the air-record attempt, the Honourable Elsie MacKay, the heiress daughter of the wealthy British shipping mogul Lord Inchcape of P&O fame. She'd put up the cash to buy the plane and had equipped the aircraft with everything that Hinchliffe wanted. Above all, though, she desperately wanted to be the first female to cross the Atlantic by air. In the end, Amelia Earhart did it, west to east, in June of that year but

MacKay would have beaten her by a few weeks as well as by doing it in the more difficult direction.

The story is a tale of bravery and foolishness – the bravery of a great flyer, his mistake in not insisting on flying with another experienced pilot, and the somewhat stubborn, brave foolishness of an ambitious and wealthy young woman who did not really understand the danger of trying such a feat with just a single, albeit experienced pilot. But it is primarily the story of Hinchliffe's wife, Emilie, who was forced to wait in increasing distress as news of the outcome of her husband's flight failed to arrive and who was consigned to poverty by the failure of the heiress to make certain that an agreed insurance policy was in place for the aviator. Hinchliffe was not rich. He was a working pilot and he naturally wanted his wife and child to be left in financial security should the flight go wrong. In exchange for Hinchliffe agreeing to take her instead of another skilled pilot, MacKay agreed to insure Hinchliffe's life for £10,000 (around £1m /$1.2m these days). There is evidence that she did try to arrange the insurance policy, but it seems that the formalities were not completed before the flight departed and then, as now, insurance companies were not terribly flexible or understanding when the small print was not adhered to.

The upshot was that, when Hinchliffe and MacKay were officially considered to have died in the attempted crossing, Mrs Emilie Hinchliffe was left with two young children and without any insurance payment. After a long fight by her friends and some of Britain's richest men, Emilie eventually received her due financial compensation – not from the insurance company but direct from Lord Inchcape. She used the money to ensure a decent life for her children and herself, but she also became convinced of the reality of the paranormal through the contacts with her dead husband that she experienced via the famous medium, Eileen Garrett. She went on to give lectures all over the world about her experiences.

It may seem as if the money was a side-issue to the tragic loss of two human beings, but Hinchliffe desperately needed to make sure his wife and children were cared for and that seems to have been the prime driver for the paranormal events which followed. Poor Emilie did not have even the small consolation of a definite, known accident or a grave beside which to mourn. The plane simply disappeared – no one witnessed it crash into the sea and therefore no-one knew where to start looking for wreckage or survivors. Emilie Hinchliffe was left for weeks hoping that her husband had managed to reach a different airfield to the one in the States that he had been aiming for, or even that he had taken to a life raft and would shortly be rescued by a passing steam ship. Slowly it became clear that the Stinson had not reached land and neither pilot nor passenger had been picked up by a ship. And throughout the hoping against hope and the grief, her extremely precarious financial position was nagging at the back of her mind. She had only their very limited savings to live on and those were rapidly running out.

Then (and one would never believe this in the wildest fiction) she was contacted out of the blue by an amateur medium named Beatrice Earl. In the 1920s, as today, there were lots of amateur mediums, and Mrs Earl often used her Ouija board to converse with spirits. On several evenings, she said she had received very brief messages purporting to be from the dead aviator about whom she had been reading in the newspapers. Mrs Earl sent the messages and a covering letter to Sir Arthur Conon Doyle whom she knew through the Society for Psychical Research and eventually, a professional medium named Eileen Garrett also became involved. Conon Doyle, the creator of Sherlock Holmes, was a steadfast believer in paranormal phenomena although he fought constantly with Harry Price and with the famous Harry Houdini over matters of paranormal detail and experimentation. It is not entirely clear whether it was Conan Doyle or Price who involved the professional medium Eileen Garrett, but she was asked to help by one or both of them.

Mrs Garrett always worked with a 'spirit guide' who went by the name Uvani and, after a number of sessions she was able to channel 'Captain Hinchliffe' to tell his story and reassure his wife. One of the most interesting things about the incident from a lay-person's point of view was that Hinchliffe's seemingly solid ghost appeared to one of two friends who were then on an ocean liner hundreds of miles from land. The men were on their way back to the UK from Africa. One night, Hinchliffe appeared in the cabin of his friend Colonel Henderson at a time that must have been immediately after the doomed aircraft crashed into the freezing waters of the North Atlantic. Henderson was so disturbed by the visit that, even though it was the middle of the night, he rushed to his fellow-traveller's cabin and told him:

> 'Hinch has just been in my cabin. Eye patch and all. He woke me up. It was ghastly. He kept repeating over and over again: 'Hendy—what am I going to do? What am I going to do? I've got this woman with me, and I'm lost. I'm lost!' Then he disappeared in front of my eyes! Just disappeared.'[2]

It was an incredible manifestation – attested to by a solid, down-to-earth soldier. One wonders how much emotional energy has to be created in order to forge a solid-looking apparition hundreds of miles away and then communicate through speech to a living human – something that ghosts are almost never able to do. Henderson was not able to tell his story until his ship arrived in England weeks later.

After that, Hinchliffe seemed to try to find other ways to communicate with the world he'd recently left. He got simple messages through to Beatrice Earl, and then a series of more detailed messages through Eileen Garrett and Uvani. In those sessions, mainly organised by Harry Price and the Society for Psychical Research (some of which were attended by Emilie Hinchliffe) he succeeded in reassuring his wife. His sole purpose, it seemed, was to make sure that Emilie was given some certainty that he was 'alright' and that his wife and children were going to be properly provided for. By that he meant that they received the financial recompense that he'd formally agreed with Elsie MacKay – no more and no less. In his communications through Uvani he told his wife, well ahead of actual events, that she would be alright, and that the money would be paid.

It took some time but, once this was accomplished, his spirit did not appear again. It is as though, following what must have been a terrifying crash into the bleak north Atlantic, he reached the 'other side' and immediately said 'Look, I know there's things to be done but just wait a bit while I make sure my wife and children are okay.' He appears then to have visited his friend Henderson in a bit of a panic before realising that Henderson could do nothing from his ocean liner. Then he managed to get a few simple word-messages through Mrs Earl, and that then prompted the more effective communication through Eileen Garrett.

Elsie MacKay died in the very same crash but her spirit did not seem to attempt to contact the living – unless Lord Inchcape knew differently. The full story is well worth reading. John Fuller tells the tale sympathetically and in detail but with due caution. Nevertheless, one cannot help but be impressed by Eileen Garrett and her improbably-named spirit guide. They knew things that only Emilie Hinchliffe and her husband would have known and they contributed greatly to Mrs Hinchliffe's peace of mind as well as helping to improve her financial circumstances. Fuller's book also links the Hinchliffe case – through Hinchliffe's friendships with the officers involved – to that even greater tragedy, the R-101 airship disaster from which similar accounts emerged and with which Harry Price, Eileen Garrett and Uvani were also involved[3].

The Last Flight of the R-101

Fuller's book is one of the best on the accident that befell the giant British airship – the R-101. It is factually accurate and deals sensitively and empathetically with the paranormal aspects of the case as well as tying the characters and events into the earlier demise of Captain Hinchliffe[4].

The R-101 was, as you will probably know, the British attempt to outbuild the Germans in airships. But, most of all, it was the key to the effort to develop a fast, comfortable, and efficient method for linking the UK with the rest of its Empire out to India and Australasia, and in other directions to central and southern Africa, Canada, central America, and the Caribbean. Even in 1930 fixed wing aircraft were still slow, of very limited range, mechanically unreliable, and were incapable of carrying decent numbers of passengers or amounts of freight.

The R-101 was a huge beast. Ground handling took at least eight teams of thirty to forty men per team. U.K. Government photo, Public Domain. https://commons.wikimedia.org/w/index.php?curid=1880365

At the time, there were those who argued persuasively that fixed wing aircraft would *never* be able to beat dirigibles. These giant airships had the ability to heft tons of freight and tens of passengers over thousands of miles. They are regarded with suspicion and derision these days but in the 1920s and 1930s airships were a convincing new technology. They were the no-brainer of future development, offering incredible range (by fixed-wing standards), lots of payload, luxurious room for a goodly number of passengers, and a supremely comfortable journey with none of the cramped seating, cold environment, and nauseas ride of the fixed wing aircraft.

The wreck of the R-101. It is not obvious from this tragic shot but the R-101 was the largest aircraft in the world at the time. Wikimedia Commons; Public Domain. https://commons.wikimedia.org/w/index.php?curid=1880377

The R-101 could lift over 150 tons. It had accommodation on two levels which included fifty sleeping cabins for passengers, a huge lounge, a beautiful dining room with sixty seats, two promenades with external views through lightweight windows, a bar, and even an asbestos-lined smoking room. In theory it could also carry tons of freight as compared to the few hundred pounds of the largest aircraft of the day.

In almost all respects airships seemed to be the most reliable, safe, comfortable, and speedy answer to long-distance travel. To the British, with their need to link Imperial possessions as far away as Canada, South Africa, India, Malaya, Hong Kong, Australia, and New Zealand, airships were the Holy Grail. So, along with the Germans, French, and Americans, the British were in a race to design and build long distance airships, a race that, in the late '20s, the British were winning. In the R-101 and its sister ship the R-100 they had the largest aircraft ever built. The promise those two airships offered was so alluring that the haste to achieve the kudos of a first spectacular flight caused a government minister and more than two score of good people to lose their lives.

Fuller's book is excellent reading and a riveting account and I won't attempt to tell the whole story or even mention all the main characters. Much of what I say below has been cross checked against the official report on the accident and against Harry Price's own writings. In the official handling of the case there was almost certainly a cover-up designed to protect the careers of certain senior people, but it is not clear whether the members who conducted the official enquiry knew of this or, if they did, whether they had enough evidence to prove it.

Suffice it to say that, after some testing and a few short journeys in the UK, the Air Ministry decided that the R-101 would undertake a highly publicised and sensational maiden voyage to India and back again. They wanted the airship to carry a load of freight and passengers out to Britain's Imperial jewel of India and then return in time for a grand Imperial conference in England. In spite of official enthusiasm, most of the RAF, Army, and Royal Navy officers who were managing the R-101's testing did not want to make that long and fateful trip. They vehemently advised against it because they did not think the airship had been properly tested. Even worse, more than a few believed it was a fundamentally flawed design. But they were all over-ruled by Lord Thompson, the Secretary of State for Air, who insisted that the airship was ready to embark on a long-range trip to India and back.

In perfect weather conditions he may have been justified in his decision – indeed the sister airship, the R-100 had completed a flight to Canada and back in July 1930 – but the conditions in which the R-101 set off for its maiden long-range journey were nowhere near perfect. In design terms the R-100 was superior to the R-101 but neither was as good as the latest German designs.

Right from the start, on that bleak October day in 1930, the trip went very wrong. The ship proved to be so heavy when it tried to leave its mooring mast at Cardington that it had to dump a large amount of water ballast to get sufficient lift to climb away from the mast. Sounds fairly innocuous, but the officers would have known that the action meant they would not have enough weight to lose later in the flight when the R-101 desperately needed to gain height. They would also have realised that it meant the aircraft was significantly too heavy. The giant airship glided off, directly into the teeth of a gathering storm. The craft was heavy enough to begin with but its canvas covering then became so soaked in water that it never achieved any real altitude. With every mile it travelled towards France it got steadily heavier as torrential rain soaked the canvas fabric of the envelope. Some experts believe that it probably sank as low as 300 feet over the English Channel and witnesses said that it was still very low when it crossed into France.

By the time it reached France, the officers had planned a small mutiny. The ship was behaving so badly that they wanted to land somewhere - which meant an airfield with a mooring mast – to sort the ship out properly before possibly carrying on to India. The R-101 was a difficult enough ship to fly even in good weather but in the storm it was handling very badly. The weather was atrocious and airships do not do well in storms. The winds tear their fabric and gas bags, the gusts make them extremely difficult to control, strong constant winds stress the framework of metal girders, the rain soaks their fabric and adds tons of unnecessary weight, and any lightning was virtually a death warrant. Many American airships of the 1930s succumbed to storms and lightning.

So, in the gathering darkness of October 4th 1930 the R-101 began its turn. The storm was raging, battering the craft with heavy rain, high winds, and violent gusts. Losing height all the time, the R-101 attempted to make a turn towards an airfield which had a mooring mast. In the course of that turn, near Beauvais, the ship lost more height, went out of control, and crashed. The speed at which it crashed was quite low – probably between about 13mph and 20mph –

but, with a gas explosion and subsequent fire, it was disastrous. The official enquiry was inconclusive, but it is likely that the steel girders and frame were simply not up to the task in the winds that were blowing that day. Some girders may have broken, the skin split, gas bags ruptured, a spark – probably from the heavy diesel engines – finished the job and, hopefully quite quickly, ended the lives of forty-six people. Only eight of those on board survived the crash and two of them died later in hospital. The survivors included a Foreman Engineer, a Wireless Operator, and four engineers from the engine cars that were hung beneath the envelope of the airship. The crash therefore cost forty-eight lives including those of all the officers and dignitaries on board (including Lord Thomson). Not for the first time, flawed design had been turned into a human tragedy by overweening political ambition.

The story of what happened next is even more gripping than that of the disaster itself. Almost immediately afterwards, Eileen Garrett, the medium who had been heavily involved in the Hinchliffe affair, began to receive messages from the newly deceased airship officers. She received the first messages in the middle of an unconnected séance with Harry Price. Out of the blue, she unexpectedly came up with a message concerning the R-101. The séance had been a mutually-agreed test of Garrett's capabilities which, coincidentally, was held on October 7th 1930 just a few days after the crash of the R-101. Her spirit guide was an ancient middle eastern character called Uvani. Through him she communicated with the dead officers and revealed to Price two facts which she could not have known beforehand. The first was one which no-one outside the RAF could know. The second referred to a virtually unknown location which was so small that even French Gazetteers did not list it. The first revelation she told Price about was that the RAF authorities were secretly thinking of adopting a mixture of hydrogen and fuel oil to power the diesel engines of airships[5]. The second was that the airship – when it got into trouble over France – almost scraped the rooftops of a place called 'Achy'. Uvani mentioned this as coming from the airship's officers, but the name was not recognised by any of the people around the séance table. In the end it turned out to be a tiny railroad halt which had not been mentioned in any of the press reports at the time, was not listed in any guide-book, and was also not on any tourist or even a large scale map of the area. Nevertheless, Garrett mentioned Achy specifically in her messages from the crew. Both of the unique messages at that first séance turned out to be absolutely correct. The RAF was then engaged in a secret project to see whether airships could travel lighter or carry more freight by using a mixture of fuel oil and hydrogen for their engines. And, in the minutes before the crash, as the airship was descending, it did pass low over the railway halt at Achy, so low that witnesses said they feared for their chimneys and rooftops.

The central character after the event was Major Oliver G G Villiers, DSO, an assistant to Air Vice Marshall Sir Sefton Brancker who had been killed in the crash. The latter, too, did not want to be on board, believing that the plan to take the R-101 to India at such an early stage in its development programme was much too risky. Villiers did most of the heavy lifting during the series of séances with Eileen Garrett, asking detailed technical questions of the deceased crew in order to test the medium but increasingly, as his confidence grew, to find out what actually happened to the R-101. At points during the séances he 'spoke' to Flight Lieutenant H C Irwin, (Captain), Lieutenant Commander Atherstone (First Officer), Sir Sefton Brancker (Director of Civil Aviation), Squadron Leader E L Johnston (Navigator), and Major G H Scott (Director of Airship Development).

If you read nothing else of Fuller's great book, please read Villiers' letter and detailed transcripts at the end. Villiers made it a condition when he gave Fuller his story that the author must include all the information verbatim. He wanted to be sure that journalistic licence would not cloud or obscure the truth. To his credit, Fuller complied with that obligation to the letter and, in their old-fashioned style, evident honesty, and correctness, Villiers' words are perhaps the most persuasive and moving parts of the book. In part, he said of the men who had died and managed to communicate ...

> *I now feel convinced that when Colmore and the others decided it was imperative that the real truth should be made available to us in this world, Brancker must have realised that since I had been forewarned I was a suitable contact and for reasons best known to themselves Irwin was asked to undertake this ...*
>
> *Once again let me wish you all success in this vitally important work you have undertaken because I am certain it will bring not only relief but great happiness to those who are so anxious to know the truth of what is commonly called Survival and to realise that there is no such thing as "Death."*[6]

The crew of the airship communicated in some way through Eileen Garrett/Uvani. Major Villiers was extremely sceptical to begin with but gradually he became so convinced that it changed his beliefs and possibly his life. The accounts the men gave through Uvani were so technical, personal, and detailed that Villiers, and several others, eventually became totally convinced that they were actually speaking to the people they'd known and worked with during their lives. The information they received was so unique and unavailable to any layperson that Villiers made numerous attempts to have elements of it formally investigated and to get it admitted into the material being considered by the official enquiry. It goes without saying that trying to get ghost testimony admitted to an official enquiry was somewhat unusual, but some of the things the dead crew said offered valuable insights into the engineering issues in the airship and the overall design. For example, Villiers was told in one séance that girders had snapped clean in two during the final turn – an indication of them being far too weak to stand up to the stress of regular flight in high winds. The deceased crew also mentioned documents and journals that would have thrown light on the issues surrounding the crash, but these somehow 'disappeared' and were therefore never taken under consideration by the enquiry into the crash.

Sir Sefton Brancker as a Major General; with Royal Flying Corps wings. Public Domain. https://commons.wikimedia.org/w/index.php?curid=23847922

At grave risk to his career Villiers spoke to the Chairman of the official enquiry and set in motion other investigations. It was a risk because senior, high-ranking officials and officers were potentially at fault for design decisions and for allowing the R-101 to undertake the fateful trip. In all eras it is personally very dangerous to undermine senior people. Villiers was never promoted beyond his then rank of

Major. The reasons could be many but one of them could be that his activities permanently annoyed certain senior people.

Nothing of what was revealed through Garrett to Villiers was ever officially taken into account by the enquiry but Villiers went to his grave believing that crucial documents had been deliberately destroyed or hidden from the board of enquiry – documents which, if they had been revealed, might have ended the careers of several living officers and officials. In the end, though, what the spirits of the officers of the R-101 seemed to desire most did come to pass. The British scrapped the sister airship the R-100 and never again built a large dirigible. The UK became the first of the western powers to abandon large airships and it was certainly a very wise decision. The airship business was left mainly to Germany and the United States. The Germans gave it up after the Hindenburg disaster of 1937 (thirty-five very public deaths) but the Americans kept trying right up to and through the Second World War, in spite of losing a world record 73 people in the 1933 crash of the USS Akron and enduring a steady stream of fatal accidents[7].

But the most powerful outcome of the R-101 disaster was that, somehow, the deceased officers were able to pass highly technical and sometimes highly secret information to Major Villiers through a medium. Villiers was a very credible and honest man who knew that Garrett could never have known or found out even a fraction of the information she passed on from the officers.

The events that followed the loss of Hinchliffe and the crash of the R-101 caused a number of initially sceptical people to revise their beliefs as to what Major Villiers called 'survival' – that is the survival of a person's essence or spirit after death. We'll look at this again later.

Eastern Airlines' Flight 401

An apparently solid ghost like that reported by Colonel Henderson from his ocean liner used to be called a revenant. It is a type of 'ghost' often regarded as being out-dated, fashionable in medieval times and in Shakespeare's plays but now rarely encountered or mentioned. However, there are reports of seemingly solid ghosts even in relatively recent times. Colonel Henderson's traumatic experience in the middle of the night was one example but an even more impressive case occurred in the 1970s.

Revenants are closely associated with very traumatic events and some writers argue that they can only manifest where there is a great deal of emotional energy. This particular type of ghost is now confused with zombies and with reports of the 'undead'. The reader is well advised to avoid the confusion and consider them as 'solid ghosts'. If zombies exist they are of a different order of paranormal phenomena than things that appear as solid ghosts.

In December 1972 a first generation wide-body aircraft – a Lockheed L-1011 Tristar (Eastern Airlines' Flight 401) – crashed into a swamp in Florida during its attempt to land at Miami after a flight from New York. Over one hundred people died including the pilot, Bob Loft, and the Flight Engineer Don Repo (there were 75 survivors).

An Eastern Airlines Lockheed L-1011 'Tristar'. Wikimedia Commons; by Jon Proctor. https://commons.wikimedia.org/w/index.php?curid=22632487

The aircraft was on finals into Miami when the crew noticed that the nose gear confirmation light was not lit. The light was supposed to illuminate when the nose gear was down and locked. It turned out that the gear was actually down and locked but the light – a tiny, inexpensive bulb – had burned out. The Captain decided to go around while they checked things and, while distracted by the issue of the warning light, the crew on the flight deck did not notice that the autopilot had been disengaged for landing and go-around. When they established their circuit they had forgotten to switch it back on. The aircraft was now losing height. From the circuit height of 2,000 feet, it did not take long to get so low that it was too late to recover. It descended under power into the alligator-infested Everglades.

In the weeks and months following the accident both Loft and Repo were reported on several Eastern Airlines flights. Their 'ghosts' looked extremely solid and lifelike. There are more than twenty such sightings on record including one involving the CEO of Eastern himself[8]. The wreck, as in many other air-crashes, was salvaged. Viable equipment was refurbished and repaired before being used as replacements for faulty equipment in other Lockheed L-1011 Tristars. John Fuller, who did some very detailed research into the crash and spoke to many Eastern Airlines staff, tells of intriguing and often frightening incidents where cabin crew and pilots saw one or both of the two men in the months after the crash. The planes in which the appearances occurred were usually those that had received spare parts from the crashed aircraft. On one occasion an Eastern staffer was told by one of the ghosts not to worry because the two men would not allow another L-1011 to crash. The ghost presumably meant another *Eastern* L-1011 because there were several other serious crashes of L-1011 aircraft after the Florida one – a Saudia Tristar crashed in 1980 leading to the deaths by fire of no less than 301 people and there were 137 fatalities in the 1985 Delta crash.

There are other compelling tales of ghosts that appear as solid and 'real'. The fire station at Temple Back in Bristol, England is said to have a ghost which seems so real that the witnesses take it for a living person[9]. The BBC did a documentary on the station in 2005 and its team of investigators saw a few very strange, unexplained things (among many others that were explicable). In the 1970s a fire controller insisted that he saw the fully armoured figure of a medieval knight descend the modern stairway.

Solid ghosts may also have connections with the way in which people report seeing people they know but in different places to where they really are. The Germans have a word for this phenomenon – a Doppelganger (a person's double). They are usually called 'fetches' in English.

American Flight 191

Apparently-solid ghosts were also reported in the weeks and months after the crash of American Flight 191 in 1979 at O'Hare International Airport, Chicago. It was an appalling crash of a DC-10 in which, due to poor maintenance procedures, the port engine was ripped from the wing on take-off. The engine completely separated from the wing and, in flipping backwards it severed fuel and hydraulic lines. The pilots were able to stabilise the flight for a minute or so but eventually the port wing dipped badly, touched the ground, and the aircraft – full of fuel – crashed and exploded. Some 273 people lost their lives in that conflagration (271 onboard the aircraft and two people on the ground).

Afterwards there were many reports of strange lights in the large field where most of the aircraft crashed. At first the police thought it was the torches of ghoulish souvenir hunters, but that theory proved false. Officers who rushed to the scene generally saw nothing, but there is some evidence that one or two police officers reported the same sorts of wandering lights.

The most intriguing tales, however, came from a trailer park near the crash site. In the months following the crash, residents complained of knocks at their doors in the night. Some residents opened their doors to find apparently solid people asking for directions or for the location of their luggage. One seemingly solid ghost appeared to a man walking his dog. The apparition reeked of aviation fuel and his clothes seemed to be smouldering as he stood there. He asked for somewhere he could make an emergency call. When the walker turned to point to the location of a phone box, the spectre disappeared.

The fascination with solid ghosts is not only about their seemingly realistic appearance but with the fact that they speak and smell. Captain Hinchliffe's solid ghost spoke to Colonel Henderson. The two ghosts of Flight 401 were said to have carried with them a slight smell of aftershave and were certainly able to speak. The possible passenger from Flight 191 carried the stink of kerosene, and we have already discussed the case of Catherine Bystock, near RAF Metheringham [10].

What all aviation ghosts tend to have in common is a traumatic death. Emotion is associated with almost everything in the paranormal, from the sex rituals of some shamans and witches to the premonitions before the sinking of the Titanic. High levels of emotional energy seem to link humans in the normal world with events and essences in the paranormal one.

CHAPTER 7
A VERY VARIED PHENOMENON

> *There is a tendency in the Twentieth Century to forget that there will be a Twenty-First Century science, and indeed a Thirtieth Century science, from which vantage points our knowledge of the universe may appear quite different. We suffer, perhaps, from temporal provincialism, a form of arrogance that has always irritated posterity.*
>
> — J ALLEN HYNEK QUOTED BY SIR PETER HORSLEY IN HIS 1997 AUTOBIOGRAPHY

Not all so-called ghosts are super-stars. While the likes of Mary, Queen of Scots and Abraham Lincoln are posing for photos on the red carpet at the brightly-lit, lavishly decorated entrance, the minor characters at the Ghost Oscars are sneaking in the back door. They never get prizes and their interviews are never splashed across the front pages the next day but they are important just the same. They are the ghosts that make all the others look credible. The 'minor characters' in my metaphor are the ghosts that are rarely spoken of – and even then only by a few individuals and in private settings. They are the 'private ghosts'.

Virtually all of us have such ghosts. Grandma once revealed at a festive lunch that – as a girl – she'd seen the apparition of a lady walking smartly through her front door. Uncle Jeff once relaxed enough after dinner to tell of the ghost of one of his workmates who appeared in the foreman's office every anniversary of a workplace accident. These sorts of stories are related by tens of thousands of ordinary people at ordinary gatherings and are almost never written about. The ranks of private ghosts extend, in their thousands, into the far distance and we have no way of analysing or even of cataloguing them. Yet they carry immense weight. Ordinary they may be, but the absence of sensationalism and financial or career motives lends them powerful credibility. No-one makes and money from them, no-one's career will be enhanced by their revelation to the world, no-one even wants them to be discussed much.

I have selected a few small examples to illustrate these points. They are all drawn from personal knowledge and from correspondents.

A Policeman's Solace

On a dark 1950s winter's night my father, then a young police constable, was on patrol in a small town in southern England. As part of his assigned beat he was required to wait at a particular 'conference point' in the High Street for a fixed period of time. In the days before personal radios the only way that a station officer could communicate with officers on the beat was if the latter stood, at a pre-arranged time, beside a designated public phone box (or a police telephone box). If there were urgent instructions, the station would call the box within the time allotted for a 'conference'. If the phone did not ring, the officer continued on his beat once the prescribed waiting time had elapsed.

On this particular night there was no urgent ringing of the telephone bell and my father simply waited out the required time standing beside the public call box which stood outside the town's post office. Across the deserted main street stood a brewery whose boundaries consisted of high brick walls. Set into the huge walls which faced the High Street was a large double gate. Its high wooden doors were shut and locked at that time of the night. In the daytime a regular stream of dray wagons and lorries passed through those gates but, at that early hour, they were simply a forbidding wooden insert in the tall, broken-glass-topped walls that surrounded the brewery.

Impatient to be moving again, if only to get the blood flowing on such a cold night, my father was stamping his feet and looking up and down the street when he suddenly became aware of a bright light. He quickly switched his gaze across the road to see that the brewery gates were now open but that, rather than a dark, empty brewery yard with parked wagons and stacked barrels, the view was of a bright, sunlit garden and a pathway that curved through flower borders almost to the gate itself. In total contrast to the real weather that night, it was a summer scene complete with flowers in full bloom. My father said that – although it may have been his imagination – he could actually smell the perfume of the flowers and the scent of cut grass.

As he looked across the street in amazement two figures came into view, walking down the path towards the gate. The first was his father (my grandfather), who had died suddenly about seven or eight years previously. The second was a young lady in a summer dress who my own father did not recognise. The two were in friendly conversation and appeared to be preoccupied in each other's company. But as they passed the gate entrance my grandfather glanced across to where my father was standing, waved a hand in greeting, and smiled. He then turned back to his companion and they continued their chat and their walk.

My father said that he blinked and the light and the vision began to disappear. Not in a flash, not immediately, but fading and disappearing gradually over a few seconds. And then all was as before – the cold, empty street, the darkness, and the glowering weight of the huge double wooden gates set in a bleak expanse of high brick wall.

The experience, as related by my father, had been both immensely uplifting and quite sad. He had been overjoyed to see his father again and remembered feeling comforted by the fact that he was 'safe' and happy. There had also been sadness and a sense of loss as the image disappeared. Nevertheless, my father emphasised that seeing his father again in such circumstances reassured him on many levels. For the rest of that shift he felt like he was walking on air.

The immediate response from a sceptic would be that this was a waking dream and that it was all in my father's head as he stood there, bored and cold, waiting for the time he'd be able to resume his beat. The explanation is used for many such visions but my father was not an idiot, he knew very well what waking dreams were and was only too aware of how people could hallucinate when tired and cold. He'd thought about the event very hard and told me that it did not feel anything like a dream. He'd been physically very active – stamping his feet, moving his legs, swinging his arms, and knew that he was pretty alert, looking up and down the street regularly and thinking about the next segment of his patrol. He had not been thinking about his own father at the time and the event seemed distinctly unworldly. The vision of the figures was extremely detailed yet none of the background was of anywhere he knew. And the second person – the young lady – was completely unknown to him. When pressed he admitted that he often daydreamed when on such duties but that his daydreams were extremely fleeting, did not involve such incredible colours and light, were never as detailed, and always disappeared in an instant.

This particular vision of what might have been the ghost of his father lasted at least a few minutes, was very detailed and bright, and faded from his view rather than instantly ceasing to exist. To the end of his life, including the next twenty-five years of policing, he never had another similar experience and he was always certain that the event was not a dream or an imagined vision. He was absolutely convinced that, whatever it was, he was able to look at the scene as in real life, that he could scan from detail to detail and then return his eyes to them exactly as he would have done when looking into a real park on a summer's day.

As a police detective he went on to participate in his fair share of night long surveillance shifts – standing watching certain places, sitting for hours in cars, and so on. He never again saw such a vision and never even had a waking dream during all those years. He was no-one's fool and – to the day of his own death – he believed that he had been granted a vision of his own father in the afterlife.

The Haunted Cottage

Another example from the 1950s involved a young naval officer and his wife. They had established themselves in a small house in the town of Arundel on the south coast of England because his Fleet Air Arm[1] posting required him to be near naval air stations in the area. The house had two bedrooms and theirs was the door directly at the top of the narrow stairs which led directly up from the front door. Their five-year old son had the second bedroom.

One night, as they slept, the couple both woke in an instant to the totally unexpected sound of their front door opening and closing. In those days people often did not lock their street doors. One can imagine their feelings. No-one was supposed to be visiting – especially at that time of night – and, if the person was a burglar, why make all that noise opening and closing a heavy street door. As the husband made moves to get out of bed to investigate, they heard the sound of heavy footsteps coming up the stairs. They hardly had time to feel afraid when the steps stopped outside and the bedroom door was opened. The wife freely admitted that, at that point, she hid under the covers. Her husband got out of bed and she expected to hear raised voices and perhaps even a fight.

But nothing happened. Her husband's baffled comment made her raise her head above the blankets. There was no-one there. They searched upstairs and downstairs but found the front door closed and no-one in the house. Finally, they checked the front door again, only to find that it had been locked and bolted all along. It was one of those totally unexpected and thoroughly mysterious events that – if it had happened when just one of them was in the house – would have quickly been dismissed as a dream. But both husband and wife had experienced it and they had both been sufficiently concerned to search their home and check all the doors and windows. But, as one does with such things, they quickly put it to the back of their minds and got on with their lives.

A few months later the couple's sleep was interrupted again. This time by their son. In the middle of the night he entered his parents' bedroom and awakened his mother by tapping her on the shoulder. When he was certain she was fully awake he calmly asked her why there was a lady in his bedroom. He went on to explain that he'd woken up to find an 'old lady' sitting on the end of his bed. She'd said nothing and he had immediately evacuated the room to find out why this unexpected guest had descended upon him. Needless to say, his parents were baffled. They had no guest and, anyway, the house only had two bedrooms both of which were occupied. They checked his bedroom and the rest of the house but – again – there was not the slightest sign of an intruder.

Footsteps, doors opening, creaking floorboards – all are a very common ways in which the paranormal intrudes upon people's lives. A similar tale is told by a friend who, on several occasions when she was a young woman visiting her mother, heard footsteps walking around her room. When she sat up in bed and put on the light, of course, there was no-one there, but her mother revealed that this often happened and that several people who had slept in that room experienced the same thing. She laughed it off as a harmless aberration, but my friend only went back to that particular house when absolutely forced to and experienced the same noises on several of those occasions.

Both that and the first Arundel example highlight noise without any visible ghostly presence, a baffling phenomenon which even the sceptics find hard to explain other than to argue that it is all in the imagination. But how does that work when two people hear the same noises having been fast asleep? The couple lived in that cottage in Arundel for four or five years and they were never again disturbed by footsteps on the stairs.

In that same span of time their young son was never again visited by the 'old lady' (a description which, from a five year old, could mean anyone from fifteen to eighty). Which just adds to the mystery of why a ghost should appear just once in a bedroom of a tiny cottage. Scholars of the paranormal might propose that the cottage was some sort of hub for such activity but if that were the case why did strange things happen on only two occasions, one of which was witnessed by a child?

Great-Grandmother in the Pantry

High quality, semi-detached houses of the sort that were built in the UK in the 1920s and 1930s, were relatively large and well fitted compared to the flimsy, modern shoe-boxes which pass for homes a century later. Their ceilings were high, the rooms large by British standards, and fitted cupboards and utility rooms were the norm. Among the latter was usually a large pantry. In the days before refrigerators, households kept fresh food in a cool pantry. It was shelved and usually had a large marble worktop on which foods like raw meat, fish, and milk could be stored so that they lasted longer. There were usually no windows through which the sun could heat the room. It was almost always built as an interior room with just a single door leading from the kitchen. My wife's grandmother lived in precisely that sort of house.

One day, when my wife's teenage sister was visiting her grandmother she had reason to walk into the pantry from the kitchen. As soon as she passed through the door she was shocked to find her great-grandmother standing there. It was a major shock because her great-grandmother had died several years previously. The girl gasped and left the room, closing the door behind her. She called for her grandmother and when they opened the door again the apparition had gone.

The ghost had seemed very solid and real to the young girl, not at all like a diaphanous ghost, so was more like a revenant. But the strange thing is that there was no rational explanation for the appearance. The girl had not been thinking about her great-grandmother, the appearance coincided with no anniversary of birth, marriage, or death, and there was certainly no apparent reason why the ghost should have appeared in a pantry of all places. And it never appeared again.

This is a story from personal experience but it is probably matched by thousands of similar incidents in scores of other countries. Why do such highly credible apparitions appear to such a wide variety of fairly ordinary people and then never or rarely happen again?

Ghost or Time Window?

Back in the 1960s the author was a regular evening customer at a medieval pub in one of England's most ancient of cities. The city's history goes back probably to the very earliest times, beyond Roman times. There had been a pub on the same site for at least four hundred years and almost certainly much longer. The street on which the pub stands was probably old even two thousand years ago.

The 1960s pub was atmospheric and cosy. Roaring fires always burned in the fireplaces in the three bars - the Public Bar, the Saloon Bar, and the 'Snug' - except on the warmest of summer days. Being a regular, I was accustomed to having frequent chats with the then landlord and many of those talks, in the last half hour or so before closing (and often long afterwards) would turn to the many ghost stories which abound in an ancient city. One of the other regulars had been a tin miner in Cornwall in his youth and brought equivalent tales from the far southwest to chill our bones. He told one story of a ghost that haunted the wheelhouse of the famous Levant mine at which he worked. The Levant – dating at least as far back as the Romans – was mainly a copper and tin mine.

Evidently twice during his five-year spell at the mine the cage that lifted the miners back to the surface failed to arrive. On both occasions it eventually arrived – about half an hour late – due, the miners were told, to the wheel-house operator having fled from the wheelhouse when confronted by a ghost. As far as our friend could recall, the ghost looked like a miner and appeared somehow 'lost'. The explanation was that it was the ghost of a miner who had been killed in the terrible accident of 1919 when the links to the lift-cage broke and thirty-nine men were killed when it fell to the bottom of the shaft.

One winter evening the pub was very quiet and I was the only customer left. The staff had cleared most of the evening's empties away and were busy in the wash-room. It was just me, my half-finished pint, and the landlord taking a rest after a long day. With a narrowing of his eyes, he cleared his throat and took a swig of his own pint. Then, with obvious embarrassment, he cleared his throat again and informed me that he had not told anyone of this event other than his wife but that it had scared him to the core and he needed to tell someone who would not immediately laugh at him. He then turned on his heels and motioned me to follow him down to the cellars, which I did even though it meant going into the coldest parts of the building. In time-honoured fashion, the cellars were an untidy mess. Their main purpose was to store beer, snacks, and other drink for the pub but they were also the place where old furniture was left before being thrown out, and where piles of boxes of crisps and snacks and empty beer crates lined two walls.

He led me through two or three underground rooms until we reached one that I knew was underneath the Snug where I had been warm and cosy just a few minutes earlier and where I hoped to return as quickly as possible. The room was extremely cold but, apart from that, it was an unremarkable space of whitewashed brick, lit by bare lightbulbs casting a stark light on the 'in-use' barrels ranged on a wooden rack against one wall, their pipes leading up to the pumps in several bars upstairs. In the middle stood full barrels awaiting their turn and a little towards the other long wall stood the empties ready to be hoisted out of the hatchway which led up to the street.

The landlord pointed at the wall against which the empty barrels were positioned and then up at the ceiling. 'There,' he said. I gazed at the dirty whitewash and flaking plaster which was coming away in small patches where the wall met the ceiling. In the middle of the ceiling on that wall was a pair of huge wooden doors, barred and padlocked on the inside. These, I realised, were the cellar-doors which opened upwards into the street above to allow stores and beer to be run down a ramp into the cellar. I looked back at him, puzzled. He gave me a wry grin. 'Don't look much now but that's where I saw them.' I waited, my gaze wandering from his pale features to the long wall which I knew ran beneath and alongside the cobbled street outside. He let out a huge sigh.

'A couple of months ago I came down here at about midnight to change a couple of barrels so that I didn't need to do it the next morning. We'd finished clearing up and everyone had gone home. My wife had gone to bed. I'd only got the one light on, but as I worked I became aware of the cellar getting brighter. There was much more light than we normally get from those bulbs. It was like daylight. When I turned around from where I was working it was as though the top of the street wall had suddenly developed a row of windows about three or four feet down from the ceiling. Through these 'windows' I could see people walking in broad daylight.'

'Problem is, I could only see the lower parts of people's legs. Everyone was wearing sandals and some had leather thongs up their calves. I thought I was having a seizure – stood transfixed like a statue. I watched as three or four pairs of legs wearing heavy sandals and thongs went past and a couple of what were obviously women with long, tatty, skirts. On the men I could see what I thought were the lower bits of swords or daggers against leather kilts.'

I asked him how long this lasted, to which he replied only about four or five minutes at the most before the light began to fade and soon he was back in virtual darkness in his cellar. 'It took me a week before I could come down here again,' he said, 'and even then I brought one of the barmen to help me even though it weren't strictly necessary.'

We talked about his experience a lot over the following weeks but the best we could do to explain the vision was that it must have been a sort of time slip – a vision of a period when the street level had been three or four feet lower than in modern times. Intrigued by the tale I checked with local archaeologists. They confirmed that the street level had been at that height between about 30 BCE and about 100 CE when their excavations showed that it had received the next major resurfacing. It seemed that what the landlord had seen, therefore, were the legs and feet of passers-by during Roman times – somewhere around 1,900 years before our cosy chat over a pint or two.

I have often wondered at that vision. I have not the slightest doubt that the landlord was telling the truth. He was far too wary about me telling anyone else for it to be a prank and no-one ever did a 'gotcha' on me. I met him again a few years later and he was still keeping the story to himself although he did say that some of his customers over the years had mentioned similar sightings elsewhere in the ancient city.

The tale is all the more compelling because it was never used to attract custom to the pub. Now that the landlord and his wife have passed on, I believe that I am the only person alive who knows the tale (with the exception, now, of you, dear reader). But let's face it – the story is not exactly going to turn the world of ghost hunting on its head. Ancient cities across the world have hundreds of similar legends. I include this one because I believed the landlord and because it illustrates how utterly bizarre some 'ghost' incidents can be. This one was a view into an ancient street from a cellar in which only the lower legs and footwear of the 'ghosts' could be seen.

Why? What was it that prompted the vision? Your guess is as good as anyone's but my own take on the incident is that it was not a ghost sighting at all but a time-slip – a completely isolated and possibly random window which opened and then closed between two points in time. Why did it open? Again a guess, but I think it was dependent on the landlord. He told me that he had, several years previously, seen a ghost in one of the front bedrooms of the pub. A man wearing what appeared to him to be nineteenth-century clothing was standing in the room when the landlord entered. The apparition was 'see through' but strong enough for the landlord to watch the man pick up his hat and look directly at the landlord before walking through the closed door into the corridor.

So, it might be that my friend the landlord may have had whatever it takes for a human to connect with the cosmos, with whatever we might call the Force. He obviously could not control it but that is the only explanation I can give for him experiencing (or causing?) two time-slip visions – first when he experienced a vision of a nineteenth-century man upstairs and then, years later, the vision of the passers-by outside his cellar from what appeared to be Roman times. One might wonder, too, whether the same phenomenon (if it exists) might have caused the vision of the great-grandmother in the pantry?

My remaining questions, if these visions were time-slips, would be: Did the Victorian man 'see' the landlord? If any of those Roman Britons had looked down while they were wandering past, would they have seen a shocked and baffled twentieth-century landlord staring up at them? And did the old lady in the pantry have a vision of a young girl regarding her in total shock?

Does all this sound a little wild? Possibly, but we can also add the very definite time-slip vision experienced by Sir Victor Goddard when he saw a future airfield at Drem in Scotland in 1935 and noted details that he could not have known at the time but which came to pass.

What are they?

The circumstantial evidence for the existence of a phenomenon that we call 'ghosts' is overwhelming. Ghosts are spectacular and they certainly make money, but the people who report them most frequently are not trying to reap a financial reward or gain their fifteen minutes of fame and publicity. A very high proportion of these people would prefer never to have experienced them in the first place. What we call ghosts exist somewhere other than our physical world. This may be another dimension or realm or the images and emotions may perhaps persist in a universal consciousness. Witnesses of end-of-life events often say that they see a shadowy or misty shape leave the body of the dying person. There are even videos online of misty shapes appearing to leave the dead bodies of accident victims. Many may be faked but are all of them made up by bored humans?

Faked or not, the instances of ordinary people experiencing and even recording ghosts and associated activity are far too numerous and frequent and far too ancient - extending back to the most archaic of times – for it all to be a trivial matter of hysteria, hallucination, or trickery. At the same time, we have to guard against the temptation to conclude that all such activity is the result of a single causal factor. How can insubstantial ghosts present themselves as physical effects and noises? In the months after the terrible fire at Kings Cross Station in London in 1987 a late night traveller at the station was alone on one of the escalators when it began shaking and vibrating just as if people were running up it behind him. There was no-one there but suddenly two young girls sped by him going up the escalator. They were laughing as they went but disappeared before they'd got more than a few steps beyond the chap.

How can a diaphanous ghost cause rappings on windows, howlings in the night, footsteps on the stairs or in the corridor? How can ghosts create smells like lavender or kerosene or the horrible smell of rotting flesh, and how can they cause lights and orbs to appear? More to the point, how can they appear on photographs and sometimes in videos?

Current theories – if one ignores the unlikely possibility that millions of humans over thousands of years have all been the victims of fakes or mental aberrations – tend to fall into two broad camps. Ghosts are either spiritual appearances from beyond the grave – apparitions of dead people created by their 'essences', or they are the visions/perceptions experienced by people whose brains have a connection (permanent or temporary) with another realm or dimension or with the universal consciousness – perhaps aided by the levels of emotional energy attached to specific elements of the consciousness.

What the questions come down to is whether ghosts are independent of, or dependent upon, the observer, and whether what we call ghosts are really several different phenomena: noises and movements perhaps resulting from 'recurrent spontaneous psychokinesis' (RSPK), visions through links between a given mind and a wider consciousness, time-slip visions based on similar principles but involving a link to previous times, controlled energy fields, independent manifestations of emotional energy, and so on.

My own feeling is that subject of 'ghosts' has become too all-encompassing. It now combines a wide range of phenomena from a number of different causal roots. Several quite distinct phenomena are in that combination: individual links to the universal consciousness, emotional energy or energy fields, telepathic and telekinetic abilities, whatever we are to call foresight and hindsight (precognition and retrocognition), and perhaps even a link between locations in the timeline that causes us to be able to see a brief glimpse of a previous event – however mundane.

We have also to consider the 'ghosts' of objects and the apparently solid appearances of monsters and strange animals (cryptids). Are these, too, related to some sort of link between the individual and the universal consciousness or are they different phenomena entirely – perhaps more akin to us being able, on rare occasions, to see into another dimension or be visited from that dimension? Sometimes you will find such things discussed under the heading of ghosts but more often, these days, within the topic of 'para-zoology' or 'cryptids'.

Ghosts in all their varied glory certainly exist. Of this there is no doubt. The basis on which they appear to people or appear on photos is not yet known but neither do we yet understand how people can know the future, how they can communicate with their minds, how some people appear to have been reincarnated from a previous life, and how some dying people are known to commune with beings in another dimension or realm. All of these are genuine phenomena but we do not yet understand how or why they occur.

In the words of many scholars of the paranormal, from Alan Hynek and Jaques Vallée to Jack Hunter and Julie Beischel, ghosts are one aspect of 'high strangeness' – the weird extension of the paranormal that includes UFOs, aliens, cryptid monsters, visions of the future, apparitions from the past, and communication with the dead. What they do above all else, however, is link our past superstitions to Paranorm 2.0 – the new reality.

During the entire two-hundred-thousand year life of modern humanity there has been not a single perceivable break in our belief in the paranormal, whether it be the immeasurably old beliefs of the original Australasians or the modern relationship between witches and their gods and spells. But the fact is that the complexity of our history and of our involvement with the paranormal has disguised its true nature. Civilisation after civilisation, indigenous belief system after indigenous belief system, established religion after established religion have produced an intricate and convoluted cat's cradle of philosophy and practice. Layer after layer of unrecorded and recorded beliefs, hundreds of gods and demons, mountains of books written by thinkers and prophets over many, many thousands of years, scores of religions with their own detailed explanations of the paranormal realm, thousands of philosophical treatises on all of the above, each interpreting and expanding upon what has been written before. All these pronouncements, arguments, counter-arguments, interpretations, alternative interpretations, and all the debates, have been piled one upon another until the truth - if there was ever any truth – is so buried under the rubble that no-one can ever (and I mean *ever*) sort it all out in any meaningfully useful way. There is simply no possibility that the human race will be able to review and whittle down this monumental heap of thinking and preaching into anything useful. That's it. Bottom line – we'll never get to the truth by reviewing whatever has survived from twenty thousand years of humanity's most profound thinking added to whatever we can learn from sixty thousand years of the deepest unwritten beliefs of aboriginal peoples on several continents.

In just the ten thousand years during which we think humans have been civilised our belief systems have taken in a wide range of paranormal considerations and have accorded humanity a veritable armoury of psychic powers. The Sumerians used soothsayers and wizards, the Greeks had their witch-prostitutes and oracles, the ancient Egyptians had female witches and male priests who interpreted the paranormal and natural worlds, Roman civilisation depended on a wide range of witches and warlocks and on divination of signs and auspices, Hindus have always believed in reincarnation and rebirth, many societies have relied upon the advice and guidance of shamans and witches for healing.

As I inferred earlier, witchcraft is one of the aspects of the paranormal towards which humans have always been ambivalent. Those with alternative ideas – usually the established religions of this world – generally fear witchcraft. The Chinese and the Romans both executed hundreds of people for practising witchcraft, and the Christians continued to persecute witches well into the eighteenth century. The close links between witchcraft and sexual energy provide a convenient excuse – especially within the more puritanical of our religions – for painting witches and anything related to them as evil, wanton, and lustful. The contradictory attitudes towards witches are never more blatantly exposed than in art.

A Very Varied Phenomenon

The Witches' Sabbat, Luis Ricardo Falero (1880) – Note the missing toe – an alleged mark of a witch. https://commons.wikimedia.org/wiki/File:The_witches_Sabbath,_by_Luis_Ricardo_Falero.jpg

Women being hanged for witchcraft, Newcastle, England, 1655 https://commons.wikimedia.org/wiki/File: Women_hanged_for_witchcraft_Newcastle_1655.png

The ambivalence towards witchcraft is simply a reflection of humanity's deep uncertainty about the paranormal as a whole. Mainstream religions claim to have the 'correct' answers and many of them insist that anything else is heresy punishable by death. Witchcraft is just a different way of looking at the universe. To condemn it on the basis that one's own belief system is absolutely correct – that it is the final and only answer – is dogmatic, bigoted, and just plain wrong. But these attitudes have been prevalent, almost unabated since humans first walked the planet. In the modern world we have continued the work of astrologers and alchemists and attempted to use mediums to speak to the dead. In spite of all this, the bottom line remains the same: attacking the Augean Stables of what has gone before will not get us anywhere at all.

This was Paranorm 1.0 in all its contradictions and complexity, and it's why we desperately need to find a new way, one that sets all of that thinking to one side and simply asks: Is there a more productive way of looking at the paranormal?

Fundamentally, the never-ending deserts of Paranorm 1.0 lead us nowhere and simply provide ammunition for ceaseless and utterly pointless debate and conflict. That's where Paranorm 2.0 comes to the rescue. Only by starting again with modern experimental techniques and ignoring the impenetrable quagmires of past beliefs and structures can we create a clearer view of the power of the paranormal as a whole.

Paranorm 2.0 is a fresh way of seeing the paranormal but it still involves the whole range of phenomena that interested our forebears. Death and the afterlife has always been a major concern and it particularly engrossed the Egyptians. Ghosts have always enthralled people. Monsters frightened almost all our ancestors and they remain a pressing issue for many researchers. The enduring mystery of UFOs needs to be examined in an experimental fashion. And the underlying psychic abilities of humans, the focus for highly intelligent cultures like China, Persia, Greece, and Rome, form the basis for witches and adepts everywhere.

In modern times the paranormal has brought us face to face with the almost certain existence of strange objects and experiences that the afficionados call UFOs. Whatever your view on the topic it has always exhibited highly persuasive aspects of what we usually term the paranormal – telepathy, control of matter, telekinesis, and more. The following chapters focus on the key elements of Paranorm 2.0 as an introduction to this new version of the paranormal.

And what better place to begin than with the age-old subject of reincarnation – a topic which has deep roots in the past but which has now been researched in depth by modern scientists? Most westerners have been brainwashed by various established religions to believe reincarnation to be not just impossible but also totally unacceptable as a belief. To a practising Hindu or Buddhist, on the other hand, the concept is one of the rocks that underpin their belief-systems. The possibility of being reincarnated has been a central belief of humans for thousands of years but to a modern European or American it sounds totally ridiculous if not blasphemous.

Approaching the subject from the new standpoint of Paranorm 2.0 might convince them otherwise.

CHAPTER 8
REINCARNATION

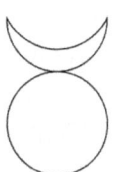

> *The statistical probability that reincarnation does in fact occur is so overwhelming ... that cumulatively the evidence is not inferior to that for most if not all branches of science, whether physics, cosmology, or Darwinian evolution.*
>
> — PROFESSOR DORIS KUHLMANN-WILSDORF, PHYSICIST, COMMENTING ON THE WORK OF DR IAN STEVENSON

Like the sensationalist visions of the future painted by fortune tellers at the seaside, the colourful horoscopes in most daily newspapers, and the extravagant antics of fake mediums, the very word 'reincarnation' evokes vivid pictures of the Victorians' obsession with the paranormal and with death. Several deities and semi-deities are said to have been brought back from the dead or reincarnated into other lives including, for a very brief period, the Christian prophet. But we also all know that it is nonsense, right? No-one can be brought back into another life after dying. When you're dead, you're dead – gone forever. Some religions insist that no one is ever reincarnated but, as far as the Christian religion is concerned this only became the case half a millennium after the death and supposed rebirth of Jesus of Nazareth. Looking back it seems shocking that, before the Second Council of Constantinople in 553 CE the Christian church assumed that reincarnation was a given for everyone. For more than five hundred years it accepted reincarnation as a core belief but it was never terribly well explained as a principle.

After the Council of Constantinople, however, reincarnation suddenly became a Christian heresy. Books and articles on the political machinations of the Christian Church would fill a library by themselves and might provide meat for a dozen great soap operas. The numerous Church Synods and Councils, attended by people with often nefarious agendas, came up with more long words, convoluted theories, and fanciful conclusions than you can shake a stick at. But, after the so-called anathematisation of Nestorianism (yet another of the scores and scores of Christian sects) in 553 CE reincarnation ceased to be a word uttered by Catholic and then Protestant Christian priests[1].

The standard modern Christian approach to the topic is that you get one shot at life after which you simply wait somewhere comfortable – or uncomfortable depending on how you have lived – until the 'Day of Judgement' when the Christian deity decides who has been good and who is on the naughty-list. Christian views on reincarnation fly in the face not only of their own original beliefs but those of other major religions and billions of people the world over.

The number of people who believe in reincarnation is staggeringly high but, nowadays, the most powerful arguments in its favour come from witness testimony and compelling empirical evidence – as alluded to by Professor Kuhlmann-Wilsdorf above. The possibility of being reborn into another life was part of ancient Egypt's beliefs as well as being a core element in modern Hindu and Buddhist teaching. Much of their philosophy is based on the concept of being made to constantly repeat life in the material world in order to somehow improve as a person. This is perhaps best illustrated by the Hindu concept of Samsara – a virtually endless circle of death, reincarnation, life, and death. The human soul is immortal and the cycle of suffering on this Earth can only be broken by an individual gathering sufficient good karma. This is the accumulation of what might be called moral stature – the gradual improvement of one's soul towards goodness and positivity. Good things bring good karma and bad ones attract the opposite. Although there are complex differences between the way Buddhists, Hindus and Jains interpret karma the basic results are similar. One can only break out of the curse of rebirth by becoming truly good and, in the Buddhist belief system, by shunning the material world and becoming one with the wider universe. The Buddhists believe that only in this way can one end the cycle of suffering and attain Nirvana. A great many early belief systems major on the belief that material things are inherently evil.

These religions teach the central role of reincarnation in the cycle of life and, today, a number of scientists and researchers agree with them to the extent that they are convinced that reincarnation as a phenomenon is real. Reincarnation, they say, is not a Victorian fantasy. It happens all the time and they have a great deal of anecdotal and circumstantial evidence to prove it (it is pretty hard to get any other kind of evidence where this topic – or any other paranormal one is concerned).

Evidence

Just a quick sidebar on 'evidence'. What exactly do we mean by that much overused word? There are many different types of 'evidence' that we humans use to judge things in different contexts – in the law, in medical research, in theoretical physics, and so on. Traditionally they range from highly scientific/quantitative types of evidence to the most qualitative and experiential.

Broadly though there are two main types:

1. **Scientific-evidence** – this is replicable, falsifiable, and usually based on experiments or observations that can be repeated with precisely the same ingredients or participants and the results tested and then compared

with other experimental results. It is essentially empirical, relying on observable facts and repeatable experiments.
2. **Experiential evidence** – evidence gained from human observation and experience, not all of it testable in a scientific manner. In quasi-scientific settings this type of evidence can sometimes be tested through statistical analysis. It can be based on anecdotal or circumstantial facts and observations.

Scientific evidence is almost always regarded as the best. If something can be repeated and verified against standard metrics then it must be true. Statisticians use a metric called Sigma – meaning standard deviations from norms. In statistical analysis a 'five sigma' result means that there is a one in a three point five million chance that the result arose by sheer chance. It could still be wrong, but the chances are incredibly low. Calculations that reach 6-Sigma eradicate a chance result in around a half billion tests.

We generally regard experiential evidence as much less reliable but for many purposes we are obliged to rely on it (e.g. in courts of law). You'll have heard people saying that 'We can infer from that ...' or 'Our deductions from this evidence are ...'. Whenever experiential evidence is presented it is necessary to deduce, induce, or abduce. The words infer and deduce mean virtually the same thing (no matter what some websites say). They relate to inductive reasoning and mean using logic to draw conclusions about a body of information. Inferences and deductions can easily be wrong if the information is insufficient or the logic is faulty. Just because the first ten people you see in the morning have brown hair does not mean that you can deduce that all people have brown hair.

One might use abductive reasoning to try to explain an event from observations of what happened. The observations might be based on human senses or perhaps electronic sensors. It attempts to come to a reasonable conclusion based on what 'could be' the causes. The academic phrase is 'abductive reasoning' – for the rest of us it is a reasonable hunch. We can be way off track with abductive reasoning because it requires a great many assumptions to be made (most of them invisible). A light appears in the night sky and appears to descend to the ground a mile or so away. Abductive reasoning might lead us to conclude that this was an alien spacecraft and then link that to some mutilated cattle discovered nearby the following morning. We may be right or we may be deluding ourselves but abductive reasoning is what many human activities are based upon.

In order to review the subject of reincarnation in sufficient detail we need to cover a lot of ground. The topic is incredibly wide and, while the evidence for people having had more than one life comes mainly from children, there are a number of persuasive cases of adults who remember past lives. One of the more interesting of the adult examples concerns a lady called Dorothy Eady whose life of extreme poverty testifies to the fact that money was most certainly not a motivating factor for her colourful claims. The litmus test of Dorothy Eady's remembrances of a previous existence lay in her uncanny ability to 'remember' where buried archaeological ruins were to be found.

Dorothy Eady

Few people these days have heard of this lady but her story reveals that sometimes the memory of a previous life may persist well into adulthood and, in fact, for a person's entire life. Dorothy Eady was apparently reincarnated over an extremely lengthy timespan, but she remembered some incredible facts from her previous life and did so for her entire life as Dorothy Eady.

A British-born archaeologist and an expert on the civilization of a key segment of Pharaonic Egypt, Dorothy Eady was never trained as an archaeologist but, nevertheless, made a string of important discoveries from memory. She believed for her entire adult life that she was the reincarnation of an ancient Egyptian temple priestess who was the illicit lover of the Pharoah Seti I (reigned around 1294-1279 BCE). She never claimed to be the reincarnation of one of the more famous female Ptolemaic or Khemetic rulers like Cleopatra VII, Neithotep,

Hatshepsut, Nefertiti, or many others – instead she claimed to be the reincarnation of a lowly temple priestess who committed suicide out of love.

In an article published on July 26th 1987, John Anthony West in the New York Times called her story

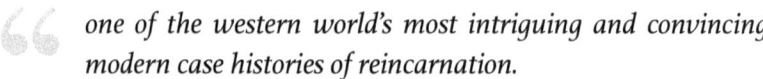
> one of the western world's most intriguing and convincing modern case histories of reincarnation.

The full story is told in Jonathan Cott and Hanny El Zeini's book published as 'The Search for Omm Sety' in the same year.

The lady was born in London in January 1904. At the tender age of three she evidently fell down some stairs at home and was so badly injured that she was pronounced dead by the doctor. That worthy then left to attend a living patient. When he returned to oversee preparations for her transport to the undertakers he found her sitting up in bed! Dorothy survived, but the accident seems to have changed her because she began having vivid dreams about a huge building with columns (a fair description of the Temple of Seti I at Abydos). She often told her parents that she wanted to go 'home' but they did not understand what she meant until, when she was four, her parents took her along on a visit they made to the British Museum. The museum as a whole was pretty boring for the four-year-old, until the family reached the Egyptian galleries. No sooner had the child entered the first Egyptian room than she became extremely animated and ran through the halls kissing the feet of the statues. Note: this is a four-year-old in 1908.

From then on she was a regular visitor to the British Museum and, later, managed to persuade the eminent Egyptologist Sir E A Wallis Budge to help her learn hieroglyphs and some of the ancient languages. Budge himself had been informally taught by experts at the museum before going up to Cambridge and this may well have been his way of repaying their generosity.

Dorothy Eady eventually married an Egyptian and gave him a son who was named Seti. But the marriage did not last – mainly, it appears, due to her constant claims of reincarnation which in an Egypt struggling to develop western credentials was an embarrassment. After the separation she stayed in Egypt fighting constantly to hold down jobs to keep her and her son alive. Eventually she found her way to the town of Abydos[2] where she said she had been called Omm Seti. She had been a virgin priestess but fell pregnant to the Pharoah. The sacrilege would, if discovered, have led to the execution of them both so, to save the man she loved, Omm Seti committed suicide.

After her divorce in 1936 Dorothy took work with the Egyptian Department of Antiquities, work which steadily revealed her mysterious ability to somehow know things about ancient Egypt and its social world as well as being able to spot where the buried remains of certain buildings at Abydos were located, before they were actually excavated.

Eady was what one might call a character. Her weird knowledge of the site at Abydos gained the respect of many professional archaeologists but she lived in the most abject poverty all her life. In spite of this she remained in Abydos and never strayed from her belief that she was the reincarnated priestess. She never budged an inch from her determination to live and die near Abydos. She died in her mud hut in a nearby village in April 1981.

Dorothy Eady's story is one of the few well-recorded examples of an adult remembering a past life, being able to provide evidence through knowledge, and holding fast to their belief for their entire life. Her story is not the only adult reincarnation case but many have been muddled and blurred by research approaches like hypnosis and poor research techniques and some have doubt heaped upon them by the money made from publications. None of this affected the Eady case. There are lots of cases of adults remembering past lives but by far the most common and best researched examples of past-lives are drawn from studies of children undertaken by two highly eminent psychiatrists.

Dr Ian Stevenson

Arguably, the first modern student of reincarnation was the famous psychiatrist, Dr Ian Stevenson. His life's work centred on child psychiatry with what was, at first, a secondary interest in children's early memories of previous lives. He held the Chair of the Department of Psychiatry at the University of Virginia. During his career of over forty years, he collected and evaluated several thousand cases of memories of previous lives.

At first sight, reincarnation is one of those things that seems impossible to prove. If someone tells you that they are the reincarnation of Mozart and they can hum a few bars of his best works, does that prove they are the reincarnated genius? Of course not, and probably not even if that person could compose music along similar lines and styles, because quite a few people can copy a musical style. But what if they could also tell you things about the composer's life that had not been printed in any biography but that could be cross-validated, or even better, could lead you straight to the hiding place of one or two previously unknown symphonies or concertos? My guess is that you would start to wonder.

To be credible, a person who claims to have lived a previous life has to show that they remember specific events, people, places, etc., that are verifiable and that cannot have been known to anyone beforehand. For an adult claiming to have been reincarnated it is very difficult to find verifiable evidence for the simple reason that the adult may have learned the facts during their life. They may even have stumbled across a previously unknown fact in the course of research or simply by accident. From the example discussed above, this person may have accidentally uncovered a lost Mozart score and hidden it again to support a bogus claim of reincarnation. Adults are incredibly difficult to verify when they claim to have been reincarnated.

Children, however, can provide compelling evidence as long as the influence of parents and other adults can be removed from the equation. Dr Stevenson managed to do this for enough cases to convince a growing number of people that reincarnation is real. In most cases Stevenson counted the statements made by the children, calculated what proportion were correct when checked, and critically examined the family backgrounds and the chances of information being transmitted to the child either wittingly or unwittingly by adults or even by TV or radio. Many of the children were very young – two or three years old. They could not read and had only limited understanding of what was being shown to them on TVs. In this way Stevenson reviewed and quantified reincarnation claims, discounted a great many, verified a few, and, thereby, built a solid case for the phenomenon[3]. Most of his work centred on overseas cases but that does not detract in any way from their credibility. He looked at societies like India because the Hindu population was more attuned to the issue of reincarnation. His careful checking and painstaking evaluation remained a key element of his approach wherever the case was located.

In 1997, Stevenson wrote up his most compelling findings in a two-volume tour-de-force which described 225 of the most convincing cases. Most of the cases involved children who had memories of a previous life as well as having birth marks or deformities which could be linked to those lives[4]. For example, one child had birth marks on the front and back of the head which matched the bullet entry and exit wounds that had killed them in their former life. There are simply too many examples from all over the world that have been exhaustively checked by Stevenson and others for anyone but the most stubborn and irrational disbeliever to ignore. There may be reasons to suspect that the phenomenon is more complicated than the straight-line life-death-life model might suggest but those reasons do not in any way undermine the immense body of evidence showing that such a process really happens, albeit in some quite astoundingly complex ways. Stevenson's work and conclusions constitute an immense step forward for the paranormal. They were, in fact, one of the first substantive elements of Paranorm 2.0.

The thought-provoking thing about reincarnation is that it is a win-win for the paranormal. Either the scientists who study it are right and the essence/soul of a person can return in another new body – even if only temporarily – or there are telepathic mechanisms that we do not yet understand that permit that essence, or part of it, to enter and reside within another human. Either way it is stunning.

Dr Ian Stevenson found that there is generally a relatively brief window in children's lives where they retain the memories of a previous existence. Usually, he says, this period lies between the ages of about two and five. That is very young, but it makes some of the memories even more impressive. From a scientific point of view children's statements that they lived in such and such a house, or were married to a given person, or were murdered by an identified individual are the very best evidence because they can easily be falsified by tracking down the locations and people to which the children are referring, or sometimes by referring to the formal court records. The age of the children also mitigates against them being trained to have memories of a previous life. Parents can, and perhaps do, try to do this on occasion but the young age of many of the children makes the fraud extremely difficult to carry off when confronted by a serious and highly skilled investigator. Stevenson rejected a huge number of potential claims for just this reason. He interviewed not just the children and their parents (at length and usually on numerous occasions) but also friends, neighbours, and relations before evaluating all the evidence and deciding whether the cases were viable.

A lot of the time, Stevenson found that, far from training their children to pretend to have previous lives, western adults tend to dismiss children's stories as being merely vivid imaginings, treating them as pure fantasy. He suspected that there are many more highly compelling cases but that they never see the light of day due to parental refusal to believe their children – or perhaps, and especially in the west, a fear of being ridiculed. He noted that Hindu parents were more relaxed about informing him of their children's claims of past lives but that American and European adults were far more defensive and secretive on the subject. The Christian refusal to countenance reincarnation may well have had a major effect. Parents who reject their children's accounts in the early stages lose the chance to record them for later investigation by people like Stevenson. Children usually remember a past life after something triggers the memory – a place, a face, a picture, an event, etc. – and this too can lead adults to dismiss the memories as fanciful. Stevenson believed that many children may have had past lives but that it is mainly those who had traumatic deaths who remember best and most accurately.

The Tucker Files

Dr James (Jim) Tucker is Professor of Psychiatry and Neurobehavioural Sciences at the University of Virginia School of Medicine[5]. He studied under Ian Stevenson and has carried the torch for reincarnation and other related phenomena since the latter's death. He also leads the Division of Perceptual Studies. His lengthy research into over 2,500 cases confirms one major conclusion reached by Stevenson: that an unnatural and violent death leads to a greater chance of children remembering a previous life.

Note that neither Stevenson nor Tucker claim that a traumatic death is *necessary* for someone to be reincarnated – only that, if you have suffered a violent end, the chances are higher that you will be able to remember bits of it in your next life. The corollary is that it is entirely likely that a large number of people will have had previous lives but do not get vivid recollections of them. Anyone who has had that feeling of having a particularly close affinity to a person, period, or a place in the past may well be vaguely remembering a past life or past lives in a fairly superficial manner. If you ask them, a proportion of one's friends and contacts may reveal that they have a feeling of closeness to certain historical characters, events, or periods. Some empathise deeply with the people who died in wars – the First World War or the Second or the Vietnam or whatever – without really understanding why. Others find certain places evocative and sometimes the source of deep emotions. I was told by a correspondent that they are moved to tears every time they see a picture of an American Civil War battle. Very few of these people actually believe that they are experiencing feelings from a previous life but there are cases on record of modern people travelling to different parts of the world – places they had never been to in their current lives – and being able to navigate them and even to identify specific buildings as the locations of certain events.

Tucker calculated that 70% of children with memories of past lives had experienced an unnatural death. He estimated the median time between death and rebirth to be seventeen months, and he invented a system of evaluating cases according to the strength of their credibility. He called it the Strength of Case Scale, based on four main criteria:

1. Whether the case involves clear physical birthmarks or defects corresponding to the alleged previous life.
2. The strength and detail of the verifiable statements about the previous life.
3. The relevant behaviours as they relate to the previous life.
4. An overall evaluation of the possibility of a connection between the child reporting a previous life and the supposed previous life.

He admits that there is no physical explanation for these phenomena but he postulates that quantum effects could be a partial mechanism – if we could actually understand them. In other words – although Dr Tucker would probably never use these words - 'the force' or whatever consciousness permeates the universe may be at the root of whatever is happening. Tucker also recognises that there may be other explanations than straightforward reincarnation. The children may be having some sort of telepathic connection with living adults who pass on their own memories, or they may be accessing the 'force' and downloading previous events and experiences. The latter might hold some water, but the former does not explain cases where the child is claiming to be the reincarnation of a person whom their parents and relations never knew, about events or a period about which they knew little or nothing prior to the child mentioning them.

One of the most famous cases in Dr Tucker's casebook is that of a Scottish child named Cameron Macaulay.

Cameron Macaulay

In 2006, Channel 5 in the UK produced a documentary called *Extraordinary People: The Boy Who Lived Before*. The programme focused on the claims of a small boy named Cameron Macaulay, who lived in Glasgow but claimed to his mother that he had lived a previous life on the island of Barra about 200 miles away, somewhere neither of his parents had ever visited. During his very early childhood the boy (who at that point had never been to the island) told his mother about his life on Barra including strange facts that his mother did not at the time believe. He asked her, for example, why their home in Glasgow only had one toilet while his previous home on Barra had three. He remembered having a black and white dog and a black car. He named his original father as Shane Robertson. Eventually Cameron's parents wrote to Jim Tucker and his subsequent investigations raised the interest of Channel 5 whose producers asked if they could do a documentary on the case. Eventually Tucker and the family agreed.

For the documentary, Professor Tucker accompanied young Cameron and his mother to Barra and, with the assistance of the boy, identified the house in which he said he'd lived in his previous existence. Almost all the facts that the lad had previously told his mother turned out to be absolutely true except that they could not find a Shane Robertson on the island or find anyone who remembered such a man. Cameron's explanation that he 'fell through a hole' from one life to the next was in line with what Tucker has heard from several other children including testimony in the US case of Gus Taylor.

Tucker covers some startling cases in his studies. In one, a boy provides strong evidence that he was, in fact, the reincarnation of his own grandfather. One theory is that our essence or soul may exist on a subatomic level – perhaps in the quantum domain – and that it persists after physical death and can enter another person. Could what we call 'consciousness' actually be this sub-atomic essence? The famous physicist Max Plank said that consciousness was probably superior to matter and that it exists almost independently of it. Sir Roger Penrose, the brilliant British physicist who worked closely with Stephen Hawking, agreed. He sees patterns in the universe that few others have spotted and he rejects the mainstream claim that quantum mechanics can have nothing to do with the brain or our minds (after all every cell in our bodies and our brains is built from quantum energy). What he firmly believes is that consciousness – whatever name people give to it – is independent of the body.

> *We need a major revolution in our understanding of the physical world in order to accommodate consciousness. The most likely place, if we're not going to go outside physics altogether, is in this big unknown—namely, making sense of quantum mechanics.*[6]

Penrose's collaborator, Stuart Hameroff, put forward the theory that such quantum effects could well be initiated within the microtubules of the brain. The science is complex but what it boils down to is that they suspect that quantum links and effects at the sub-atomic level in our brains are capable of existing (presumably as an energy form) independently of the physical brain. Put even more simply, our basic essence or being merely inhabits the physical body and is capable of moving on to other realms and other bodies after the death of our physical self. If this quantum soul exists – and these reincarnation cases seem to indicate that it does – the quantum effects might not be limited to simply a soul existing independently of the body. They might also be responsible for connections between living people (telepathy), influences on matter (telekinesis), precognitions, and much else.

Professor Tucker added a number of tests to Ian Stevenson's criteria that I listed earlier. He asks whether the parents of the child are credible – have they passed on 'memories' even unwittingly?

Could the young child have picked up the memories from TV or the radio? He says that 75% of his cases have been verified – that is, he has done the checks and critically examined the child, the parents, and the circumstances, has found verifiable records of the person from whom the child believes it has been reincarnated, and has verified statements made by the child and confirmed that these could not have been drawn from any current source.

Some cases of supposed reincarnation are initially based on regression hypnosis – taking people back to a past time or life by putting them under hypnosis. One such case involved the famous claim of a lady named Ruth Simmons (her real name was Virginia Tighe) in the 1950s. She claimed she had been reincarnated from a person called Bridey Murphy who, she said, lived in Belfast, Northern Ireland in the mid-19th century[7]. No-one could find evidence for the existence of such a person but Ruth remembered the names of two grocers from whom she said she bought food. Both were real grocers in Belfast at the time. There were many gaps in the account and, of course, it could be that Ruth Simmons did her homework and had researched the names of the two grocers. Her hypnotist, Morey Bernstein believed her story and wrote a book about the case, setting off a reincarnation craze in 1950s America. But hypnosis is a delicate and treacherous tool and most academics these days would caution against its use. The method of regressive hypnosis has been severely criticised – particularly in the case of people who claim to have been abducted by aliens but, unlike the latter, the claims of reincarnation can be checked against real-world events and people.

James Leininger

Another famous Tucker case concerned a young American lad called James Leininger, a two-year old who woke screaming in the night many times, worrying his mother greatly. His nightmares were about an aircraft crash and he kept telling his mother about a 'little man' who could not get out of the burning plane. Despite his parents' scepticism, the boy kept remembering details about World War Two fighter aircraft which no two year old should have been able to know (at little more than two years old he told his parents, for example, how the torque from a propellor could cause an aircraft to veer off the runway or a carrier deck if you were not careful[8]). He believed that he had been trapped in a burning plane, could not bail out, and was killed. His father was highly sceptical and was adamant that the boy could not be genuinely repeating facts from a past life. The parents pressed for more information. James told them the type of plane he'd flown (a Vought Corsair) and the name of the aircraft carrier he'd been flying from (the Natoma). To the amazement of experts the two-year old boy was able to tell of the Corsair's faults as an aircraft. His knowledge was tested time and again and he even confirmed that his previous name had been James, that one of his friends had been Jack Larsen, and that he'd been shot down during the Battle of Iwo Jima in 1945.

An F-4U Vought Corsair. Wikimedia Commons; Tony Hisgett. https://commons.wikimedia.org/w/index.php?curid=24198772

Through veterans' associations the parents eventually tracked down the name of the pilot who had died at Iwo Jima. Lt (JG) James Huston (USN)[9] had been shot down in flames and had not been able to bale out[10]. His plane had been hit by anti-aircraft fire and had lost its propellor and part of the engine. One of the flyer's closest buddies was another pilot named Jack Larsen. Their aircraft carrier was the USS Natoma Bay[11], and Huston had been killed in a Vought Corsair.

Some of Huston's former comrades say that James Leininger even looks like Huston.

The Leininger case is impressive because James' statements were recorded by very sceptical parents long before anyone sought to look for evidence, and they were corroborated by the subsequent investigations.

Ryan Hammons

We've seen how most reported memories of reincarnation seem to be connected to traumatic events – people being murdered or dying violent deaths, etc. and these include mass deaths such as those that occurred during the 9/11 atrocities.

Rachel Nolan's four-year-old was certain that he was a firefighter who was killed during the 9/11 emergencies. Like young James Leininger he remembered things that no young child should know – about firefighting techniques and even the make of the fire trucks that were used in 2001. There are many similar accounts – some from office workers who died and some from emergency workers. One young lad told his mother that his previous body was still buried under the rubble. There are also many people who believed they were reincarnated passengers from the Titanic tragedy but high-profile events such as this do tend to attract those among us who revel in teasing and hoaxing.

The issue of reincarnation raises a number of questions but, assuming for the moment that it is possible, perhaps the most fascinating are whether *everyone* is reincarnated or just some people, and how the numbers work out. If everyone is reincarnated, and as more and more people are born onto the planet. where do the additional essences come from?

The characteristics of past-life cases are summarised by Jim Tucker in a chapter he wrote for Leslie Kean's book on the subject[12]. They are as follows:

- Average age at which people speak about a past life – 35 months.
- Average age of ceasing to speak about a past life – 6 years (but many adults report knowing of previous lives).
- Most describe only one previous life.
- Three quarters know and can describe how they died.
- People rarely report being anyone famous – most report relatively non-descript lives but traumatic deaths.
- Reincarnation occurs almost always in the same country and usually quite nearby.
- 70% describe an unnatural death.
- Average interval between lives is 4.5 years.
- Median interval between lives is seventeen months (so half of all reported cases were shorter gaps than that and half were longer)
- Many of the memories are emotional or behavioural but children remember facts, people, and places – even types of cars or airplanes.
- 35% of the children who reported a past life had an intense fear of the mode of death suffered by their previous person (e.g. guns, heights, fire, heart attack, etc.)

One has to consider though that the type of death may have a direct effect on past life memories. The more violent and traumatic the better the chance that children will remember. What about the millions of people who die in bed or in hospital? Does the fact that the demise is not violent mean that those essences cannot be reincarnated? Or is a non-traumatic death simply something that is less vivid and therefore not remembered to the same extent?

Another father who was highly resistant to the idea of past lives was police Lieutenant Kevin Hammons. In 2009, his wife Cyndi had been struggling alone for a while with the regular nightmares experienced by their five-year-old son Ryan before she told Kevin what was happening. As part of his nightmares Ryan Hammons often woke up complaining of pains in his chest and gasping for air. Cyndi spent a lot of time with the youngster trying to understand what was going on. His nightmares were scary but the stories were consistent and detailed. She recorded what the boy said and, after the child had made an outrageous claim after seeing a picture in a bookstore window, she began reading up on past lives cases.

Passing a bookstore with his mother one day, Ryan got really excited about a book on display in the store-window. The book was about early Hollywood. It had been opened to show some of its pictures and Ryan pointed delightedly to one of them and told his mother that it was of himself and 'George'. Although it was expensive, she bought him the book. Then, one evening, in bed after that event, Cyndi asked her deeply sceptical husband to read a couple of chapters from a book on children who claimed they had experienced past lives. He read the chapters but then angrily threw the book across the room while making a comment to the effect that it was all nonsense. Ryan must have heard the angry comment because he immediately came, crying, into his parents' bedroom. His father, mortified that he had made his son cry, comforted him and agreed to Ryan's request that he take at least one look at the boy's own book. What the boy returned with was the illustrated book he'd spotted in the store window – a pictorial book about Hollywood in the nineteen-thirties and forties. Ryan opened the book for his father and turned to a picture from 1932 about the release of the George Raft, Constance Cummings, and Mae West picture *Night after Night*. It was Mae West's first film and it turned out to be the launching pad for a very successful career for her.

The five-year-old Ryan Hammons showed his father a particular page of the book and pointed to a picture of the film star George Raft with another man. Ryan pointed to the second man in the photo and told his father 'That's me and that's George; we did a picture together'. The boy could not remember his previous name and it was not mentioned in the book, but he knew he'd been friends with Hollywood stars, used to travel first class on ocean liners, lived in a big house with a swimming pool, and that (amazing detail) he'd had three children who weren't his.

A cinema board for the George Raft film – Night After Night. Wikimedia Commons; Paramount; Public Domain. https:// commons.wikimedia.org/w/index.php?curid=57178267

Although by no means convinced, Ryan's parents contacted Dr Jim Tucker and went on recording statements that their son made about events from Ryan's very adult memories (and they certainly were adult). Eventually, and much against his better judgement, Ryan's father came to fully believe that Ryan was telling the truth. After a great deal of work in interviewing the boy and his parents and travelling with them to California, Tucker was also convinced and, as a final test, was able to present Ryan with a series of sets of photos. All of them were unmarked and the pictures in each set were carefully selected to be very similar. Nevertheless, from the first set, Ryan picked out his previous wife from a set of photos of four similar-looking women. From another set of photos selected for their similarity within the group he picked out his previous self at a younger age. Then Tucker had Ryan's father slowly read out four names and asked Ryan to tell him which was his own name in the previous life (Ryan's father did not then know the correct answer). The names were John Johnson, Willy Wilson, Marty Martyn, and Robert Robertson. Ryan did not need much thinking time before he identified the third as his previous name. Tucker then confirmed that Marty

Martyn, whose real name had been Kolinsky, was the other man in the original George Raft photo – the one Ryan had said was him. Martyn had run a famous Hollywood talent agency and had been as rich and famous as the boy had claimed.

Leslie Kean mentions in her book that James Leininger had had twelve of his recorded statements verified. For Ryan Hammons she listed forty-seven – which, if the eight statements that had been previously recorded by Ryan's mother were added, made no less than fifty-six pre-recorded things that Ryan had said that were eventually verified. In reality of course Ryan Hammons said a great many things about his past life, but some were very personal and impossible to verify. Kean's account of the case is carefully analytical and detailed, yet the reader can also feel the heartache that it caused to Ryan and his family. At times, Kean says, Ryan and Marty Martyn were the same person. His parents and particularly his mother found his adult memories and attitudes extremely unnerving and upsetting. At five years old Ryan acted and thought like a puzzled, angry sixty-one-year-old film agent who thoroughly resented the fact that he had lost a great life full of wealth, women, luxurious cars, and first-class travel.

The age at which Martyn had died was another important and compelling aspect of the case. Ryan insisted throughout that Marty Martyn had been sixty-one when he died. He'd been quite offended that Marty had been taken so young and then somehow forced to come back as a baby in what he considered a poor household. But the records, including death certificates, showed that Marty Martyn had been fifty-nine when he died in 1964 (i.e. born in 1905). In spite of this documentary evidence and the insistence of the grown-ups, Ryan stuck to the fact that he'd been sixty-one when he died. It was one of those things that made the adults doubt the whole story but, in the end it was the clincher for his reincarnation. The boy had been absolutely correct and the official records of death had been wrong. Kolinsky's year of birth was traced, with a great deal of trouble, through census records and from steamship passenger lists as being 1903[13].

Jim Tucker's studies – of mainly US and European reports – revealed that the subjects were generally intelligent and highly verbal. He stressed that one reason he focused on western youngsters was that he wanted to compare western experiences with those recorded by his colleague and mentor, Ian Stevenson. He found that western families tended to keep the matter very much to themselves, and that they could often be embarrassed by their children's statements. Indian and other eastern families tended to be more attuned to reincarnation and therefore were rarely embarrassed or secretive. Notwithstanding those differences, the western and eastern cases in themselves were remarkably similar. Tucker felt sure that the reason that reincarnation appeared to be more common in India and Asia probably had a great deal to do with the readiness of parents in those regions to be open about their children having such stories to tell, while western parents were prone to cover them up and hide the embarrassing, un-Christian tales that their children were telling.

Tucker's chapter in Leslie Kean's book contains this summary from him:

I am now ready to say we have good evidence that some young children have memories of a life from the past. Precisely what this says about survival after death and the ultimate nature of our existence is less clear to me.

Balanced and honest as always, Tucker also has some intriguing things to say about what happens between one life and the next. It seems that one in five children who have memories of a past life also have memories of the bit in-between dying and being reborn – Tucker calls them 'intermission memories'. They include 'falling through holes into new bodies' and 'waiting somewhere else'.

Reading Stevenson's, Tucker's, and Kean's books is a sobering but somehow exciting experience. Sobering because they illustrate the virtual certainty of some sort of continuation of one's 'essence' after physical death, and exciting because the possibilities seem endless and the implications for the rest of what I call Paranorm 2.0 are immense.

What I have yet to read, however, in any of these discussions is any account or analysis of the ethical/moral differences between the various souls who are reportedly reincarnated. Most of the ones that have been reported are of generally 'good' people who are slightly peeved at dying violently, being murdered, or being taken at a relatively early age when they did not want to go. What happens to the evil members of our society – the cold-blooded murderers, the serial rapists, the serial killers, the torturers? Can they be reincarnated to repeat or expand on their crimes? The Buddhists and Hindus and others would argue that 'karma' is the answer and some of them believe that truly evil deeds send the soul immediately to 'hell' – wherever and whatever that might be.

One might also ask: Is there a sense that reincarnation is only permitted/possible for those who really did not want to die when they did? Or does everyone get reincarnated but not everyone remembers their past life as distinctly, perhaps only retaining a 'feeling' for the era or location? If so, how many times does one get reincarnated? Are the Hindus right and the process is repeated time after time until one achieves some sort of higher and better state of grace? The questions will probably never be answered in this world, but scholars like Drs Stevenson and Tucker are providing some tantalising and compelling insights into the issue.

The wider evidence for reincarnation or for some even stranger connection between the living and the dead, is almost unarguable. Stevenson not only researched and catalogued, he analysed in great depth. For example, he identified over three hundred cases in which birth marks and handicaps were related to injuries and accidents in a reported past life[14]. In one case he confirmed links between a set of chest birthmarks on a boy to a fatal shotgun wound that had been received in his alleged previous life.

He summed things up as follows:

- Reincarnation memories seem to be strongest where the previous death was violent or traumatic.

- Reincarnation never seems to be immediate – the gaps is almost always at least a few years.
- Most cases seem to be local – that is, the person is reincarnated within a few miles of their original life. This could be a reflection of the type of death – i.e. those who suffer traumatic deaths want to return to the scene or to confront the murderer.
- Fears and habits from the previous life seem to be transferred into the new life. A fear of water or of heights might well become part of the character in the new life.
- The memories of a past life seem to surface between two and five years of age on average. Some may remain longer but most dissipate with increasing age or sometimes after solving a traumatic issue from the previous life.

So, are what some people remember as past lives a link to a genuine life that they lived in previous ages? The evidence seems to indicate that this is so. Some scholars have argued that these 'memories' could have been transmitted somehow from whatever force or consciousness exists in the wider universe. This would certainly explain why some past lives seem to be experienced by more than one person and by other anomalies, but it probably does not explain the birth marks or the fears.

The phenomenon of reincarnation may not be as simple as we have been led to believe by traditional views on the matter. I will be looking at a number of aspects of Paranorm 2.0 in the pages and chapters that follow and many of them exhibit strong signs of being a lot more complex than the vocabulary would suggest. In the case of reincarnation, it may be that there are several phenomena being exhibited: some cases that are 'classical' reincarnations, some that are actually some form of telepathy, perhaps even some that have elements of both.

CHAPTER 9
DEATH – THE FINAL FRONTIER?

 'Don't think of it as dying', said Death. 'Just think of it as leaving early to avoid the rush.'

— TERRY PRATCHETT

In many of the cases recorded by Drs Stevenson and Tucker the subjects recalled bits of what they thought were the in-between periods – those which separated their previous life from their current one. They described feelings of 'falling through holes into a new life' and a perception of time spent waiting for a new life to come around.

All of which has a direct connection to the ways in which living humans report out-of-body experiences (OBEs), near death experiences (NDEs), and end of life experiences (ELEs). For all of these we have a string of eminent medics to thank for painstaking research and compelling results.

Out of Body Experiences (OBEs)

Lots of people report experiencing periods during anaesthesia or unconsciousness when they seemed to be elsewhere, watching and listening to events. Most medics regard OBEs as mental aberrations while under anaesthetics or in comas. They call them 'dissociative experiences' and explain them as the brain creating realistic sights and sounds connected with the person's current location. Some believe them to be wishful dreams – i.e. dreams in which the person sees a different future for themselves. Both are plausible and may explain certain reports but there are many accounts which cannot be rationalised in these ways. There is the famous case in which a patient had an OBE in which they 'saw' an old shoe on a ledge outside a window which was a) not visible from inside the building, and b) was several rooms away from that in which the witness was located. Similar OBEs – impossible to explain in conventional terms – are reported by many people – including such things as knowing what instruments were on a table which was above their head and invisible to them even if they have their eyes open. OBEs can also be unconnected with medical conditions and hospitals. A good many people claim to be able to leave their bodies at will.

From the work on reincarnation discussed in the previous section we can see that consciousness appears to survive death and is not dependent on the brain or any other physical object. Feelings, memories, emotions, personality ... they all seem to be part of what, hitherto, we have called the 'soul' – some essence which exists independently of our physical bodies and the physical world.

People who are in medical emergencies and cannot know (in conventional ways) what is happening around them, sometimes regain consciousness to tell of details 'seen' while they were unconscious or in surgery that they could not possibly have been able to intuit or to know. Such events are called veridical out of body experiences – meaning an OBE which it is possible to verify after the event. Leslie Kean tells the story of Vicki Noratuk whose optic nerves were destroyed shortly after she was born. She was, in other words, profoundly blind. After a car crash when she was twenty-two she 'saw' herself on the operating table, was able to describe who was there and what they did.

OBEs have been studied in great depth and are now a virtually proven phenomenon. Many highly competent medical professionals have looked into the matter over the years and have discounted theories that the person was not fully unconscious or was able even through an anaesthetic to hear conversations. Dr Sam Parnia led the most extensive study of experiences during resuscitation covering over two thousand patients in hospitals in the US, the UK, and Austria. The research team used a three-stage vetting process which was extremely tough in its criteria for the phenomenon. The analysis produced just over one hundred people who got through to the third round. One of them – a social worker from Southampton, UK – watched his own resuscitation from the corner of the room. He told Parnia's team that a female up there in the corner had beckoned him and that he then watched his nurse and a bald doctor trying to resuscitate him. Parnia checked the circumstances carefully and concluded that this had been a genuine OBE and that there had been a period of three minutes during which the patient had been clinically dead.

The distinction between out-of-body and near-death experiences is pretty blurred. Out of body experiences can happen to almost anyone and many scientists believe they are actually lucid dreams – i.e. extremely realistic dreams about things around you while you sleep. Others think they are straightforward hallucinations. The most compelling, in the sense that they are most easily verified, are usually the ones that happen to people while they are unconscious in hospital.

Dr Parnia ran a study from Southampton Hospital in England, called AWARE. It was set up in 2008 as a global study designed to examine all aspects of alleged OBEs and NDEs. Most of the participating hospitals installed shelves in coronary, intensive care, and emergency rooms. There were around a thousand shelves installed and each had a small 'target' object placed on it which was not visible from below. Yes, a *thousand* shelves in different hospitals and facilities. Sounds like a good experimental set-up but the subjects are all in an extremely bad way – so, by definition, the pool of potential OBE/NDE experiencers is reduced during the actual process. There is a large proportion of what one can only call missed subjects. Cardiac arrests are just that – the heart completely stops beating. Staff resuscitate a high proportion – probably around 40% to 50% - but there is a high mortality rate for the survivors and only a tiny proportion can be interviewed as to whether they had an OBE or NDE. To put it bluntly - a lot of good potential subjects for research are lost due to death. The report on the study was published in the medical journal 'Resuscitation' in 2014.

In all, the study covered over 2,060 cardiac arrests from which only 330 people (16%) survived and only 140 were eventually able to be interviewed (just under 7%). Fifty-five of the survivors said that they had had conscious experiences during their cardiac arrest (39%). Of these, nine patients reported experiences which were categorised as near-death experiences (6.4%)[1]

A second AWARE study ran between 2014 and 2017. It studied a further 465 cardiac arrests leading to twenty-one interviews and four patients who reported specific memories. For AWARE-2 the in-room stimulus was an upturned iPad which could not be seen from the bed in which the patient was being treated. None of the twenty-one people reported seeing the iPad. The study has been criticised for expecting such unconnected stimuli to be noticed by someone in the midst of a cardiac arrest and at a time when they were probably more concerned with watching what was going on than studying the room for random stimuli. Interestingly the memories that were reported were mainly about a feeling of 'peace and joy', seeing 'light' or a tunnel, and sometimes a review of the person's life (akin to the old saying about seeing one's life flash before one's eyes). With only four patients being able to report memories while effectively dead, the statistical basis of the study is impossibly fragile but a subsequent unofficial analysis of the audio cues that were played for the patients (they wore Wi-Fi headphones feeding them a selection of sounds) showed that no-one heard the audio. However, the results also showed that some patients heard and could accurately report conversations going on in the emergency room that they should not have been able to hear these through the audio being played into their ears. Somehow, seriously ill patients who were clinically dead and had noise being played into their ears through headphones managed to hear and accurately report conversations between doctors and nurses which could be verified afterwards.

Parnia's series of studies are not the only attempts to research OBEs and NDEs. One recent one was the COOL programme established in Montreal around 2011. It studied patients in deep hypothermic cardio circulatory arrest. It studied thirty-three cases and returned a total of just under 10% who remembered something while clinically dead. COOL also came up with a single verified instance of an OBE – a young pregnant woman who was able to accurately describe a number of medical instruments that had been laid out behind her head. Her account of the instruments was verified by hospital staff.

A small but impressive number of people claim the ability to leave their body at will. One young woman said she developed the talent after becoming bored at school. Others develop it through meditation but many more seem to have a single experience of apparently leaving their body, being frightened, and then never having that experience again. There are thousands of examples online but the most convincing are those that can be verified by doctors and nurses.

Technically an OBE is different from a near-death experience in the sense that the latter generally includes aspects which are beyond the material world – another dimension usually described by the person as the afterlife. But, in scientific studies it is extremely difficult to separate the two. One major problem for researchers (and for the patients) is that a very high proportion of cardiac arrests result in death. Around 85% die either during the cardiac arrest incident or shortly after resuscitation. The survivors often do not wish to be interviewed about their experiences. This leaves a tiny sample of people who don't mind giving an interview and this could skew the sample and the results considerably. If the 'reporters' are self-selected *because* they had an experience, the stats are ignoring a reasonably high proportion of people who went through the cardiac arrest and resuscitation without any form of vision or experiences. Conversely, researchers have to be aware that some proportion of the 85% who do not survive may have had experiences but did not live to tell of them.

Near Death Experiences (NDE)

There are many convincing accounts of near-death experiences which seem to demonstrate the separation of 'essence' and body but, as we have just discussed, experts tend to separate things called 'out of body experiences' from 'near death experiences'. The former occur when a person is not expected to die but may be deeply unconscious or in a coma. The latter term refers to experiences of those who doctors believe (that is, are pretty certain) are about to die. Leslie Kean says that these NDEs are reported by between 10% and 20% of people in resuscitation across the world.

One of the world's leading NDE researchers is a chap called Bruce Greyson, who was also one of the first to point out (in a very constructive way) the problems with the stimuli used in the AWARE studies. In 2021 he was the Chester Carlson Professor Emeritus of Psychiatry and Neurobehavioral Sciences at the University of Virginia. He has a lifetime of scholarly study of NDE behind him, having become interested in the subject almost immediately after leaving medical school. His website explains that, as a very new doctor, he treated a deeply unconscious lady in the emergency room and that she stunned him the next day with her memories of what had gone on. That event led the young doctor to begin what became a lifetime academic study of NDE[2]. He argues persuasively that NDEs are linked to past lives memories too.

> *The young children that Ian Stevenson and other researchers have investigated not only have memories of a past life, but often show behaviors, such as phobias or preferences, that are unusual within the context of their own family and can't be explained by any current life events*[3].

Greyson points out that reincarnation may not be as simple as it appears – i.e. a direct transmission of someone's soul or essence into a young child. There are some recorded cases of multiple children claiming to be the reincarnation of the same person. In other strange cases a child can 'remember' the lives of two separate people and in at least one case Greyson reports that a child reported a past life of someone who did not die until after the child was born. All this indicates a far more complex phenomenon than the traditional straight-line reincarnation process would imply.

One particular patient reported after emerging from what the doctors had originally thought was certain decline into death:

> *I was made to understand that, as tests had been taken for my organ functions and the results were not out yet, that if I chose life, the results would show that my organs were functioning normally. If I chose death, the result would show organ failure due to cancer as the cause of death. I made my choice, and as I started to wake up in a very confused state, as I could not at that time tell which side of the veil I was on, the doctors came rushing into the room with big smiles on their faces, saying to my family, 'Good news: we got the results and her organs are functioning; we can't believe it! Her body really did seem like it had shut down!*[4]

Greyson also points out anecdotal evidence that NDE experiencers can report an 'other world' in which time is not sequential but is completely present in the same place.

> *It's as though our earthly minds convert what happens around us into a sequence; but in actuality, when we're not expressing through our bodies, everything occurs simultaneously, whether past, present, or future.*[5]

For the reader, the subject of reincarnation and near-death experiences is steeped in the same fundamental issue as all things paranormal: the lack of hard science. Time and again I have seen comments online and in newspapers scorning paranormal incidents because the reports lack scientific credibility. Most go along the lines of 'there's no proof, it's all subjective and anecdotal'. There is no getting away from the fact that what these critics say is absolutely true. Take Dr Greyson's book as an example. It is a very good piece of work, and I would recommend it to anyone interested in the subject but, in essence, it consists of a series of anecdotes interspersed with intelligent discussion and consideration. And this is really as it should be. As with almost everything to do with the paranormal there is no 'scientific', testable, falsifiable proof and this is because there could probably never be scientific proof of anything that lies outside the physical world. We can never prove or disprove the existence of any given deity, we can never offer more than limited scientific proof of the causes of happiness or despair, we cannot 'prove' the state of a quantum particle in the time before we actually observe it, and we can never discover scientific proof of something so literally existential as a near death experience.

By insisting on 'scientific proof' we are ignoring the fact that our lives are largely governed by non-provable phenomena – love, hate, desire, faith, belief, jealousy, and so on. We cannot *prove* any of those things, but they certainly exist and have a massive influence on what we do. Humans get around the problem of proof by accepting circumstantial or even partial evidence. In most instances where a crime is committed it is totally impossible to know to 100% certainty who did it. So we accept the fact that three or four witnesses who testify to seeing the culprit break the window are sufficient to convict him of criminal damage. Even the testimony of a single, credible witness can end in a conviction. Similarly, with NDEs and reincarnation. There will never be any scientific proof but, if someone of credibility stacks up dozens or hundreds of carefully checked and verified examples, that, for me at least, is sufficient circumstantial evidence that there is a phenomenon of which we need to take serious notice, to think deeply about, and on which we should do more detailed research.

Circumstantial evidence is not our preference but, if it is all we've got and there is enough of it, we tend to accept it. However, there is another avenue – that of 'negative proof'. It's not possible, but if you could show that no other person in the world could possibly have broken that window, you'd be left with incontrovertible proof that your defendant must have done it. Some medical practitioners have spent many very constructive years trying to 'negatively prove' the phenomenon of near-death experiences. One example is Dr Pim van Lommel, the famous Dutch cardiologist who, with his colleagues, has examined in detail a wide range of other potential factors around NDE such as gender, ethnicity, drugs being taken at the time, age, religious conviction, mental state, level of education, types of treatment, time under anaesthetic, severity of cardiac arrest, urban/rural location, and so on. Incredibly, they found no statistically-significant correlations for *any* of these factors to link them to NDE. Put simply, near death experiences are not dependent on any human characteristic or treatment that the researchers could measure. Your age, gender, socio-economic group, religion, level of intelligence, and medical factors have not the slightest impact on whether or not you undergo an NDE.

In one study van Lommel and his collaborators looked at 344 cardiac arrest patients who had, at one point during their attack, been clinically dead:

- 82% had no memories of the period they were unconscious (this ties in with Dr Sam Parnia's findings)
- 18% said they'd experienced 'something', of whom two-thirds had had a 'deep' experience.

The forty-plus deep experiences included seeing a light or people they had known and who had since died. Feelings of peace and calm were commonly mentioned too. The medical researchers could find no common factor among those who had had an NDE but they did wonder whether, as there was clearly a gradient from quite profound and deep NDEs to very mild experiences, some of the 82% who said they had not experienced anything might simply have forgotten it[6].

Van Lommel's findings and conclusions are well worth a detailed read. He thinks that the evidence shows that the human brain does not produce consciousness – it *receives* it from somewhere else. This conclusion leads to some interesting corollaries. For example, if it were the case that humans were the only truly conscious entities on the planet it might explain why the monsters and strange animals on the Skinwalker Ranch in the USA would attack and kill animals but never humans. Van Lommel supports the theory that there is something called 'non-local consciousness' – that our consciousness is not located in our brains but exists outside them – and he is far from being alone in that idea. The closest analogy is to a TV. When switched on, the TV can show pictures and produce sound. When switched off, the TV is dead and shows no pictures, but the pictures and sound still exist in the electromagnetic spectrum all around.

If there is such a thing, then non-local consciousness might go some way towards explaining such things as remote viewing and precognition. There is intriguing evidence to suggest that some people have a way of accessing wider fields of information than are provided by their five senses. Perhaps we all have the capability but most of us choose not to use it? Just as some people report experiencing an OBE but being scared and never doing it again, perhaps we all have the capability to access the paranormal but most of us are too frightened to do so. Later on we will be discussing the strange power of 'belief'. It has been shown by scientists that people who 'believe' in certain things are more likely to experience them. This applies to a number of paranormal phenomena as well as to many who witness UFOs/UAP.

End of Life Experiences (ELE)

I cannot imagine that anyone with an open mind who has read the two sections on OBE and NDE's above and who has perhaps delved into the books on the subjects by top-rate scientists can have any reservations as to the reality of these phenomena. But if you do, then what follows will answer all remaining qualms. End-of-Life Experiences, like Out-of-Body and Near-Death experiences, are not readily explicable in conventional terms. People who are very close to death can report seeing relatives and friends who are already dead. They say that they are visited by these deceased people who offer them comfort.

A good proportion of medical practitioners believe that these experiences are genuine although they do not attempt to explain them (at least not in public) and many nurses accept them, again without necessarily telling their colleagues. But sceptics explain them as the wanderings of a dying brain, hallucinations, and dreams. The fact that the patients are otherwise lucid and that carers are perfectly capable of distinguishing between ramblings and rational thought does not seem to count. Doctors, nurses, and relatives can sometimes actually see the effects of these visitations and witness the associated events. This, too, is largely ignored by sceptics in favour of outright denial.

The sceptics' arguments have, in fact, long since been discounted, not least by a chap called Sir William Barrett. He was a physicist and parapsychologist who, in 1926, wrote a major treatise on ELE called 'Deathbed Visions'. It summarised one of the earliest empirical studies of the subject, detailing numerous cases of otherwise lucid and rational people reporting being visited by dead relatives. But the most stunning element of his findings – one which has been validated many times in modern studies – is that, in a small minority of cases, doctors, nurses, and living relatives who were present in the sick room also saw the visions[7]. It is certainly not uncommon for modern doctors and nurses to report seeing wisps of 'smoke' or even full ghostly apparitions in the days and hours prior to a patient's death. We have no way of knowing how many modern medics and nurses see other things but keep them to themselves.

The nearest modern equivalent to Barrett is the eminent neuropsychologist Dr Peter Fenwick, who specialises in epilepsy and has also come to believe that human consciousness is not resident in the brain. He has studied over 300 cases and is now convinced that what he and others have found tends to point to some sort of separation between the physical brain and individual consciousness – that the brain is simply a temporary residence for one's 'spirit'. His cases mirror those reported by Barrett and by non-scientists – of people in care, nearing death, seeing their relatives, and being visited by dead friends, and of medical staff and relatives in the room sometimes (but not always) seeing light and even 'ghosts' at the moment of death[8]. Fenwick's conclusions – on the basis of considerable numbers of examples and detailed study of cases in English and Dutch hospitals – indicate that over half of those who die while conscious seem to be helped on their way by those who are already dead. One fascinating addition to the standard phenomenon is that he has found that the experience of death is sometimes extended and multi-faceted. He describes a wide range of phenomena including premonitions, clocks stopping, dogs behaving in uncharacteristic ways, lights in the death room, and even of shapes seen leaving the body. Like Van Lommel, who we met earlier, Fenwick thinks that the end-of-life experience is about non-local consciousness.

The scholars of this topic have also come to some surprising conclusions as to how long death actually takes. We usually assume that death is a relatively quick transition from life to non-life – a period of perhaps a few minutes when the body finally shuts down. The brain is supposed to continue to operate for about thirty to forty-five seconds after the heart stops beating or the blood is otherwise cut off. Almost all the experts who study the subject, however, seem to believe that death is not something that happens within a few minutes but that it involves a period when the conscious self begins to depart from the brain and the body. The length of that period can be days or minutes, but the process seems to be similar for everyone – one of dipping into and out of whatever exists beyond this life.

Two nurses attended a dying person in the early morning. The patient evidently wanted to thank them for taking care of him. But, as he was doing so, he looked over the shoulder of one of the nurses and said 'Hang on a moment. I just want to thank these nurses.' The chap then expressed his thanks directly to the nurses and then died. In another case – said by Fenwick to be typical - a very frail dying lady sat bolt upright in bed with a broad smile on her face thanking her dead husband for coming to see her. Fenwick says that the most common visitors are parents, spouses, and other relatives. Sometimes the patients see a person whom they believe to be still alive when in fact that person has already died.

One study mentioned by Peter Fenwick found that almost 80% of dying patients had experienced such visions, *but that these phenomena were only mentioned in 8% of the hospital case notes.* There would appear to be a reluctance in western culture to put into writing that a person had an NDE or an ELE. The reluctance may be about attaching one's name to such a statement in a set of official notes. Fenwick is very clear that things like culture and religion can affect the way a dying person *explains* the occurrences but that the actual substance of the events seems to be the same regardless of who the dying person is. He says that people can have Near Death Experiences days or even weeks prior to their deaths. Generally, light appears to be a major feature and people report the whole thing as being calm, warm, and comforting.

As to the shapes and lights that witnesses sometimes report as leaving the body, Leslie Kean described some ELE events in the following way:

> *What is seen has been described to us variously as a 'smoke,' a 'gray mist,' a 'white mist,' a 'very wispy white shape,' seen leaving the body, usually from the chest or through the head. Some describe the air being wavy, like the heat haze of a mirage. It can also be an almost solid white form.*[9]

There may also be a form of telepathy involved in the process of dying, for Peter Fenwick says that relatives can sometimes 'know' when someone has died even though they were nowhere near the place at which the person passed away. In his book he discounts the possibility that the relative expected the person to die and therefore retrospectively rationalised their experience around that time. He explains that, in many cases, the people reporting such knowledge did not even know the person was ill.

All of this meticulously-collected evidence changes the widely accepted and rarely questioned assumption that we all make about death – that it is a black and white affair. One minute, whether unconscious or conscious, you are alive and in this world, the next you are dead and gone forever. All the evidence now points to a much more prolonged transition (for at least some people) between what we call life and what we think of as death. Case after case shows that we probably go through a protracted process of transfer between two states of consciousness – one linked to the material world and the other released from it and existing in a different dimension or realm. Could this be why sudden death – the unexpected separation of the 'spirit' and the body – might be so traumatic and why it might cause the person to want to return quickly to another life or to somehow hang around the site of their demise? Could it even explain why some ghosts are reported as not believing they are dead?

CHAPTER 10
PAST AND FUTURE

> *I must admit to being a bit perverse for, as a psychiatrist, I believe that anything that can be a big blow to the human ego can only be a good thing in terms of our collective development. Such shocks can perhaps help us to grow as a species.*
>
> — DR JOHN MACK

Being able to see the past is not something that immediately strikes one as being a valuable ability, but it has its strengths. In effect it is a 'vision' of something that happened in the past and (like precognition) is akin to other psi visions such as those of ghosts and out-of-body experiences. We mentioned the alleged events at Borley Rectory earlier and one might wonder whether witnesses who saw a nun, or those who witnessed an ordinary horse-drawn carriage (as opposed to the one driven by headless drivers) were seeing ghosts or were having a retrocognitive vision of something that really happened in the past. That friend of mine, the landlord of the old pub had the late-night vision of sandal-shod legs walking by his cellar. The cellar had no windows and the landlord was an intelligent person. Although his vision would have been called ghostly in times gone by it appears to have been more like a time-slip or retrocognition which somehow allows a person a glimpse of something that happened in the past. It can come in one's waking life or in dreams and can sometimes be shown in laboratory experiments. Usually, the visions are very short-lived. There are a few good examples of retrocognition including the controversial one in which two English women said they saw people from pre-revolutionary France at Versailles in 1901.

Versailles

A lady named Charlotte Anne Moberly with her younger colleague Eleanor Jourdain were visiting the famous French Palace of Versailles on August 10th 1901. They were respectively the Principal and Vice-Principal of St Hugh's College, Oxford, on a leisure trip to the French capital. Like all educated tourists, they wished to view the wonders of the magnificent palace. If you have ever had the pleasure of visiting Versailles you will be well aware how extensive the grounds are and how numerous the buildings. The Palace itself is huge but there are scores of other grand buildings, immense ornamental gardens, water features extending to a kilometre in length, as well as a large arboretum and other gardens and grounds. It is a place you need days to take in properly. Among many other beautiful buildings is one they call the Petit Trianon (because there is also a 'Grand' one). It is closely associated with Marie-Antoinette and is not to be missed if you enjoy the grandeur of neo-classical architecture and incredible Marie-Antoinette furnishings and gilded carvings.

Our two English academics wanted to see the Petit Trianon but, in the confusion of parks and gardens and buildings, they found it extremely difficult to locate. They asked for directions but soon realised they had become lost. Suddenly, they said, they both felt a sense of depression at the same time as the air became very still. Things did not look real. The colours were different and sounds seemed to have retreated to the background. They reported people in 'old-fashioned' clothes and saw what they described as old equipment (a horse-drawn plough) alongside a rough track in the gardens. They asked directions from two men dressed in 'long greyish-green coats with small three-cornered hats' and, near a gazebo, were stared at 'unpleasantly' by a man whose face was ravaged by smallpox. The women went on to claim that they encountered several women in very old-fashioned garb from whom they received further directions. They then walked over a bridge and eventually reached the Petit Trianon. There one of them saw a woman sitting outside sketching on an easel. She was dressed in an old-fashioned dress with a pale-green scarf. The feeling of intense depression was still with the two tourists when they saw a man dressed as a footman emerge from a door in a nearby building and slam it behind him. The two ladies attracted his attention and asked where the main entrance was. When they reached the front they were returned to the modern world in which they found a wedding party waiting to enter. They also noted that the feeling of deep depression lifted. Things appeared to have returned to normal. Colours and sounds were back and they knew they were back in the early twentieth century.

Naturally, the two talked about that experience and one very strange fact emerged – that Moberly had seen the sketching woman, but Jourdain had not. In further chats, they came to the conclusion that they had actually been in the France of 1789 and decided to write a book about the incident which they, somewhat unimaginatively, called 'An Adventure'. The book, which was not published until 1911 – ten years after their visit – hit the streets under the pseudonyms of Elizabeth Morison and Frances Lamont. It was an instant success and caused much controversy. Naturally the sceptics discounted what the women claimed and, to prove it, pointed to a map of the area at the time on which no bridge was to be seen. Luckily another map had been discovered at Versailles, hidden in an old chimney. That map showed that there had, indeed, been an ornamental a bridge where they had said it was. The men they saw in grey-green coats and small tricorn hats were dressed in the uniform of the Swiss Guard and, if they were genuine apparitions, they would probably have been killed during the massacre of the Guard by a mob during the Paris Commune in 1792. The pockmarked man who gazed at the two women so malevolently at the gazebo could have been the infamous Comte de Vaudreuil – a cultured and intelligent man, known as a bit of a womaniser and as having little love for the Queen.

The Moberly-Jourdain story can never be proved. Those two young college teachers would have been very familiar with the history of France under Louis XVI and could have spotted the chance to write a best-seller from what might have been a fictional story made up during their walk around Versailles. The map element is compelling – if true – but the whole experience was unique in that they seemed to be able to interact with their vision and receive directions from late eighteenth-century citizens even though the two were presumably speaking modern French.

The odds are that the whole thing was made up and the girls simply saw a way of making a few bob to supplement their academic salaries. Almost anyone with knowledge could have made up the majority of the story. The fly in the ointment is the bridge. The story was out and published well before the second map was discovered – so how did the two women know about it when all the experts in 1911 were certain that the bridge did not exist? If you were going to make up such a story the least you would ensure was that you did not claim to have seen a bridge when all the current maps and books showed gardens without such a structure.

And, if the event did happen exactly as the two ladies allege, what was it? They claim to have seen and felt the past and they even say that they spoke to and heard responses from people of the time. In some ways, stemming from the physical aspects of the experience, it was 'time travel' – the transfer of present-day humans into a past event – but in most aspects it was a vision of the past. The bridge is certainly a powerful element in any quest to believe the ladies but there is also the very honest way in which they admitted that one or the other of them did not witness what the other did. This is most marked in the case of the sketching lady (who they came to think had been Marie-Antoinette) but they also noted other people that one or the other of them had not seen.

I have mentioned the power of emotion in paranormal incidents on many occasions and here too there may be an 'energy' issue. Apart from incidental characters, all the people the two women met or saw were involved in the intrigue and violence of the French Revolution and we know that Marie-Antoinette, who was to meet her death in 1793 under the guillotine was particularly fond of the Petit Trianon. She was there when she heard that the Parisian mob was approaching.

Nebraskan Library

A credible example of retrocognition occurred in 1963 when a young Coleen Buterbaugh, a secretary at Nebraska Wesleyan University, walked into an office in the music building. She immediately smelled a strong and unusual odour and saw a tall woman with old fashioned clothes reaching up to a bookshelf. She sensed a man sitting to one side and when she looked out of the window she saw, to her great surprise, the campus as it had appeared roughly half a century previously. Afterwards, together with Sam Dahl, the Academic Dean, she identified the woman from an old yearbook as being a Miss Urania Mills who had been a music teacher from 1912 until her sudden death in the late 1930s.

In this case Coleen did not phone the newspapers or write a book. She tried to forget the experience by leaving her job and moving to Colorado. The library incident carries no apparent motive for the witness to fabricate a psychic event. It is modest and lacks sensationalism. The case also emphasises the difference between retrocognition and the sighting of a ghost. If what Coleen had seen was the ghost of Miss Mills, the library would have been the 1963 one, the external view also of the 1963 campus, and the apparition would have been perhaps less solid. The smell that assailed her as she entered the room would possibly have accompanied either a ghost or another psychic event but the vivid nature of the surroundings and the fact that she saw a quite different campus through the library window (it was missing one or two important buildings), plus the fact that she identified a person who had been at the University in that period are all suggestive of a retrocognitive event.

Pictish Battle

Another well-known retrocognition case concerns the Battle of Nechtansmere, which took place on May 20, 685 near Forfar in Scotland. It was an important turning point in the Northumbrian incursions into what is now Scotland. At that time a good part of what is now eastern Scotland was Northumbrian territory. The Scots were not involved. The battle was between a Pictish army under King Brude mac Beli, and the Northumbrians (who were mainly Angles), led by King Ecgfrith.

The affair, now usually called the Battle of Dunnichen (Dun Nechtain), was an overwhelming victory for the Picts. They lured the opposing army into wetlands, encircled and slaughtered the Northumbrian cavalry, and finished up by doing the same to the foot-soldiers. King Ecgfrith and his entire royal bodyguard were killed and only a small proportion of his army fled back to Northumbrian territory south of the Firth of Forth.

The retrocognition incident occurred well over a thousand years later when, on January 2nd 1950, a lady named E F Smith was walking back to the village of Letham (near Dunnichen Hill) late one snowy night after her car had slid off the road into a ditch. She explained that, as she walked, she felt 'nervous' before seeing a mass of lights on her left towards the Hill. She was surprised because there were very few homes in that direction. She looked closer and saw figures carrying torches who appeared to be examining bodies on the ground. They were turning them over and she felt they were searching for known faces – presumably spouses, relatives, or neighbours. Miss Smith's dog barked throughout the entire ten-minute episode.

She was more than a little frightened so walked quickly back home. She later explained that she had been extremely tired, as well as a little shocked by her car accident, and had tried not to think too much about her experience until she woke up next morning. From her descriptions, the Society for Psychical Research suspected that she had seen the 'ghosts' of long dead Picts searching the battlefield. It was normal practice in those hard-pressed days for locals to scour the scene immediately after a battle in order to strip the dead (after slitting the throats of any enemy who had the temerity to be still alive) and take any valuables. They also, of course, retrieved their own dead and wounded from the field.

Miss Smith did not profit from her reports and her visions would certainly qualify as retrocognition rather than a vision of ghosts. Two questions seem to stand out: Why would such a scene be re-enacted over 1,200 years later solely for the benefit of a cold, shocked, and possibly frightened lady? And what is it about animals that they seem to have a very powerful sense of the paranormal and often 'see' or sense things that humans do not? Deborah Hatswell's database (referenced elsewhere) contains an interesting account about a cat appearing to see invisible people in a room while refusing to take any notice of its owner. Cats, of course, were revered by the Egyptians as being able to travel between this world and the next at will and they are also known as 'familiars' for witches. Dogs, too, are said to have telepathic or psychic powers to be able to tell when their owners are about to arrive home or when they are ill and to sense natural phenomena well before humans. There are lots of theories concerning the psychic abilities of animals but only J B Rhine and his wife appear to have undertaken serious scientific work on the topic.

In the case of Miss Smith, the possibility of retrocognition is very high. There was no fame or fortune involved in her report and the event itself was of only fleeting interest to the press. In fact, it was quickly forgotten by almost everyone. The fact that she saw a full scene tends to weigh against her simply seeing ghosts and the fact that she had had a severe shock shortly before the experience may indicate a high degree of emotion accompanying the sighting.

Precognition, the opposite of retrocognition, is the ability to sense the future in some way. Some scientists call it *'anomalous anticipatory activity'*, but it comes down to sensing, or even knowing exactly, something that has not yet happened. Sometimes it occurs through vague 'hunches' or 'feelings', at other times people get full-blown premonitions through dreams or while fully awake and active. As a psi power it tends to get more attention than retrocognition for the simple reason that the latter is theoretically capable of being researched and memorised before being regaled to the waiting press and public. Precognitive incidents are capable of being tested – as long as the witnesses record things properly.

One very famous example is Abraham Lincoln. The US President is said, by his long-standing friend Ward Hill Lamon, to have dreamed that he attended a funeral in the White House and that, when he asked a soldier who they were mourning, the response was 'The President. He was assassinated.' Lincoln told Lamon of this dream ten days prior to his assassination and thereby verified the prediction. A large number of people have precognitive dreams every year.

The issue is one of huge importance. If a person can see the future, it may mean that the future has either already happened or is happening simultaneously with the present (and possible the past). It throws up mind-bending conundrums which make the cat's cradle events in *'Back to the Future'* seem simple by comparison. If I can somehow sense or see that something bad is going to happen does that mean that the event is predetermined – that it *must* happen no matter what anyone does in the meantime – or is it a connection with one of a range of possible futures (even with a range of possible parallel universes) which permit current actors to somehow change the outcomes? The case of the Dakota crash and of people avoiding death by acting on premonitions would seem to indicate that premonitions can be partly accurate and partly not and that would seem to argue against the deterministic theory of time. But in that case, we would have to accept that the future has not already happened.

The Drem Incident

Air Marshall Sir Robert Victor Goddard, who we encountered in the case of Bobby Capel's photo, might well have had psi abilities. He was certainly a deep and intelligent thinker about the paranormal. During his life he studied it and wrote a very good book on the subject alongside a highly successful career in the RAF. He had three encounters with the paranormal but only one could be positively ascribed to his own psi-ability. The famous case of the photographic ghost at Cranwell only came to his attention in the 1970s but, before Bobby Capel related her puzzlement at the ghost of 'Freddy Jackson', Goddard had had at least two other paranormal experiences – one of which was turned into a good film.

In 1935 he was possibly not aware of having psi powers, but it was in that year that he had the first of two experiences with precognition. In this case it was his own, but later, in 1947, it was through someone else's precognitive dream. To keep the narrative brief, in 1935 Goddard was a Wing Commander (USAF equivalent Lieutenant-Colonel) and his duties in the period in question required him to fly from the south of England to Edinburgh. He piloted an open cockpit Hawker Hart biplane which, at that time, was quite new although rapidly becoming obsolete (much of its design went into the subsequent Hawker Fury and the future Hawker Hurricane of Battle of Britain fame). Goddard spent a few days in Edinburgh on RAF business during which he visited the abandoned and derelict RAF airfield at a place called Drem – to the east of the city. The reason for his visit is not in the public record but I suspect that it had something to do with seeing how much work would be required to reinstate the base in the event of renewed hostilities with Germany.

When he had completed his tasks, Goddard began his return flight south from RAF Turnhouse, (now Edinburgh's International Airport). The weather was poor when he took off and it quickly became appalling. In the rain and cloud Goddard soon got lost and disorientated. With reference points invisible in the mist – those aircraft possessed only the most rudimentary instruments – he lost control of the aircraft. He said that at one point he was unsure whether he was even up the right way! The plane went into a spin which he only just recovered before crashing into the Firth of Forth. So, breathing a heavy sigh of relief, he steadied the plane, waited for his heart to slow down again, and looked around to establish his position. He was to the east of Edinburgh and, as soon as he confirmed that fact, he spotted the airfield at Drem. As he did so the weather suddenly changed completely. The rain and clouds disappeared to be replaced by bright sunshine.

Goddard turned the biplane towards for the airfield, presumably in order to give himself a new and known 'point of departure' for his navigation south. He flew the aircraft over the airfield at Drem expecting, of course, to see the deserted and dilapidated place he'd visited on the ground only a few days previously. But he was stunned by what he saw. The airfield was totally different – it was a fully functioning RAF base, repaired and operational. Its hangars had been completely repaired, there were new fuel tanks and defences, and on the airfield below he saw three Avro 504N trainer biplanes, all painted yellow, and a fourth monoplane aircraft of a type he did not recognise – also painted yellow. The 504s were very familiar to Goddard. They had been in use as initial trainers for many years. Nevertheless, he was sorely puzzled because they were all painted yellow and were being maintained by mechanics in blue overalls none of whom reacted to his overflight.

The Wing Commander was shocked and surprised, but he was all too aware of the fuel he must have used during his recent troubles. He had a long way to go to get back to his home base. He turned south, knowing that there were high hills just to the south of Drem, but the weather seemed fine, and he'd easily see the hills and be able to get above or around. But, as soon as he left the vicinity of the airfield, the weather closed in again, the storm returned in all its original ferocity, and visibility became very poor once more. Goddard had his work cut out to avoid the hills and make his way through the storm. It was many miles before he had the time to consider what he had seen.

When he had visited it recently, RAF Drem had been totally derelict and empty. Yet he'd just seen the airbase in a fully operational state. He was even more puzzled however because what he had seen was nothing like the RAF airfields he was used to. All the aircraft he saw were yellow – a colour in which no RAF aircraft was painted in 1935 – and the mechanics were wearing blue overalls which, again, were not regulation issue in 1935. All RAF mechanics in 1935 were still wearing the brown overalls that had been regulation issue since World War I and training aircraft were not painted at all.

After receiving some very strange looks when he told his colleagues about his experience, Goddard decided to keep his paranormal experiences to himself in future. Even so, he had gone through a precognitive experience which had a profound effect upon the officer. A few years later the RAF (and this was not a decision in which an officer at his rank had any say) decided that all training aircraft would be painted yellow in order to make them eminently visible for safety's sake. A parallel change of policy was that RAF mechanics were provided with blue overalls – presumably to distinguish them from Army mechanics.

The fact that Goddard's precognitive experience was fully vindicated a few years later makes the whole issue totally credible. He saw a renovated airfield, yellow-painted training aircraft, and another type – a Miles Magister – that did not exist in 1935 (the type did not have its first flight for another two years). He told his colleagues what he had seen. They did not believe him but, by telling them, he had established a verification point well in advance of the RAF's change if policy.

The Dakota Crash

The Air Marshall kept his paranormal interests to himself for many years until a second precognitive event occurred which almost cost him his life. This time it was not something of which he himself had a premonition; he was the subject of another person's precognitive dream. In 1946, Goddard was in Shanghai on RAF business. Like many senior officers, he kept his flying hours current by piloting occasional flights himself. He'd therefore put himself down to fly an RAF DC-3 Dakota to Tokyo. On the night before the flight, he was at a party, enjoying drinks and exchanging good-natured banter with the other guests. While speaking to someone he happened to overhear two other officers talking behind him. One was telling the other that he had had a dream the previous night in which Goddard's plane had crashed and Goddard had been killed. He went on to tell his companion that the aircraft was carrying Goddard, with two other men and a woman. It ran into difficulties when it became iced up. The plane became unmanageable and crashed on a pebbled beach near mountains. The man ended by saying that Goddard was killed in the crash.

Victor Goddard overheard this conversation early in the evening and did not give it much credence. There were to be no passengers on the flight. However, later that same night, the RAF bigwigs at Shanghai asked Goddard to take with him on the trip to Tokyo two men and a woman. He agreed, in spite of the implications of the dream he'd overheard. Part of his reason was that he knew his scheduled route was across warm seas, so there was almost no chance of icing.

A DC-3 Dakota of the RAF. This one is carrying D-Day markings. Wikipedia Commons; Tony Hisgett; https://commons.wikimedia.org/w/index.php?curid=64156164

The long trip was not uneventful, however. After an overnight stop half-way, the navigator became lost in cloud on the way to Japan. For modern pilots this is usually not an issue because they have GPS to pinpoint their position in real time. But in 1946 navigators had to be able to get a visual fix on landmarks or stars. If they got such a fix they then had to navigate by dead-reckoning through the clouds. The meant understanding the rough direction of flight and somehow allowing for drift due to side winds. Given that their last definite fix was many hundreds of miles in the past and that the clouds were dense within the aircraft's flight envelope (it was not a pressurised plane) the aircraft became completely lost and was well off course to the north when the wings and control surfaces started to ice up. The conditions worsened until the aircraft became almost impossible to fly. In-flight de-icing equipment on aircraft was in its infancy in those days. Today, most civil aircraft use one or more de-icing and anti-icing systems (so called 'boots', and bleed air systems being the most common) but in 1946 the only real solution to heavy icing in flight was to descend into what you hoped might be warmer air or trust to luck. Either you had sufficient altitude to be able to descend into warmer air and the ice melted – or you crash landed. Even modern aircraft are not immune – one of the most recent crashes due to ice was an ATR commuter aircraft in Canada in 2017. In 2020 a Wideroe Dash-8 aircraft lost both engines due to heavy icing as it was descending into Bergen, Norway. Only the fact that they descended into slightly warmer air, and the automatic restart functions on modern gas turbine engines saved the aircraft, its crew, and fourteen passengers. The main problem with ice is that it can build up on aerodynamic surfaces and cause the aircraft to lose lift. It can also jam the control surfaces and even cause engine flame outs.

Losing height fast Goddard emerged from very low cloud to see a mountainous island. Going inland was not an option so he managed to crash land the Dakota on the beach of a Japanese island called Sado (off the mainland city of Niigata), well to the north and west of where they should have been. Luckily, no-one was killed or even badly injured. It had been extremely skilful flying although the aircraft was a write-off. The story was first told in the *Saturday Evening Post* of May 26, 1951. Then, in 1955, a successful film was released, based on Goddard's experience. It was called *The Night My Number Came Up*, and starred Michael Redgrave. It's a good film.

Air Marshall Sir Robert Victor Goddard was a brave man – and I mean that not only because he was a flyer in the years when aircraft were wood and fabric contraptions powered by highly unreliable engines. He was brave as a flyer and because he actually did something about his studies into the paranormal (including UFOs/UAP). He was a persuasive force in setting up Sir George Trevelyan's Wrekin Trust in 1971 (a spiritual education charity), he supported Bobby Capel by telling her story in his book, he studied the paranormal and UFOs and wrote other books on the subject. There are few people who have had such eminent careers who take those sorts of risks with their reputations.

Goddard's second brush with precognition was just as compelling as his first. In the Dakota case, all the criteria for a valid premonition were satisfied and we are left with yet more hard evidence of psychic powers displayed by fairly ordinary human beings.

The Criteria for Premonitions

We are all intelligent creatures. We have the ability to put two and two together and occasionally come up with the right answer. If you go to a small modern airfield and see rusty tools lying all over the place, dirty rags stuffed into corners, and bits of engines lying around for dust and rain to get into, you would not be having a premonition if you chose not to fly in any of their planes. You would simply be assessing the evidence and being entirely sensible.

A premonition requires more than the application of brainpower to your surroundings. For something to be categorised as a valid premonition the event has to meet a number of criteria:

1. The incident should not be predictable in the normal course of events by the application of logic.

2. There must be at least two distinct 'elements' to the prediction. That is two or three from the event or events, a sequence, the time, the place, the people involved, etc.
3. There should be a reasonably short interval in time between the prediction and the event.
4. The prediction should be written down or attested-to by independent witnesses *before* the event.
5. The question must be asked as to whether anyone has acted on the prediction to their benefit.

So, an incident must not be capable of being predicted – even unconsciously – in the normal course of events. There should be at least two aspects of the event that have been predicted – preferably more. For example, simply thinking that a particular wall is going to collapse is not necessarily a precognitive event. Your sub-conscious mind may have noted the small cracks, the soggy ground, and the precarious condition of the garage on the other side. But predicting the day and time at which it would collapse and the fact that a lady pushing a pram was going to be the victim would seal it as precognition if that was what actually happened.

Most parapsychologists also require that there be a reasonably short time interval between the anticipation and the event. After all, saying that a train carrying lots of people is going to crash somewhere, does not count as precognition if there is no timeframe. The event is virtually certain to happen somewhere within the next five to ten years. However, if the prediction is that it will happen in Italy and in the next week, that's close to a full-on precognitive statement. If the prediction also included the facts that it will happen in a wood in bright sunshine near a river, then that is the stuff of warnings to be acted upon if at all possible.

The litmus test for precognition is putting it in writing and giving the written account to a third party or having independent witnesses to an oral prediction. Lots of people say they predicted things and many probably did, but because they did not write their predictions down or tell other people well in advance, we have to treat their statements with a huge amount of caution. A final test could be whether someone acts on their precognition after telling someone or writing it down. That is, did someone act on the premonition in order to benefit from it. Many people appear to have had premonitions concerning the 9/11 tragedy. Some claim to have acted upon them and thereby saved their lives.

In the case of the Dakota crash the prediction was based on a third-party dream and was heard not only by the person the chap was speaking to but by Goddard himself. The prediction contained a number of elements that neither the dreamer nor Goddard could know or predict logically at the time. Goddard's flight was planned for a warm-water (and warm air) journey to Tokyo without passengers. Neither the dreamer nor Goddard could have predicted that the flight would unexpectedly have to carry two men and a woman, that the plane would end up so far off course that a crash would be caused by icing, and that the crash would be on a pebbled beach near mountains. The dreamer also predicted that Goddard would be killed in the crash. That's four or perhaps five predictive elements of which the dreamer got only one wrong. For me that's a cast-iron example of precognition.

CHAPTER 11
DREAMS

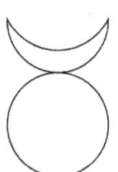

> *There is a theory which states that if ever anybody discovers exactly what the Universe is for and why it is here, it will instantly disappear and be replaced by something even more bizarre and inexplicable. There is another theory which states that this has already happened.*
>
> — DOUGLAS ADAMS THE HITCHHIKER'S GUIDE TO THE GALAXY

The Titanic

Certain disasters have become notorious for being the focus for precognitive experiences. The loss of the White Star liner Titanic in April 1912 is an event that produced some of the most compelling stories. Having said that, it also produced hundreds of not-so-compelling accounts of paranormal foresight. Most of these were opportunistic and sometimes financially motivated (pretty much as we find on social media today) but a few are well worth considering. A fairly large number of passengers who were booked on the Titanic for that fateful voyage from Southampton, Cherbourg, and Queenstown (now Cobh near Cork, Eire) had paid for their tickets but changed their minds and either did not travel at all or re-booked on other ships. We have no way of knowing how many of these cancellations resulted from conscious or unconscious presentiments of danger but, the weird fact is that, unlike almost all the other liners that sailed around that time, the Titanic was not full. Quite a few of the crew deserted or simply failed to join the ship. Again, there is no way of knowing whether some or all had presentiments of disaster and whether the proportion of deserters and no-shows was higher than normal before a major, highly publicised voyage on a brand-new ship.

We do know, though, that some people listened to their premonitions while others ignored warnings and travelled anyway. A high proportion of the latter group (but not all) died in the freezing waters of the North Atlantic. The following examples illustrate some of the stronger cases for precognition over periods that are longer than those demonstrated in laboratory experiments.

Around 1,500 people lost their lives when the Titanic sank on its maiden voyage. Wikimedia Commons; by Willy Stöwer - Magazine Die Gartenlaube; Public Domain; https://commons.wikimedia.org/w/index.php?curid=97646

One account is based on a number of articles in New York newspapers[1] shortly after the couple in question returned to the States on the RMS Mauretania. Mr. and Mrs. Edward W. Bill, from Philadelphia, had been in Europe in early 1912 and were looking to return to America. The husband dearly wanted to try the Titanic – it was brand-new and was then the largest and most luxurious liner in the world. The maiden voyage was bound to attract the richest and best-known celebrities in the world. Would *you* have given that up?

Mr. Bill's desire would be readily understood by those today who strive to be among the 'early adopters' of any innovative technology or at the front of the queue for a first flight, cruise, novel vehicle, or spaceflight. In the days leading up to the departure of the new liner the couple stayed at the Cecil Hotel on the Strand in London. However, as the date for the trip grew closer, Mrs. Bill began to have increasingly strong feelings that a disaster was about to occur very soon. For all married couples, the battle of wills that ensued between the two parties is very familiar. After many unsuccessful attempts to persuade him to abandon the trip, Mrs. Bill eventually wore him down. With great reluctance he swapped their tickets to the Cunard liner, Mauretania, which arrived in New York several days after the Titanic had encountered its fateful iceberg. After their arrival in New York, Mr. Bill gave an interview to the newspapers:

> *I had chosen our cabins on the Titanic, and I told my wife that it would be interesting to be on the biggest ship in the world for her maiden voyage. Mrs. Bill was not very enthusiastic and, as I was about to go to the White Star Line office to collect the tickets, she begged me not to go. She told me she didn't know why, but that she didn't want to go on the Titanic. I had never seen her before oppose a travel plan, but this time she was adamant, and I had to reluctantly give in to her desire.*

The 32-year-old Norwegian musician Daniel Danielsen Gronnestad and his brother Bertil had been making one of their quite frequent visits from the USA to visit to family in Norway. When it was time for them to return from their 1912 trip Daniel booked himself 3rd Class on the Titanic for £8 15s 6d (around £830 in 2023 money) the millionaire Astor family paid £224 10s 6d for their party – roughly £20,000 today². Daniel's brother Bertil, however, had experienced a premonition and tried to dissuade Daniel from sailing on the Titanic. But Daniel was determined to travel, and the brothers split up. Bertil stayed on in Norway for a while longer before returning on another ship. Daniel boarded the Titanic alone and shared a four-berth cabin with three other Scandinavians. He died in the sinking of the 'unsinkable' Titanic.

The Adelmans, from Seattle, had an experience not unlike that of Mr. and Mrs. Bill. Franck Adelman was a violinist. He'd booked tickets for himself and his wife to return to America on the Titanic. A few days before departure, Mrs. Adelman had a strong premonition of danger and begged her husband to cancel the trip. After a lengthy discussion at the end of which they had failed to agree a course of action, Mr. Adelman agreed to flip a coin to decide if they would travel as planned or wait. It was Mrs. Adelman who won the coin toss and the couple canceled their reservation on the Titanic. Was she telekinetic as well as precognitive?

Perhaps the best-known precognitive incident from the Titanic tragedy concerns Lucy Christiana, Lady Duff-Gordon, the groundbreaking British fashion designer. Her brand 'Lucille' was perhaps the first global fashion brand. She had offices in Paris, London, New York, and Chicago. Such a business demanded that Lady Duff-Gordon travelled a great deal, and her growing fame in the USA meant that she regularly took the famous liners across the Atlantic. In the spring of 1912, she had to visit the New York branch and her secretary 'Franks' (Laura Mabel Francatelli) therefore booked herself and her boss on Titanic's maiden voyage.

Lady Duff-Gordon – who always travelled under the alias 'Morgan' – was, however, unusually worried about traveling on the new ship. The business in New York could not be avoided or delayed, so she asked for the reservations to be switched to another ship. 'Franks' tried her best to comply with the requests but found that the Titanic was the only option to get them to New York within the necessary timeframe³. Lady Duff-Gordon had strong feelings that 'something' was going to happen and discussed her fears with her husband, Sir Cosmo Duff Gordon. Her fears must have been very compelling because, although he did not normally travel with her, he agreed to accompany her on this occasion to allay her concerns. So, Mr. and Mrs. Morgan boarded the ship with Miss Francatelli.

Lady Lucy Duff-Gordon clearly had a keen sense of style even as a young lady. Wikimedia Commons; by Khang17092004; https://commons.wikimedia.org/w/index.php?curid=65755338

During the trip, her Ladyship continued to be uncharacteristically anxious. She refused to undress completely at night. Her jewelry box and some of her very precious belongings and papers were placed on a table in the bedroom ready for a quick exit. Her outdoor coat, scarves, gloves, hat, and so on were always placed ready for action. Not surprisingly, when the order was given to abandon ship, the couple and their secretary took no time leaving their cabin and were among the very first on deck, queuing up for the lifeboats. Lady Duff-Gordon was apparently wearing two dressing gowns over her clothes as well as her warmest hat – which she called her 'motoring hat'. Because they were so early the group was able to line up for Lifeboat Number 1 which could seat around forty people.

When their turn came to board the lifeboat, Sir Cosmo and his wife both asked the officer in charge of the lifeboat station whether he could board with the two ladies, who would otherwise be unaccompanied. The officer agreed. This may (or may not) have run counter to the Captain's alleged order that only women and children should board the lifeboats, but it was certainly not an order that was universally followed.

Lifeboat #1 was one of the first to leave the liner. Due to the increasing list on the vessel only a few were ever able to be launched. It was absolutely no fault of the Duff-Gordons, but Lifeboat #1 departed with just twelve people on board – seven of whom were crew assigned to it as oarsmen and coxswain. At the time at which the boat was hastily launched the Titanic was beginning to list severely. The unsinkable liner was already down by the bows, well on its way to sinking. For the officer in charge of Lifeboat #1 it was a major dilemma. If he launched it too early, people still on board the liner would not get the chance to conveniently board the lifeboat. If he left it too late, the list on the ship would, in the very immediate future, prevent the boat launching at all. He decided to launch the boat while it was still feasible. The lifeboat would then be free of the liner and able to collect more people from the increasing numbers of passengers and crew already floundering in the ice-cold water.

The Duff-Gordons and their secretary survived the tragedy, but Sir Cosmo came under severe criticism at home, not so much for being a male in a lifeboat when the alleged orders were women and children first, as for apparently failing to demand that the crew returned to pick up people in the water. He was even falsely accused of bribing the lifeboat crew to ignore people in the water.

Lady Duff-Gordon's premonition of disaster was, like several others reported by Titanic survivors a feeling that had been oppressing her for a long time before and during the voyage. She was very reluctant to take the ship in the first place, persuaded her husband to accompany her when he never normally did so, and maintained a remarkably elevated level of awareness and readiness during the voyage itself.

A Scottish MP and King's Counsel (senior attorney) booked the Titanic for the maiden voyage. Norman Carlyle Craig had evidently decided to make the trip on a bit of a whim - 'for a blow of fresh air', he said. He had paid for his ticket and was on the passenger list. After the Titanic sank there was a wide assumption that he had been aboard, and his body had not been recovered. However, he never made the trip. He explained afterwards to the papers:

> *I suddenly decided not to sail, I cannot tell you why; there was simply no reason for it. I had no mysterious premonitions or visions of any kind, nor did I dream of any disaster. But I do know that, at practically the last moment, I did not want to go.*

The experts these days would call this an unconscious premonition. Craig went on to become a Royal Naval Volunteer Reserve Lieutenant Commander during World War One and, sadly, died in 1919 from complications following an operation.

These are just a few accounts among a large number of claimed precognitions relating to a single, highly traumatic event. All are fascinating insights into people's feelings prior to the event and several were from regular trans-Atlantic travellers like Bertil Gronnestad, Lady Duff-Gordon, and the Bills – people who did not hesitate to travel on other ships at other times. Mrs. Bill happily sailed on the Mauretania and the Adelmans and Bertil also found their way back to the States in other liners.

Precognition can be demonstrated in the laboratory, but it seems to be heightened where harrowing events are concerned. It is as though the event sends emotional shock waves back into the past which are picked up by those with the right psychic ability. It could be that the shock waves affect all of us but that only people with developed psi talents receive them at a volume sufficient to stimulate fear and action.

The World Trade Centre

One account from immediately prior to the terrible tragedy at the World Trade Centre in New York in September 2001, tells of a lady named Holly Winter whose mother strangely insisted upon her daughter visiting her instead of going to New York to the Twin Towers with her friends (as they did every year around that time). Holly Winter later said that her mother had never before been so insistent on her coming to visit her without prior arrangement. She obliged her mother and did not join her two friends, both of whom were among the 2,977 who died in the combined 9/11 terrorist attacks.

That same horrendous event is associated with many tales of people who did not visit the buildings as planned on September 11th. Some ran late when they never did before, some simply changed their minds at the last moment, while others felt unwell and stayed away. One chap claimed to have had unconscious premonitions of two separate disasters at the World Trade Centre. Barrett Naylor claims to have avoided the 1993 bombing at the Trade Centre after he had a bad feeling while he was on his way to work in the Centre. He had travelled by train into New York City and was in Grand Central Station when he said he had a 'sense that he could not describe'. Something, he said, was telling him that he should turn around and go home. He did exactly that and, thereby, avoided the deaths, injuries, and turmoil that followed the explosion of a terrorist bomb in the lower parking levels of the North Tower. Islamic terrorists packed a van with over 1,000 lbs of explosives and detonated it at 12.18pm. The explosion was intended to bring down both Towers. It killed six people and injured thousands. Smoke filled the lifts and stairwells of the entire North Tower, power was cut off to the building, people were evacuated from the roof, and many were trapped in lifts/elevators for hours. The plan was that the North Tower would be brought down and would fall onto the South Tower killing thousands. That it did not work was, according to the FBI, probably down to the fact that the van was not positioned closely enough to a major concrete foundation.

Then, on that terrible morning in 2001, Naylor had the same feeling of fear and foreboding and also paid attention to it. He said that he felt a sense of great unease as he went to catch his train. The feeling was that this journey – one he'd taken on weekdays for years – was somehow wrong. Again, he returned home, and was safely there when he watched, distraught, as the TV coverage showed the Twin Towers burn and collapse. Unfortunately, there is no corroboration of Mr. Naylor's unconscious premonition, but he did say that he felt both relieved at avoiding the disaster and guilty that he had not attempted to warn others.

There are many accounts of premonitions and what might be termed 'pre-awareness' of the tragedy – one author details over two hundred of them – but few are corroborated in any way. A good example is the harrowing tale of David McCourt. He lost his wife and four-year old daughter when United Flight 175 (scheduled from Boston to Los Angeles) was hijacked by the terrorists and deliberately crashed into the South Tower. He had spoken to his wife and daughter before they boarded the aircraft and wished them a safe flight but, as he put the phone down, he said he said he experienced a bright and powerful flash in his head which actually threw him back onto the bed[4]. He said later that, at that point, he just knew that there would be a crash. But it was too late. Without a mobile phone (and few had them in 2001) it was impossible for him to contact his wife.

Flight 191

In the section on solid or revenant ghosts we discussed the air-crash at Chicago O'Hare in 1979 after which local residents were disturbed night after night by apparitions and knocks and ghosts smelling of aviation fuel. That accident is also the focus for a fascinating tale of the man who predicted it.

It is one of the best examples of a premonition which met almost all the tests and criteria. David Booth was living in Cincinnati in 1979 when he dreamt, ten nights in a row, of an air-crash. He was so disturbed by the dreams – by their consistency and vividness – that he eventually called the Federal Aviation Administration (FAA) and described as much as possible of his dream premonitions. He told them that his dream was of a plane veering off the runway before it flipped over and burst into flames. The FAA took his story seriously and, based on his detailed descriptions, narrowed-down the possible planes to either an American Airlines Boeing 727 or an American Airlines Douglas DC-10. They now knew roughly what type of aircraft would be involved and how it would crash, but Booth could not give them a location, date, or time. Booth's last, identical, nightmare was on the night of May 24th, 1979.

On May 25th American Airlines Flight 191 – a DC-10 – had just left the ground on its way from Chicago O'Hare to Los Angeles when its left engine broke off the wing. The wing pylon for the engine had been improperly removed and reinstated during maintenance some weeks previously. The stresses occasioned by that rushed engine replacement eventually caused attachments to shear. The failures happened because the engines were at take-off power and the stress fractures finally gave way. The aircraft was completely destabilised and the pilots did not stand a chance at that incredibly delicate point in the flight. They did their absolute best, but they simply could not keep the left wing up at that speed. Within moments the DC-10 flipped almost completely over just to the left and above the runway and it crashed, killing all 271 people on board plus two people on the ground. The crash was due to poor maintenance but neither the FBI nor the FAA could believe that David Booth had predicted it in such accurate detail. Neither could he but the major issue here was that the traumatic crash came through to him very clearly in his dreams but the location and date did not. Again, the 'shock wave' theory seems to apply.

Perhaps more people experienced the premonition but did not report it.

Winning the Lottery

All the preceding cases are solid examples of people being aware of a future event before it occurred – human beings being able to see into the future. It seems that the more traumatic the event the more likely it is that someone will be able to anticipate it. If that were the standard rule we could rest on our laurels as having linked premonitions to highly charged, emotional events. Yet premonitions can also involve much less traumatic incidents. Sometimes it seems that people can see into the future where much less charged, even mundane, events are concerned. One of the examples we have already looked into is the vision of a future airfield at Drem in Scotland by then RAF Wing Commander Victor Goddard. There is also an even more ordinary example – of a man who predicted a lottery outcome.

In January 2018 a computer programmer in Virginia, USA had a dream. He said afterwards that he had never had a dream like it before in his life. He dreamed of some numbers. They were 3-10-17-26-32. In the morning he was extremely puzzled, but he wrote the numbers down and then went out and bought four identical lottery tickets, each using those five numbers. Each ticket won him $100,000 for a total prize of $400,000. The tests for precognition are all met. There was no way he could have logically deduced the numbers and the odds against a random concurrence of the numbers are astronomical. He had an anomalous anticipatory event. The time between the prediction and the event was extremely short and the chap, Victor Amole, recorded his prediction by buying those numbers on the lottery ticket before the draw was made. On top of that he was so confident of five random numbers that came to him in a dream that he bought four separate but identical tickets. In the past he'd have been accused of witchcraft but would probably have kept his mouth shut or said that it was an angel who came to him in the dream.

The Power of Dreams

The odds against Victor stumbling on five winning numbers in his dream are equivalent to him making up five numbers every night for around 762 years before getting a winning set (with all the associated costs of buying well over a million lottery tickets). In this case he was so confident that something important had happened that he did not hedge his bets as most of us do with lottery tickets. He did not enter for multiple sets of numbers based on all sorts of 'lucky' dates and times, house numbers, elevator floors, or whatever. He dreamed five numbers in that order and bought four identical lottery tickets.

Seeing the future in dreams is one of the main ways in which people experience precognitive events. In the past it was regarded as total fiction but, as some of the events described above illustrate, we now know that precognitive dreaming is a very real phenomenon. It may well be linked to the theory that dreaming can be a connection between the individual consciousness and a wider universal consciousness – that sleep is the time when our consciousness plays with the universe.

A British aeronautical engineer called J. W. Dunne wrote a book in 1927 called *An Experiment with Time*. It dealt primarily with the precognitive powers of people's dreams which he regarded as a very real phenomenon supported anecdotally by a whole raft of examples. Julius Caesar's assassination was said to have been foretold in a dream. Defeat at Waterloo was predicted by Napoleon himself in one of his dreams. Abraham Lincoln, as we have seen, dreamed of the funeral following his own assassination. There are several examples of people predicting the San Francisco earthquake in their dreams, and we have records of people predicting or anticipating the sinking of the Titanic, Victor Goddard's crash in Japan, the 9/11 attacks, and the accident to Flight 191 to name but a few.

For sceptics who can criticise laboratory psychic experiments (often with some justification) the task of debunking precognition – particularly in dreams – is almost impossible. True, much of the evidence is anecdotal but its weight, when combined with the pre-recorded examples (such as David Booth and the American Airlines crash of 1979) is more than sufficient to convince. There is no doubt that some people, under certain conditions, can receive feelings or messages from things that are yet to happen. All of which seems to imply that what modern physicists suspect – that all time and matter is actually bound up together in one place and that the past, present and future coexist alongside one another – is actually entirely possible. The 2009 book by Dr Larry Dossey sums up the issue of premonitions in a very balanced way[5].

One of the most important starting points for anyone who has a serious interest in parapsychology and the paranormal is the work of a husband a wife team of academics, Dr J B Rhine and his wife Dr Louisa E Rhine.

Dr J B Rhine (left) Wikimedia Commons; by Francis Wickware - Life Magazine. April. 15, 1940, Public Domain, https://commons.wikimedia.org/w/index.php?curid=57851900

Dr Louisa E Rhine. Unknown photographer. Wikimedia Commons; Public Domain, https://commons.wikimedia.org/w/index.php?curid= 61762650

They were early scientific investigators of the paranormal and were key figures in the development of Duke University's Parapsychology Laboratory. J B Rhine specialised in ESP and psychokinesis (known as PK but also better recognised these days as telekinesis). Louisa Rhine painstakingly put together real-life examples of a range of types of extra-sensory perception – including those of ghosts and apparitions – which contained a very large number of dream-related precognitions. Her work accumulated around 7,000 accounts and – while anecdotal – it forms an incredible dataset for all researchers of precognitive phenomena. She wrote a number of major texts over a twenty-year period which were bookended by *'Hidden Channels of the Mind'* (1961) and *'The Invisible Picture'* (1981). Her work can be criticised on a number of levels, but it has remained part of the bedrock of Psi research for over sixty years.

In 1988 an Atlanta psychologist called David Ryback published a book called *'Dreams that came true'*. In it he describes an experiment he conducted with the aid of students at the university. As an initial step he issued a questionnaire which received over 430 responses. Almost 300 of these included claims of different forms of predictive dreaming. He then analysed these carefully and critically. As a result, he discounted most as being either intuition (a sort of informed guess) or forms of post-hoc argument (e.g. after the event a person interprets a vaguely related dream as being a premonition – as in 'I tripped over a kerbstone and only then remembered that I'd dreamed the night before of walking along a sidewalk'). When Ryback had finished removing the doubtful cases he was left with just under 9% - around 38 cases – which, he argued, showed that the people had experienced genuine precognitive dreams. Almost one in ten seems a high proportion but that was from a sample of people who had self-selected themselves to answer the questionnaire. His work is open to similar criticisms as that of Louisa Rhine but, as with many things paranormal, the weight of circumstantial and anecdotal evidence is extremely compelling[6].

So, we have a massive amount of empirical and anecdotal evidence that precognition is a genuine phenomenon, but we also have a mountain of critical argument which attempts to debunk the whole thing. How can we judge whether something is genuine precognition or not? A chap named Guy William Lambert was one of the longest serving members of the Society for Psychical Research (SPR) whose headquarters are in London, England. He was an eminent civil servant who gave his time to the SPR for around 70 years. He was the Society's President for two years in the 1950s. His stance was always intelligently sceptical but open minded. He proposed five criteria to be met before an account of a precognitive dream could be regarded as credible:

1. The dream should be reported to a credible witness before the event predicted in the dream.
2. The time interval between the dream and the event should be short.
3. The event should be unexpected at the time of the dream (i.e., it should not be possible for anyone to have logically

predicted it).
4. The description should be of an event destined literally, and not symbolically, to happen.
5. The details of dream and event should tally.

In spite of being penned seventy years ago these remain excellent tests of a precognitive dream and link tightly to the standard 'precognition criteria' that we discussed earlier. The dream of the man who predicted Victor Goddard's crash landing, Victor Amole's lottery dream, and dreams of David Booth all meet these criteria. The Wikipedia article on the subject says, quite rightly:

> *A great deal of evidence for precognition has been put forward, both as witnessed anecdotes and as experimental results, but none has yet been accepted as rigorous scientific proof of the phenomenon.*

All very true. But the problem is whether there can *ever* be 'rigorous scientific proof' for any psi-phenomenon. The core question is how one can set up a scientific experiment or test for something that cannot be controlled? The quest for scientific proof is also a bit of a distraction. For example, we have three examples in this book alone which prove that it happens.

Another persuasive experiment into precognition was carried out at the University of Colorado, Boulder, by Christopher Carson Smith, Darrell Laham, and Garret Moddel. In 2010 the researchers carried out a simple but pretty impressive experiment. They took ten students, untrained in any form of clairvoyance or remote viewing, and asked them to predict stock market futures. They then placed small amounts of money on those predictions. The group of students got seven predictions out of seven absolutely correct and the process yielded a decent stock market profit. The researchers admitted that the predictive process was probably degrading as it went on, but they could deduce no clear reasons for that drop-off in performance (Carson Smith, et al., 2010).

CHAPTER 12
THE POWER OF THE MIND

 To the mind that is still, the whole universe surrenders.

— LAO TZU

Controlling things with our minds without physical or electronic means has been a major theme of the paranormal for thousands of years. Shamans and witches claimed the power to use their minds to cure ailments, control the weather, curse, and sometimes kill. Some said they had the power to move things without touching them and some shamans and witches were said to be able to fly using just their minds to cast the right spells. There are a few quite credible accounts from recent times of Buddhist monks being able to move large rocks by chanting.

Today, mind over matter is usually called telekinesis or paranormal healing. Both have their supporters, and both are naturally labelled as pseudoscience by many scientists. Telepathy and remote viewing are not mind to matter powers – they are mind-to-mind or even just the mind set free to roam. Usually, these days the whole subject is combined into the field of Extra-Sensory Perception (ESP) which has been defined as:

anomalous processes of information or energy transfer, processes such as telepathy... that are currently unexplained in terms of known physical or biological mechanisms.

— BEM & HONORTON, 1994

Mind over body

Let's be clear right at the start. If someone was able to heal a disease without medicine or other physical intervention 'something' would have caused a physical change in the body which killed the virus, bacteria, or cancer cells. As all the latter are physical objects, the act of killing them is physical and any effects of a person's mind on them would be 'mind over matter'.

Healing people has not always been a professional pursuit of specialist scientists. For most of our history as a species the task fell to witches, shamans, and priests whose knowledge was passed down from generation to generation in oral tradition or secret texts. Some of it was based on lengthy experience in the use of plants and herbs whose constituents doctors today know are effective against certain ailments. Willow bark contains the main ingredient of aspirin and has been used to alleviate pain for many centuries. But other types of healing were based on the patient's *belief* in the person doing the healing and, amazingly, that is still the case to this day.

There is supposed to be no scientific proof that healing due to belief works and yet scientists have a mountain of evidence that the placebo effect and its opposite – the nocebo effect – are very real and that the patient's belief in the powers of the person prescribing the treatment is often critical to success. It would probably not be considered ethical, but it would be interesting to see the effects on people if drugs and medicines that we know to be effective were, instead of being prescribed by white-coated physicians, were rebranded, reboxed and touted by local shopkeepers or perhaps bar staff under names like 'Pain-B-Gone' or 'Bacteria-Killer'. We would effectively be testing the reverse of the placebo effect – the nocebo effect. Would the customers of these non-medical outlets respond in the same way to these medicines as they might to a clinic or hospital-based prescription?

Perhaps even more profoundly – are we missing a lot by ignoring the belief effect? Could doctors and nurses do even greater good if they worked a bit harder at gaining even more credibility and trust? The counter thought is to ask what harm may be being done by the press publicising the errors of medical staff? The evidence that a person's belief significantly influences the effectiveness of treatment is now overwhelming. Perhaps it is time we took some action to enhance and support belief even at the cost of what we are pleased to call 'transparency'.

The placebo effect occurs when a person is given a perfectly innocuous remedy or treatment whose effect on the disease or ailment in question has not the slightest basis in science. Yet it works and we'll be looking at a few experiments in this area later. Scientists have come up with a number of 'could be' possibilities, but no one has yet satisfactorily shown how the placebo actually works to counter an ailment. But one thing is absolutely carved in stone – trust in the expertise and effectiveness of the person or organisation (preferably both) prescribing the placebo. In a statistically significant proportion of cases, the treatment actually works.

The effect can also be demonstrated where patients are given the same placebo by different people or even with different labels. If the placebo is recommended and given to the patient by an ordinary person dressed in everyday clothes, the effects are much less pronounced than if an identically packaged and named placebo is given in a hospital or a doctor's surgery by someone in a white coat wearing a stethoscope. Belief – the role of the mind – seems therefore to be a powerful thing and it probably accounts for the relative success of ancient healers.

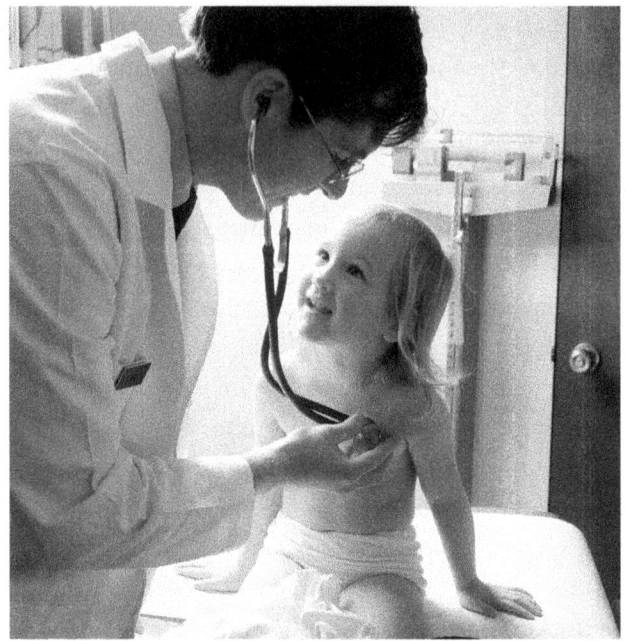

A patient with total belief in their white-coated physician. Wikimedia Commons; Unknown author; Public Domain, https://commons.wikimedia.org/w/index.php?curid=9783736

Our modern priests dress in white coats and carry stethoscopes but the power of appearance, location, and reputation to effect medical results is very powerful.

The use of the word 'mind' is also important. What is it that acts as the location of belief? It is not the brain because almost all brains are identical in structure and yet one person can respond to a placebo while another will not. Belief is in the 'mind' and this seems to act independently to – or at least irrespective of – the physical brain. It's as though the mind in its crucial roles acts separately to the brain. It needs the brain as a locus (possibly a temporary one) but each broadly identical physical brain somehow hosts an independent and very different mind.

Ritual and appearances matter a great deal in their ability to underpin faith in a medic. If sufficient ritual can be designed and followed, if the provider creates an aura of power, reputation, and status, if the medicine sounds and looks sufficiently weird and wonderful, the 'remedy', whatever it is, can have a beneficial effect on the body. Nobody knows how this works any more than they can explain music-induced analgesia – the way that listening to music you love can have a real and measurable effect on pain[1]. In the midst of all this scientific scepticism, the power of belief is taken completely for granted by most religions. If you have faith and truly believe, miracles can happen. The question is whether this is a function of a specific religion and deity or whether it works in any situation in which the conditions for belief are fulfilled – ritual, appearance, belief. It certainly seems to be the latter. Belief can make things happen whatever religion or belief system you adopt. Just about every religion in the world has its stories of miracles and the strength of belief in voodoo cultures is famous for its effectiveness for both good and evil. The effectiveness of belief is almost certainly completely independent of specific religions or systems so why are we not using it in a more organised and effective way?

The scientist Dr Ted Kaptchuk of the Beth Israel Deaconess Medical Center (affiliated to Harvard University) has long focused his research on the placebo effect. An expert scholar in oriental medicine, he is pretty sure that placebos will not cure major diseases but has shown them to be very effective for conditions like pain management, stress-related insomnia, and cancer treatment side effects like fatigue and nausea[2].

> *You have to go to a clinic at certain times and be examined by medical professionals in white coats. You receive all kinds of exotic pills and undergo strange procedures. All this can have a profound impact on how the body perceives symptoms because you feel you are getting attention and care.*

He speaks of 'the body' in perceiving symptoms but what he really means is the mind. In 2014 he proved that a totally useless pill could reduce pain in half of his patients. In a paper published in Science Translational Medicine in 2014 he described a study in which he divided a group of patients who suffered migraines into three groups. He gave one group a placebo medicine marked with the official name of the migraine drug. The medicine for the second group was labelled 'Placebo', and the third group took nothing. Migraines were reduced in the first group. They were reduced in half of the second group but not reduced at all in the third. Kaptchuk believes that the simple act of taking a pill – any pill – can produce effects. The prescribing of a medicine by a scientific-looking doctor means that people associate the taking of that pill with positive effects[3].

In another experiment he gave half of a different group what they thought was a pain relief pill but was a placebo and the other half were treated to what they were told was acupuncture. The result was that acupuncture worked better than the medicine. The only problem, of course, was that neither treatment was real – the pill was a placebo and the acupuncture needles never penetrated the skin – they were retractable. Nevertheless, the acupuncture group, having received what they believed to be a more exotic treatment, reported real pain relief. Even some of the pill group got relief. Kaptchuk was astounded that a third of both groups reported side effects. Neither intervention was real yet a third of both groups reported the sort of side effects that the doctors had 'warned' them about before the treatments began – sluggishness from the pills and red blotches and swelling on the skin from the 'acupuncture'.

Pain still baffles scientists. We are taught that it is a warning of damage. In some minor cases it can be just that – for example when you get a paper cut – but it actually has little value for larger injuries and no value at all for long-term illnesses. Why on earth would you need incredible pain to warn you that your arm has just been severed at the elbow in a car crash? Why do cancer patients suffer agonies for years when they already know about the disease? So, what is pain and why do we suffer from it? The other puzzle is that, if pain is supposed to be a warning, why does it often take its time before appearing? Military physicians are very aware that soldiers can suffer the most appalling injuries but not feel the slightest pain for quite a long time. Then, suddenly, and quite redundantly, the severe pain begins. Why? What possible purpose does it fulfil?

An Andrew Brown article in The Guardian[4] in 2009 told the story (which he attributed to the famous neuroscientist Professor Patrick Wall) of a surgeon who was practising in a field unit during the Korean War (1950-53). The surgeon came down with appendicitis just as a mass of casualties was arriving from the front. He chose to treat the wounded before he had his own operation and, in order to cope with the pain of appendicitis (which everyone knows is considerable), he ordered one of his nurses to give him a dose of morphine. It worked and he continued to operate on the injured soldiers until eventually he was able to finish and submit to his own appendectomy. It was not until he was back in the recovery ward and had regained consciousness that he found out that the supplies of morphine had run out well before his request. The nurse had given him an injection of saline solution. In spite of getting a treatment which was, medically, totally useless with respect to pain, his excessive pain from appendicitis was dulled and he was able to operate on the wounded soldiers. He knew how morphine was supposed to work, so his body blocked the pain – simply because he *believed* that he had been given morphine.

There are physiological reasons for pain and the ways that it can be ameliorated but scientists still do not understand how the mind can sometimes succumb to pain and, at other times, can reduce it or even ignore it, both without scientific or medical interventions. There are some who argue that the only reason that placebos are ineffective against severe diseases like cancer is simply because modern people have been deeply conditioned to believe that cancer is a very major disease and that it is incurable – or at least only partially curable after a significant amount of 'high-tech' treatment. What would happen, they ask, if people were to be *genuinely* persuaded that a specific pill regime could completely cure ninety-nine percent of instances of their type of cancer?

The mind-over-body effects discussed above are easy to pigeonhole into a medical category. They appear to be effects which are physical and that could have nice, neat scientific causes. If a placebo works then, the sceptics reason, it must be some sort of influence that the brain has on hormones or other biological processes. The really important question is HOW the mind does this and why it does it for substances that are not medically effective? Most of us are totally sold on the scientific and medical view of the human body as an electro-biological object. It may be called biological but the fundamental scientific and medical paradigm rests on a mechanical relationship between electro-chemical reactions and cells. But could it be that we have become enmeshed in the wrong paradigm based on years of exposure to the dominant belief system - science?

You have a disease and the tests in the laboratory show that a chemical (or more likely a cocktail of chemicals) of some sort has a beneficial effect on it. Consequently, that treatment becomes a standard part of the doctor's kit. The use of very fancy Latin words might help but essentially the chemical cocktail might work only because a reasonable proportion of patients are convinced by the associated medical shenanigans that it will.

The human body is made up of countless cell-types from brain neurons to skin cells, from the electro-optical cone cells in the eye to the entirely different digestive cells in the gut. Each cell has a number of different parts plus a nucleus to control it through extremely subtle chemical processes. The DNA and mRNA in each cell do the controlling and the whole thing is set in motion by the tiny strands of DNA and mRNA in the fertilised human egg. The immense complexity of a human body comes from that almost invisible egg after mating with a sperm. Scientists are still grappling with how it all works and how stem cells create all that complexity. And here is something else to think about. Our scientists do not yet understand why people look different. In theory our DNA should create a human but we have no idea how it works to create different face shapes and the variation in bone length and so on. Why it all works to make a human being actually look like a human being and to look slightly different to their parents and siblings is a mystery.

Scientific understanding today is greater by at least an order of magnitude to that of the medics of the early twentieth century but doctors still do not really understand more than about half of everything that needs to be understood about our basic physiology. What causes cancer and why does it spread? How can we best deal with viruses like those associated with various diseases? Most particularly why can we not instantly stop a virus like the coronaviruses that cause so much death and heartache? Why does one, apparently healthy, human being succumb to Covid-19 while another shrugs it off like the flu? How does pain work? Why can the liver regrow and skin and muscle repair themselves, but the same does not apply to faulty cells in the kidney or brain, and a severed finger or hand will not regrow? We have partial – chemical and mechanical – answers to all these questions but we still do not know for sure in spite of around two centuries of study.

Quite apart from all the things we have just been talking about, doctors are now totally convinced of the power of positive thought and happiness to help people live longer. How does this work? Why exactly should a happy person live longer than an unhappy one? They both have the same physical and electro-mechanical, bodies which respond to the environment in the same way. But, somehow, it makes a statistical difference if you are a positive and happy person. If the mind can really do this – and doctors are now convinced that it can – what other benefits are we missing? Are we missing the possibility that deep and genuine belief in modern medics and their cures would have the effect of making those cures much more effective?

Each atom of each cell of the human body comprises the well-known larger particles including electrons, protons, and neutrons. What we almost always forget in imagining the little solar systems of atoms is that the so-called 'particles' are not particles at all. They are not matter in the sense of a speck of dust, they are electro-magnetic charges. And each of those 'particles' consists of even smaller ones. Those, in turn, are made up of – well ... nothing. At the quantum level exist some very strange things of which we are only just beginning to be vaguely aware. The weird connection between two 'entangled' quantum particles has now been proved in practice by communication and cryptology experiments and we know, through the new experimental quantum computers, that a qbit (part of a quantum byte) can be in two different states at the same time! The practical effects of the latter are to enable extremely powerful quantum computing, those of the former may permit us to develop theoretically unbreakable codes.

So, we have a few really weird effects but what all of us need to remember is that human bodies and brains are made up of these very same quantum weirdnesses. The brain may look like a physical thing and we may operate on it as though it is, but it really does not exist. Every particle of every cell in the brain is just an electro-magnetic charge. In any materialist sense it does not exist and we have not the slightest clue how it relates to the mind.

The mind is a powerful thing and not all its powers are explicable in purely physiological terms. All human beings are almost identical in DNA terms. Their bodies work in the same ways from a purely mechanical and medical perspective with the same chemicals, hormones, neuron connections, and so on. But they react to different things in very different ways and somehow (again the medics and scientists do not understand quite how) virtually identical strands of DNA result in a wide range of very different creatures – humans, elephants, cows, dolphins, and so on. At the macro level it is still a mystery and at the quantum level no-one has the slightest clue how quantum effects may influence human life. There is no scientific reason, for example, why a cell in one human brain cannot be 'entangled' in some way with a cell in another brain, we still do not know whether quantum entanglement could not operate perfectly effectively between different dimensions, and there seems to be no reason in principle why quantum effects cannot link the universe and its stars and planets, with human life on Earth.

The Power of Belief

There is a long-established saying in the world of paranormal experimentation: sceptics are goats, believers are sheep. Dean L Radin's book repeats the rule and provides much evidence to support it. The bottom line is that if you already 'believe' in the paranormal (if you are a sheep) you are more likely to score highly in paranormal experiments[5]. On the face of it that seems like a sceptic's dream – a bias towards the paranormal means that people are bound to score highly, therefore we can ignore the results. But think about it for a moment. *Why* should the scores be dependent on belief? What mechanism is at work that makes believers score higher on paranormal tests when the experimenters themselves have no vested interest in making anyone score more highly than anyone else? Why aren't other variables having an impact – why don't women score more highly than men, or younger people achieve better scores than old-timers, or tall people more highly than short ones?

None of these seem to be key variables, yet simple belief has a measureable effect on experiments. Belief makes medicines out of placebos, apparently makes it more likely that you witness a UFO/UAP, and more likely that a curse from a witch will affect your life and health. There is also evidence that the levels of belief in paranormal phenomena in the scientist undertaking an experiment can directly affect the outcomes. But what is belief but a predisposition to accept the truth and power of something that cannot be scientifically demonstrated to exist. Religious belief lends strength to millions of people around the world, no matter what the religion actually is, and there is strong evidence that belief in a particular person or job role can minimise or even cure illness. Faith healers are often dismissed as charlatans and some undoubtedly are, but there are powerful examples of strong belief achieving quite extraordinary things – like a doctor able to continue working through severe appendicitis solely because he believed that he had been given a strong pain killer. Or patients experiencing a genuine reduction in migraines when prescribed a placebo or given a fake course of acupuncture.

Feelings of optimism and happiness also seem to be powerful medicines. Happily married men live longer than unhappily married ones, optimistic people seem to deal with disease and illness better than pessimistic ones, and so on. The opposite seems also to be true. People who are pessimistic and prone to depression and despair seem to be more likely to die of the same diseases and illnesses that happy, optimistic people can battle through.

Belief operates outside the materialist world. It cannot be tested by science and cannot be falsified, yet we have very strong proof of its effectiveness in all sorts of environments and subjects. Whatever we are talking about – happiness, optimism, belief, faith – they are all attributes of the human mind, they are not stitched into chemicals, hormones, DNA, or flesh and bones, they are not an immutable part of everyone's brain. All of them are mind – that incredible, non-physical phenomenon that I doubt any scientist will ever be able to pin down.

To put it bluntly, there are powers in the human mind that are real but cannot be explained by science. I often wonder what would happen if we announced that our wonderful medical scientists had cured cancer. If everyone truly and deeply believed that the disease had been cured by a course of clever pills involving some mumbo-jumbo about nano-crystals, mRNA, or stem cells and with long-Latin names, what would happen to the recovery rates? Could scepticism or our modern cynicism about medicine turn out to be the most powerful dangers to our health and well-being?

Telekinesis

Of all the mind-over-matter powers, none has captured the human imagination quite like the ability to move or change objects by the force of human will. Psychokinesis (PK) is probably one of the most studied of the paranormal powers but has rarely been convincingly proved to exist in scientific experiments. Even when proof has been claimed, it is always disputed by sceptics. The spoon bending exhibitions of the famous Israeli-British psychic Uri Geller were demonstrated to be possible without exerting PK powers. Sceptics showed that subtle use of force using one's fingers could bend spoons and other implements in a similar way to that exhibited by Geller.

We should understand, however, that just because it is possible to bend a fork or a spoon using gentle manual force, this does not necessarily mean that there is not another way – a mind-centred way – of doing it. In 2017 the CIA released a set of hitherto secret files and admitted, publicly, on its own website that Uri Geller had been tested by them, had worked for them, and had *'Demonstrated his paranormal perceptual ability in a convincing and unambiguous manner'*. The revelations were almost certainly the result of legal pressure on the agency, but they are stunning nevertheless. The Central Intelligence Agency admitted that Geller had been totally convincing in his demonstrations of *paranormal* perceptual ability. They were not admitting to PK ability but the CIA most certainly testified that Geller had used his powers of paranormal perception in *a convincing and unambiguous manner*.

A controlled experiment with an Indian Yogi called Swami Rama, in 1970, recorded him moving a knitting needle five feet. The air vents in the room were covered and Rama was wearing a medical mask and a full gown to prevent him subtly blowing on the needle. The British psychic Matthew Manning was shown in the 1970s to have telekinetic abilities to a level above chance. But his efforts have also been heavily criticised by sceptics.

The question, as always with the paranormal, is: Are scientific tests ever going to be able to demonstrate something that could be a uniquely human and unscientific – i.e. paranormal – ability? Scientists would argue that this is precisely the point. If paranormal abilities cannot be demonstrated and replicated scientifically then they simply do not exist. Does this apply to the placebo effect? Hundreds of tests show that it works but it cannot be replicated scientifically – that is it cannot be falsified. And would this apply to deities too? A large number of scientists are religious – so clearly there are exceptions to the rule. My view is that humans have become far too enamoured of the scientific method. It is extremely valuable in many ways but we must at least consider the possibility that there is much more to the universe than that.

Laboratory experiments often focus on basic feats of PK like trying to make dice land on a certain number at an above-chance rate or influencing a computerized random number generator. There is some quite compelling evidence that humans can do both of these things to rates that beat pure chance, but there are also strong reasons for asking whether the scientific approach is ever going to work.

A séance involving table levitation. Photo by Jules Courtier - donated to Wikimedia Commons as part of a project by the Metropolitan Museum of Art; https://commons.wikimedia.org/w/index.php?curid=60494961

In 2015, Leslie Kean joined a group led by Dr Stephen Braude[6] which was evaluating table levitations and other forms of telekinesis as performed by a German medium named Kai. Kean's book contains a detailed description of the events. People, in association with the medium, were able to raise a table several feet in the air - something that the British SPR has also demonstrated. She says the groups also experienced raps and bangs from objects that no-one around the table could reach (all doors were locked so no-one could get into the room to create the noises). Stephen Braude said of this exercise:

> *I think it would be hasty to conclude that there was only one agent. Some of the participants felt tense enough for the emotions to have yielded a poltergeist effect. Kai may well have been the repository of most of the tension and the likely (paranormal) cause of the drum thwack and some other phenomena.*

He could not explain the significant movement of the table but nevertheless thought that everything was probably the result of telekinetic powers (PK) and not what he calls 'discarnates' (ghosts). An emotionally charged atmosphere is probably familiar to all readers who have held séances at college or in their own living rooms. Things can happen in such conditions and no one knows why or how, but the levels of emotion seem to have a definite effect.

Braude was quoted by Kean as saying ...

> *I am hardly comfortable about announcing to my academic colleagues that I believe, for example, that accordions can float in mid-air playing melodies, or that hands may materialize, move objects, and then dissolve or disappear... But I have reached my present position only after satisfying myself that no reasonable options remain. Actually, I find that my discomfort tends to diminish as I discern more clearly how little the most derisive and condescending skeptics really know about the evidence and how their apparent confidence in their opinions is little more than posturing and dishonest bluffing.*[7]

Another physical effect that has often baffled researcher is the noise that accompanies some paranormal effects. Dr Barrie G Colvin of the Society for Psychical Research (SPR[8]) in London published a paper in 2010 in which he electronically-analysed ten noises (raps and knocks) said to have been caused by verified poltergeists during séances. The noises had been recorded during the events and the resulting computer files sent to the SPR. Colvin assessed the noises using advanced audio software against equivalent recordings of similar noises that had been verified as being made by humans. The human raps and knocks had been made on the same materials as the ones from purported ghosts. What he found was very interesting. In all cases he found that the human raps were at their loudest at the moment the sound started – for example, at the moment a knuckle rapped on a door or a stick banged a drum. The sound intensity/frequency then tailed off and died away in a smooth curve. The alleged poltergeist raps, on the other hand, began faintly and gradually rose to their loudest pitch at the end of the sound clip. Colvin could not explain this. He said that the closest he could come to an explanation was that the non-human sounds resulted from the gradual build-up of stress in the material itself as though the molecules were being vibrated and the vibrations gradually increased. He has since established a dedicated poltergeist research group within the SPR.

These findings from acoustic investigations support to an extent the testimony of some witnesses who describe noises produced by what they believe might be ghosts or poltergeists. Anecdotal evidence is that the sounds seem 'strange' and unlike equivalent noises heard in everyday contexts. What Dr Colvin has found may well explain why humans find the noises strange and unusual while being unable to explain the difference. A possibly unconnected but very similar phenomenon occurs with UFO/UAP sightings. Many witnesses describe colours either on or within the objects, but they frequently say that the colours are not 'natural', that they are somehow more intense or different to the same colour in normal life. One wonders whether the explanation may lie in a similar process to the acoustic differences discovered by Dr Colvin.

Older experiments in psychokinesis were heavily criticised by academics as being influenced in a variety of ways by the experimenter. Modern research into PK rests more heavily on complex statistical analyses – extending across multiple different studies. In practical terms, the issue these days is not so much whether a person could bend a spoon, move a knitting needle, or knock a glass over with their minds, but whether quite large samples of people can make a coin come up heads significantly above 50 percent of the time over the course of 1,000 trials or significantly influence the fall of a die above chance. Modern studies work to mitigate any bias from individual experimenters or experimental design by averaging the results across many similar studies and using sophisticated statistics to test the outcomes.

A further issue, as mentioned previously, is the potential impact of a laboratory setting on psychic abilities. As we will see below, the effects demonstrated in many experiments are relatively small and many researchers admit that the data fall short of what might be termed scientific standards of proof. The famous researcher, Russell Targ, acknowledges that *'the evidence for laboratory psychokinesis is quite weak'* but his immense volume of work in the area of extrasensory perception (ESP) is unrivalled and entirely convincing[9]. Targ has the sort of physics track-record that most professional scientists can only dream of. He has produced ground-breaking work on lasers and plasma physics for a multitude of organisations including NASA and Lockheed Martin but has also written some well-researched books looking into ESP and was part of the CIA trials of remote viewing and other paranormal effects at the Stanford Research Institute.

Telekinesis is undoubtedly possible but, as with most other paranormal phenomena – it is probably impossible to prove scientifically.

Telepathy

Telepathy is one of the super-stars of the paranormal. It is almost as widely promoted and written about as witchcraft. The internet offers hundreds of sites purporting to explain and improve your telepathic skills and there is an equal number of sites containing alleged examples of telepathic communication between twins, mothers and children, people in love, and even those in danger.

Please forgive me if you already know what a Ganzfeld experiment is, but many readers may not have heard of them. The idea is to take two people and place them in two well separated rooms in comfortable environments. In a theoretical attempt to mimic a state of altered consciousness the first person (the 'receiver') has their eyes covered with half-ping-pong balls while the room is lit with a gentle red light. Their ears are covered with earphones through which mild white noise it played. In the other room the 'transmitter' person is shown random pictures and is asked to concentrate on them and try to transmit them to the receiver in their distant room.

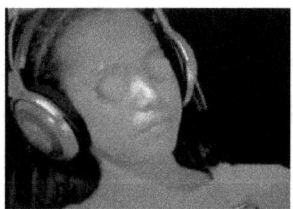

A Ganzfeld Subject with earphones, covered eyes, and red-light environment; by Nealparr; Wikimedia Commons; Public Domain
https://commons.wikimedia.org/w/index.php?curid=3181503

After each attempt, the receiver is asked to identify – from four photos or images – which one the transmitter/sender was looking at. A large number of experiments show that they can usually do this at well above the level expected by pure chance – which would be 25 per cent of the time. A meta-analysis by parapsychologist Charles Honorton and sceptic Ray Hyman examined twenty-eight studies which took place between 1974 and 1981. They reported an average hit rate of 35 per cent (Honorton, 1985). The 10 per cent excess over pure chance may seem relatively small but, over so many trials, this is a very strong finding. The studies also showed an impressive 'effect size' of 0.63 (Bem & Honorton, 1994) where 0.5 is normally considered a medium-sized effect in the social sciences. Ray Hymen later wrote that the findings were suspect due to what he described as 'sensory leakage' and poor randomisation of the images. It is not at all clear what he really meant by the vague term 'sensory leakage'.

A later study of the experiment by the US National Research Council in the 1980s accepted what Hymen said but still found that the effect was so consistent as to be unlikely to have been caused by pure chance. Following the criticism directed at the first tests, a new and more stringent set were designed with fully automatic randomisation and selection of the senders' images. Daryl Bem and the late Charles Honorton published findings in 1994 based on eleven fully automated studies consisting of 354 sessions. They found a significant hit rate of 32 per cent.

So, two major meta studies of different sets of multiple tests by different scientists showed results well above pure chance, yet the criticisms kept coming. In 2001 Bem and Palmer published the results of a meta-analysis of forty studies revealing an average hit rate of 30%. Other studies have found that belief and mood seem to have an impact on results. Participants who believe in ESP seem to do better, and those who are happy and optimistic also perform better. The level of someone's education has a positive correlation with belief in ESP. Put simply, the more highly educated people are, the more they seem to believe that there may be such a thing as Extra-Sensory Perception and the higher the belief and the happier and more optimistic a person is, the more likely they appear to be to succeed at telekinetic and telepathic tests[10].

There is little doubt that the transfer of feelings and ideas between minds is possible under certain experimental conditions but 'real world' anecdotes seem to indicate that a much stronger link is possible. Comparing the two might indicate that the testing of people in laboratory conditions is not terribly effective and that 'real life' anecdotes actually provide more reliable guidelines.

Telephone telepathy is the name given to the ability to 'know' who is calling on the phone before you pick it up. The problem is separating out pure intuition (i.e. logical inference) from any genuinely unique mental connection between the caller and the receiver. Dr Rupert Sheldrake performed tests on 'telephone telepathy' which revealed that, on 45 per cent of occasions, the receiver knew exactly who was calling. His results have (of course) come into serious question. The Rhine Research Center, one of the most respected psychic research groups in the world, has carried out a great deal of research into telepathy. Their reports contain a case of a mother who was on a trip without her children. Early in the trip she experienced intense 'feelings of danger and concern' centred on her youngest son. When she called home, she discovered he had been taken to hospital with a very high fever.

Twins – especially identical ones – may also be susceptible to telepathic links. In fact, there is probably not a single set of twins in the world who cannot tell you of instances where they 'know' that the other is feeling unwell or is in trouble. These instances are particularly compelling when the twins are separated by a great distance and therefore cannot read each other's subtle non-verbal messages. Female twins can often tell when one is going into labour even though they are separated by hundreds or even thousands of miles. The anecdotal stories are legion but there appears to be little in the way of an empirical study of the phenomenon.

In 2005 Rupert Sheldrake and Pam Smith gathered fifty subjects and had them predict which of four potential emailers would send them a message. The subjects had to submit their predictions one minute *before* the email was sent and the predictions were kept very separate to the people making the decisions on email senders. In 552 experiments the subjects predicted the correct emailer for 43% of the emails – very significantly above the 25% statistically likely for pure chance.

The research is always questioned by the sceptics but, over the years, there have been so many studies, by so many scientists, that have shown greater-than-chance probabilities that humans can feel or predict the future (i.e. the people who would contact them) that I would argue that we are either at, or closely approaching, a level of circumstantial certainty and in some cases high levels of statistical probability that psi powers exist.

So, can we receive messages from other people via the mind?

Looked at from a purely practical standpoint the whole thing seems impossible. How can a brain send a sufficiently powerful signal by mind power alone? How come other people do not pick up the same signal?

Wikipedia calls telepathy the

purported vicarious transmission of information from one person to another without using any known human sensory channels or physical interaction.

The Wikipedia article goes on to say that there is no proof because experiments have been criticised for 'lack of proper controls and repeatability'. Predictably, it ends by calling telepathy a pseudoscience. Yet there can be very few people who do NOT believe that telepathy exists. Almost everyone has had direct or secondary knowledge of instances where – at the very least – people had 'feelings' that turned out to be what other people were actually going through at the time. There are countless stories of siblings, parents, and lovers who 'know' something is happening to the other party at the same time it is occurring miles away.

How long are scientists going to be allowed to get away with criticising individual psi powers as pseudoscience? Ghosts, NDEs, telepathy, telekinesis, healing through belief, OBEs, UFOs – all are branded as pseudoscience and written off but the overwhelming evidence for all of them is indisputable. One science fiction author once pondered the subject and ended up wondering whether we are all capable of telepathy but that we have developed, over the millennia, a way of cloaking our minds to prevent messages and feelings getting through.

Remote Viewing/Clairvoyance

Clairvoyance is the old term for the power to perceive events and situations at a distance purely with the power of one's mind. It differs from precognition and retrocognition only in the fact that remote viewing is usually focused on the current world and not on past or future events. Back in the 1960s the Americans (and probably the British, too) were concerned with reports that the Soviets were developing talented psychics to be able to 'see' into US bases and military programmes. It was one of those moments that leaders hate. Do nothing and you get panned by history, do something and you risk becoming a laughing-stock. The powers-that-be decided to do something but to keep it under wraps. They recruited a couple of eminent scientists who had the courage to address the issue, Russell Targ and Harold Puthoff, and they began to experiment with what became known as remote viewing. The work, sometimes called the Stargate Program, went on for many years. It identified suitable talented people and used them to test the viability of remote viewing. It's generally thought that the work was successful but that it was also highly dependent upon the 'viewer' and a range of personal characteristics and attitudes. In the end the decision was taken to end the programme.

Professor Jessica Utts, chair of the statistics department at the University of California, Irvine is an expert statistician who has done a lot of work in the psi field. Part of that work was spent under contract to the US Government looking into whether psi abilities could be used in intelligence work – mainly focused on remote viewing. Dean Radin, in his 2018 book, *Real Magic*, quotes her as saying that the statistical evidence for precognition, and perhaps other psi phenomena, is strong.

> *Using the standards applied to any other area of science, it is concluded that psychic functioning has been well established. Arguments that these results could be due to methodological flaws in the experiments are soundly refuted. Effects of similar magnitude to those found in government-sponsored research ... have been replicated at a number of laboratories across the world. Such consistency cannot be readily explained by claims of flaws or fraud* [11]

Radin went on in his book to discuss eight different psi experiments which have been tested in different labs multiple times over the years, The results of six of them show that the probability of getting the psi-positive results by chance are less than one in a billion (in one case – one in a trillion)[12].

Six out of eight important scientific studies show that psi abilities are real.

One of the most interesting outcomes from research and practice with respect to remote viewing is that it seems to be extremely intuitive and that it has little to do with one's rational expectations or logical thinking. One comment was that a good remote viewing session is almost always one where the viewer does not really understand what they have done or how accurate it is. It seems that the more confident a remote viewer is that they have delivered the goods the less likely it is that they are correct. Nevertheless, Dean Radin believes that the talent is there in all humans.

As with the 2010 experiment with stock market futures that we discussed earlier, work on remote viewing has also found a degree of drop-off in the effectiveness of practitioners. The degradation of remote viewer capabilities is attested to in much of the literature, but no-one understands why this happens. During the Stargate project some viewers became bored with what they were being asked to do, some simply 'went off the boil', and others refused to carry on. There is little doubt that individual motivation and personal character and attitudes make a great deal of difference and, again, this may well be why ESP experiments in laboratory settings sometimes fail to detect an effect or only find mild effects. The person, the situation, and the general emotional and motivational atmosphere may be critical. This is the crux of what I call the 'experimental conundrum' but it is not the only problem.

Personality, motivation, and the character of the experimental subjects appear to have a profound effect on results. We know that belief and optimism are important. We also know that the psychic influence of the experimenter can almost certainly affect the outcomes of studies. The mind is a strange and still unknown land. What is worse is that we seem unwilling to explore it other than as a mechanical contrivance based in the brain – one whose powers we assume are purely physical. But if there is one message that the material in this book conveys above all others it is that there is a huge and growing body of evidence that the mind is far more than just a temporary thing which resides in the brain, does a few calculations, and remembers faces, birthdays, and where the office is located. The message shouts loudly that we must begin to examine the powers of the mind outside the walls of laboratories and that we may need to be bold in our experimentation.

CHAPTER 13
IMPOSSIBLE EXPERIMENTS

> *We stand at the edge of reality ... The edge of reality is also the edge of knowledge. But beyond this edge is another science and another knowledge.*
>
> — HYNEK, J. ALLEN. THE EDGE OF REALITY: A PROGRESS REPORT ON UNIDENTIFIED FLYING OBJECTS

Allen Hynek and Jacques Vallée did some of the very best thinking about the phenomenon we call UFOs. The subject took over their lives as they explored the rabbit warren of unidentified objects, psi-effects, aliens, abductions, and government misdirection, and cover-up. Filing cabinets were filled and book followed book as they were drawn down the tunnels, gradually testing theories and ideas, until the pair of them ended up staring at something that was very different to the anomaly they thought they were investigating. They'd started their long journey in the days when everyone, governments included, thought that UFOs were advanced metal spaceships carrying little green men from outer space (or, alternatively, advanced Soviet aircraft). They eventually came to the conclusion that this was not the case – although they admitted that it could still be *part* of the case. Instead, they realised that UFOs were another extremely complex aspect of the paranormal universe, and that they and the associated phenomena were far more mysterious and much closer to the intangible paranormal than they'd originally believed.

Their journey has strong parallels with the one that we have been on in this book. Hynek and Vallée journeyed from purely physical UFOs and a very comfortable 'us against them' paradigm, to a paranormal realm in which human consciousness plays the key, perhaps even the only, role. On our own road we have come from a relatively simplistic view of paranormal phenomena as being isolated topics, each comfortingly colourful and familiar, to a viewpoint from which we can see that we are actually dealing with fully interconnected and interdependent phenomena.

Dr Edgar Mitchell, the Apollo 14 astronaut and the sixth human to walk on the Moon, had what he called a transformational-moment in the Apollo Command capsule as it travelled back to Earth in 1971. He said that, while watching the blue and white globe of the Earth, the realisation that the molecules in his body and those of the Earth came from the same ancient stars gave him an ecstatic sense of the oneness of everything and the immense value of the planet.

> *I realized that the story of ourselves as told by science—our cosmology, our religion—was incomplete and likely flawed. I recognized that the Newtonian idea of separate, independent, discrete things in the universe wasn't a fully accurate description. What was needed was a new story of who we are and what we are capable of becoming.*

He developed a belief that the universe itself is a conscious entity and that, rather than matter being the fundamental reality, consciousness is the basis of everything and matter is simply an illusion – a product of consciousness. He also believed that the quantum attributes of entanglement, coherence, resonance, and non-locality are the key and that they lie at the base of hitherto paranormal phenomena like telepathy, remote viewing, psychic healing, and telekinesis. He cited the strange contact possible between mothers and children and between identical twins and sometimes between psychics and dead people as possible features of what we currently call zero-point energy[1].

In a very real sense, Mitchell's belief in 'god(s)-in-everything' rather than in the interpretation of any single religion is not a million miles from the beliefs of the native American tribes, the Australasian aborigines, the ancient Britons and Druids, and the Saami people of northern Scandinavia who all believed that every part of nature was a part of the whole, that aspects of 'the gods' inhabit the Earth, the waters, the animals, and the trees, and that mankind is just a small – but integral – part of the whole. Against that background some 'modern' religions could be seen as narrow, divisive, antagonistic, and even shallow - creating antipathy, conflict, and discord rather than peace and harmony.

We depend on rationalism and logic and the sad fact is the neither may apply to the paranormal. We have always believed that there is 'something' beyond our physical world. In the past this has been encapsulated in a wide variety of religions and belief systems ranging from the exciting, sex-filled Valhalla of the Norsemen and the soap opera realms of the Greek and Roman gods and goddesses, to the dour and unexciting Heaven of the Christians and the somewhat more complex realms envisaged by Buddhist and Hindu scholars.

In recent times science has encountered its own Waterloo. Its old belief-system of materialism and mechanistic answers has come up against the weird, illogical, and definitely non-material conundrums represented by dark energy and the quantum domain. The uncertainty and lack of predictability in modern physics is leading even the most stalwart of scientists to consider how the universe really works. If it is not a clockwork mechanism as envisaged by Newton and has much more mysterious aspects than those conceptualised by Einstein, how does it all work? If the body is not an electro-biological machine, where does human consciousness originate? More and more philosophers and scientists are coming to ponder the reality and location of consciousness.

We don't know what being 'conscious' means, but there are a number of theories ranging from a simple extension of the mechanical, neuro-biological processes that take place in any brain, to the transcendental possibilities inherent in the theories of non-local consciousness and universal consciousness. The latter sound highly academic and, if you read up on them, you will encounter more long words and convoluted logic than you ever want to see. They all end up with the implied phrase – 'we just don't know'. The only consensus appears to be that we suspect that merely being sentient or self-aware is not enough. We are pretty lost from that point on, but we do know one very important thing: that consciousness is science's brick wall, its Waterloo. It is the question that finally defeats the scientific method and, while that did not matter fifty years ago because it could be shunted off as something to be discussed by the philosophers, it most certainly does matter now that we have realised that there are huge aspects of the working of the universe about which we can never be completely certain. It is irrational and illogical that a computer byte can be in two different states at the same time, it's illogical that, without electronic connections, two entangled 'particles' can communicate across vast distances, it is baffling that a beam of particles can go through two different slits at the same time, it's mind-bending that a phenomenon like light can be a particle and a wave at the same time, and the fact that the universe will expand forever goes way beyond logic. So, rationality fails and we must begin to consider the fact that an irrational, non-logical approach may take us a lot further.

Only a few humans currently realise this, but we are living through one of the most exciting and profound changes in human history. The old clockwork model of the universe has been consigned to the scrapheap. Even the Einsteinian model is fast being superseded. The model that is replacing them is so close to what we call the paranormal that you could not slip a sheet of paper between them.

Science has brought humanity a long way in material terms in three hundred years, but its priests are now battling demons who do not obey its laws. These foes will never overturn what science has accomplished, or indeed what it may accomplish in the centuries to come, but they represent a boundary between pure materialism and a future in which that is seen to be less important than attempts to engage with the paranormal force that underpins the universe.

The most pervasive neuro-biological theories of consciousness propose that it is a direct outcome of the workings of the physical human brain. There is no more scientific proof of this than there is of the man in the Moon but, because the theories are wrapped in scientific jargon and accompanied by EEG and CAT scans, they receive a lot of attention. The materialist hypothesis, once highly compelling, has been weakened a great deal by the ever-growing proof of human psi capabilities. Human minds can receive feelings and even specific information from the future and the past, and there is a growing body of evidence around telepathy and remote viewing. None of this appears to feature on CAT scans.

The most convincing evidence that undermines the materialist hypothesis comes from some of the best minds in the world. The men and women who have come to the conclusion that consciousness is non-local - that it exists independently of the brain and that said consciousness underpins everything. Dr Pim Van Lommel is one such scientist, as are renowned and reputable scholars such as Eugene Wigner, John Bell, and Roger Penrose, who have proposed the idea that consciousness could be a quantum phenomenon. The idea is gaining traction all the time.

How might it work? It's difficult for practical humans (that is all of us who are rooted to the scientific method and its material world) to imagine how we connect to a wider consciousness. It's easy for us to put it all down to New Age nonsense. Consciousness does not pay the bills or fill the car with gas or electricity, it does not keep kids safe at school or make it easier to run a successful business. It may be existentially important but we all tend to ignore it in our everyday lives. And science cannot really help us with consciousness – there is no way it can prove anything to do with such an inherently immaterial, paranormal capability. It may be able to demonstrate the mechanisms behind the brain controlling an arm or a leg but it does not even get close to explaining how the brain interfaces with love, rage, hate, jealousy, humour.

Exploring the boundary between the material world and consciousness is not easy. It has close parallels to the current dilemmas facing science where the material/quantum boundary is concerned. We cannot use the scientific method but, being material creatures we have no choice but to depend either upon science or upon the collection of anecdotal and empirical data. Put more simply we either carry out scientific experiments under the strict rules of the scientific method or we attempt to use observation and to acquire circumstantial information. It's the basis for a major conundrum.

The Experimental Conundrum

The experimental conundrum is actually a series of fundamentally critical conundrums. Academics have been attempting to investigate the paranormal for at least the last hundred and fifty years, but the majority simply write the whole topic off as pseudoscience. If one were to accept the definition of pseudoscience as given on Wikipedia we might as well all pack up and go home:

> *Pseudoscience consists of statements, beliefs, or practices that claim to be both scientific and factual but are incompatible with the scientific method. Pseudoscience is often characterized by contradictory, exaggerated or unfalsifiable claims; reliance on confirmation bias rather than rigorous attempts at refutation; lack of openness to evaluation by other experts; absence of systematic practices when developing hypotheses; and continued adherence long after the pseudoscientific hypotheses have been experimentally discredited.*

All very valid – if one accepts that the scientific method is all-powerful and of universal application. There is too much evidence, though, that this is not the case and there is therefore the very serious possibility that scientists are coming at paranormal abilities from entirely the wrong angle. For a good half-century between 1950 and 2004 the US government decried and disparaged all claims by people who said they'd seen UFOs. People who saw UFOs were either mistaken or they were fraudsters. Black and white. Nothing in between. The paranormal phenomenon comprising UFO sightings and experiences was denigrated for decades and a good part of the rationale was that UFOs could not be falsified through experimental means, so they could not exist. This all changed between about 2004 and 2020 when the US government changed its tune and a string of verified sightings by humans and military sensors became the bedrock for significant and ongoing official investigations. The Department of Defense admitted that the phenomenon existed and changed service rules to make it easier for pilots and others to report anomalous encounters.

I seriously doubt that any purely scientific investigations will be successful but the example serves to illustrate how things are changing and how even governments are coming to see that paranormal phenomena have to be investigated. But, if we want to investigate, there is an experimental conundrum the size of a skyscraper standing smack in the centre of our road.

It represents two critical concerns: the distribution of psi powers, and the conditions under which such powers might best be displayed. From these a number of critical questions emerge:

- Is it justifiable to assume that, if telepathy exists, *everyone* will be able to do it and to the same levels of competence?
- Are we confident that it can be demonstrated in an identical and consistent way every time one conducts a given experiment?
- Can scientists be certain that their experimental method is compatible with effective investigation of the paranormal?

Just for the sake of argument, assume for a moment that telepathy is possible but can only be performed by people in a particular mental state and perhaps even with the correct mix of genes – possibly a small minority of the species. How would experimenters identify such people if they wanted to test telepathy in the lab? The same consideration applies to most paranormal powers. If such abilities are only available to certain people, or if only a miniscule number of people have genuinely significant abilities, or they can only be exhibited in certain circumstances or conditions, how can scientists test them?

Consider a couple of examples. If scientists test a thousand randomly selected individuals for the ability to solve a difficult intellectual puzzle the results might show that it could be solved in an average of five minutes. But, if the test were restricted to only those of extremely high IQ, we might find that it can be solved in under two minutes. The way that psi experiments are conducted makes the crucial assumptions that all humans are alike in psychic abilities and that psi powers need only a warm, comfortable environment to be successfully demonstrated. Inherent capabilities are one issue but emotion and circumstance may well be even more important. I'll come to those in a moment.

Virtually all human abilities are dependent on individual characteristics. A lot of people can run fast. A tiny proportion can run extremely fast, and a vanishingly small proportion can break Olympic records. Some humans possess innate mathematical abilities at a very high level and a tiny few are maths geniuses. Human abilities in such things as athletics and mathematics are not spread evenly across the species and high-level skills are extremely rare. If we were to select 1,000 people at random, we might be incredibly lucky and find, within that sample, a mathematical or physics genius. But my guess is that we would not and that we might not with the next sample of 1,000 or the sample after that or even in the thousand samples that might follow. And, if we did not find someone with those abilities in the million or so people in the test samples, would we be justified in assuming that the necessary skills are an impossible dream – that mathematical genius is simply not possible? So, why should psi abilities be susceptible to testing of relatively small groups of people drawn at random from large populations?

The point is that exceptional psi powers may well be as rare as exceptional powers in other human abilities. Psi powers might be extremely poor or even non-existent in the majority of the population. Scientific experiments on psi might therefore be picking up only weak psi abilities for the simple reason that their samples miss the truly gifted (or perhaps the truly gifted avoid the experiments in the first place). Should it be that psi ability is restricted to certain people – some of whom may not even know they have it and perhaps some of whom do not wish their ability to be known – how can representative test and control groups be formed?

Even if psi ability is not restricted to a tiny proportion of the population, it could be that we are trying to experimentally investigate a paranormal skill that requires specific attributes or conditions in which to operate successfully. Time and again in this book we've seen that emotion, stress, trauma, even ecstasy are vital components of some psi experiences. It is therefore entirely possible that a scientific laboratory does not constitute the most conducive environment for the minds of subjects to engage in paranormal activities. Both possibilities may sound like I am making an attempt to sidestep a lack of clear scientific proof that psi abilities are genuine phenomena but, once again, we have to ask whether the scientific method is sufficient when exploring certain aspects of reality. There are things that science cannot explain or predict.

A panel commissioned by the US National Research Council to study paranormal claims concluded that:

> 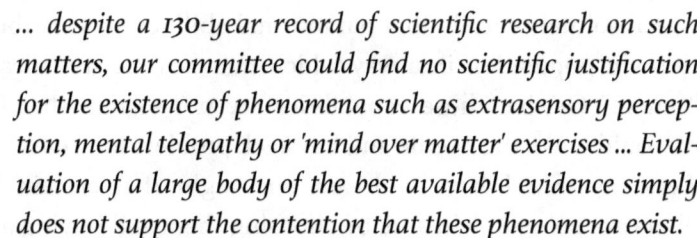 ... despite a 130-year record of scientific research on such matters, our committee could find no scientific justification for the existence of phenomena such as extrasensory perception, mental telepathy or 'mind over matter' exercises ... Evaluation of a large body of the best available evidence simply does not support the contention that these phenomena exist.

All very true. Yet a great many scientists have studied the subject closely, many still do, and a growing number believe that there is, indeed, convincing empirical and statistical evidence of paranormal abilities. That is not the same thing as scientific proof, but it is compelling evidence. Scientifically-minded researchers such as Sigmund Freud did not rule out the existence of telepathy but he seems not to have made his view very public. Freud evidently believed that there had been telepathic communication between himself and his daughter at one point[2]. Unfortunately for the National Research Council, a good number of eminent scientists, while agreeing with the words, disagree with the spirit of its findings.

The problem is that it is not true that, if you cannot prove something, it cannot exist. A lot of negatives in that sentence – let's put it the other way around – things can exist or be true even when scientists cannot prove them. Professor Brian Josephson (Nobel Prize in Physics, 1973) argues that telepathy is real and that quantum physics may have something to do with it. In 2001 he caused an incredible storm when he said just that in a booklet which accompanied a UK Royal Mail postage stamp issue. Scientists absolutely fought each other to join the line of people expressing their high-brow, academic outrage[3], but not a single one of them was able to disprove the phenomenon. It reminded me forcibly of the eminent scientists who fought each other to be the first to condemn Einstein's theories.

It's convenient for scientists to be able to say that something cannot exist unless it is subject to scientific replicability and falsification, but can we be absolutely sure that we are experimenting with the right people, in the right way, and that the circumstances and surroundings do not negatively influence the results? Can we be sure that any given paranormal phenomenon is mechanically replicable? Are we absolutely certain that paranormal abilities are distributed in the human population in a way which matches the statistical 'normal' curve? Or that those capabilities are not so rare that finding them would make the needle and haystack problem look easy?

Let's say that I have a dream one night that certain lottery numbers are going to win and, by choosing them and buying a ticket,

I rake in a small fortune. As long as I recorded the numbers on the day before the draw and told people that they came from my dream, that would count as a solid paranormal event. Yet, before science can recognise it as paranormal it has to pass the scientific method tests of replicability and falsifiability. It would have to be replicated every night or at least regularly afterwards. Scientists would have to be able to count the number of times I succeeded and failed at dreaming up lottery numbers.

I am certain the paranormal does not work like that and part of the reason is that science does not have any truck with emotion. Paranormal phenomena don't conform to the mechanistic worldview of science but does that negate any possibility that they might be genuine phenomena? An article by the semi-sceptic John Horgan in Scientific American (July 20th, 2012[4]) noted a number of senior scientists whom he considered to be open-minded about various aspects of the paranormal. Note that his list does not even begin to touch the scientists and academics mentioned already in this book. Horgan's 'open minded' group included: Alan Turing who had been impressed by Dr J B Rhine's card reading tests, Carl Jung who believed in synchronicity and said that such events are 'meaningful coincidences' if they occur with no causal relationship yet seem to be meaningfully related. Sigmund Freud, Brian Josephson and Freeman Dyson also made the list.

The eminent physicist Freeman Dyson, who died in 2020, was one of the most highly admired and innovative minds in the post-war world. He revelled in his ability to be 'subversive' in science and was definitely more open minded than the average scientist. He undertook an incredible amount of cutting-edge work but also expanded the boundaries of physics in many ways which will be cited and tested for many years to come. These include such concepts as 'Dyson Spheres', 'Dyson Trees', and 'Dyson's Eternal Intelligence'[5]. He was a long-serving member of the US Government's top scientific advisory group – JASON – but surprisingly (at least to the innocent outsider) never won a Nobel prize. Of this he once said:

I think it's almost true without exception if you want to win a Nobel Prize, you should have a long attention span, get hold of some deep and important problem and stay with it for ten years. That wasn't my style.

He also argued that paranormal phenomena are real but that they lie outside the limits of science. He was open to the possibility that psi phenomena do not submit to science because he believed that they only occur when humans are emotional or stressed in some way.

If you listen to the scientific establishment, another whom they dismiss as 'rogue' is Dr Rupert Sheldrake[6]. This brilliant Cambridge and Harvard-trained biologist, who is to biology what Dyson was to physics, came up with the theory of Morphic Resonance and has developed his career into paranormal studies. Naturally, he attracts the usual Wikipedia criticisms of his findings as being 'suspect' and his work mere 'pseudoscience' – yet the man is a highly capable scientist and one would presume that he is therefore at liberty to propose a fascinating theory which says that life – i.e. any self-organising system – inherits memories from previous similar systems. Sheldrake's website clarifies this by saying that, essentially, the laws of nature are actually just habits. The theory of Morphic Resonance proposes that biological inheritance need not come only from genes. It is a sort of collective memory from previous members of the species.

Sheldrake says that genetic chemistry cannot explain everything. He points out that genes control proteins but do not control form. That is, a gene can tell a human cell to contain or produce certain proteins but it cannot tell that cell what the organism should *look* like. He points out that we share a huge amount of genetic code with most other animals but that we do not look like them. To explain this Sheldrake has come up with the idea of Morphic Fields which effectively tell a tree to look like a tree and which evolve and change over time. His book on the subject was updated with new experiments and republished in 2009[7]. A Morphic Field is a force lying outside our current understanding of the way in which information is transmitted from the past to the present and within species. Sheldrake argues that certain experiments have already shown its existence – for example by rats in other parts of the world learning tricks that other rats in (say) New York have learned.

In the introduction to his 2012 book *'The Science Delusion'*, Sheldrake wrote[8]:

> *I have spent all my adult life as a scientist and I strongly believe in the importance of the scientific approach. Yet I have become increasingly convinced that the sciences have lost much of their vigour, vitality and curiosity. Dogmatic ideology, fear-based conformity, and institutional inertia are inhibiting scientific creativity.*

The book is most definitely pro-science but Sheldrake believes that science must shrug off centuries of false beliefs and dogmas and open up to new ideas. The greatest delusion that science suffers, he argues, is that it thinks it knows all the answers, that only the details are left to be uncovered.

The law of averages would dictate that not every scientist who develops an interest in the paranormal necessarily comes up with correct ideas and results. But it does seem strange that they are *all* discounted as indulging in 'magical thinking' and pseudoscience and that such conclusions are sufficient to consign them to the nether regions of scientific hell. It takes a very brave scientist these days to be as subversive and creative as people like Sheldrake and Dyson. For younger physicists and biologists it is a sobering choice. Follow the standard dogma and stand a chance of a Professorship in a decade or so or think openly and boldly and find yourself side-lined and perhaps even jobless. Perhaps scientists did more productive work when they were independently wealthy and could ignore the dictates of the god 'Career'?

It may be that a lack of falsifiability is a crucial weakness and a psi-dealbreaker but, could it not also be at least possible that science cannot explain everything and that consciousness and belief open doors to many other phenomena that are just as 'real' as the technologies produced by science? Sheldrake's experiments into 'telephone telepathy', were mentioned earlier. The sceptics point to what they believe are weaknesses in the scientific method but this eminent biologist has been designing and conducting experiments all his life and the results are pretty spectacular[9] [10]. Sheldrake believes that telepathy has evolved in many species in the same way as other biological abilities. That is, through natural selection. Like many other investigators he comes to the conclusion that telepathy works best when the emotional bonds between people are strong – as with mothers and their children, close spouses, twins and triplets, and close friends. Freeman Dyson, Sigmund Freud, Brian Josephson, J B Rhine, Louisa Rhine, Alan Turing, and Carl Jung all agreed that:

1. telepathy is possible under certain circumstances, and,
2. that the emotional state of the recipient or the level of trauma in the environment seem to be key factors.

The greatest variable that scientists almost never take into account when experimenting is the emotional state of the subjects.

Emotion is King

We use the word all the time. 'You're being too emotional', 'He let his emotions get the better of him', 'It's been an emotional time.' But what exactly is it? Broadly speaking it is possible to list a huge range of emotions. One dictionary definition reads:

> *A mental state that arises spontaneously rather than through conscious effort and is often accompanied by physiological changes; a feeling.*

Wikipedia keeps its 'Silliest Definitions' crown unsullied with the following:

Emotions are mental states brought on by neurophysiological changes, variously associated with thoughts, feelings, behavioral responses, and a degree of pleasure or displeasure. There is currently no scientific consensus on a definition.

Discounting the fact that this is partially a circular definition – emotions are states brought about by feelings (like pleasure/displeasure?) which are emotions, how does that particular author know that emotions are 'brought on by neurophysiological changes'? The questions to ask anyone who tries that one on you are: 'What is it that brings about the physiological changes in the first place?' – according to this definition feelings /emotions bring about physiological changes which then create emotions. The final sentence is disarmingly honest, though. Put another way, it says, scientists haven't a clue what emotion is.

What is very certain is that emotion, stress, and trauma seem to be important in most psi-phenomena. The phenomena we group under the term 'ghosts'–are often associated with unnatural and violent death, mediums seem to be able to communicate with the dead more easily if the dead person has had an unjust or traumatic demise, reincarnation appears to be more readily recognised when there has been a violent death, precognition may operate particularly well when a violent event is about to occur, the highly-charged emotional state of some teenagers seems to be a cause of 'poltergeist' activity, telepathy might work best when the circumstances are emotionally-charged, and so on.

Most scientists believe firmly that the mind is a function of the brain and cannot exist without it, even though a good number of scientists are religious and therefore believe that the essence of a person can outlive the physical body. The scientific understanding seems to be that all functions of the brain are revealed on brain scans and the location of movement, thoughts, and even decisions can be physically pinpointed and given distinct locations in the head. But how does science explain the power of belief to effect cures and pain control, the ability of the mind to see the future, the repeatedly proven ability of two minds to connect at critical times? There is absolutely no doubt that such things are possible – there are countless examples – yet the bulk of our scientists continues to insist that it is all either faked or misunderstood.

Earlier we looked at the example of traumatic events leading people to 'feel' the future and at the ability of genuine mediums to pass on messages from the dead (e.g. the airmen who died in the R-101 disaster). This may also be an important factor in assessing the credibility of the results from ESP experiments. The critics call this *'post-hoc rationalisation of experimental ESP failings'*. Their argument is that, because ESP experiments show only relatively small effects, supporters try to rationalise them after the event. But we cannot throw out psi-experimental results simply because they show weak effects. There are strong reasons to doubt that such experiments could show anything other than weak results. And we certainly cannot discount and discredit paranormal research simply because it does not conform to our current, hidebound scientific model.

Almost all the circumstantial evidence we have on paranormal phenomena points to high emotional states as being a powerful factor. Events such as air crashes, 9/11, and the sinking of the Titanic – seem to create massive psychic waves but these examples should not blind us to the probability that similar waves may be present everywhere, all the time, and that ordinary people, leading quiet, everyday lives in an essentially unemotional environment might be able to experience psi-events that are just as real.

History also tells us that shamans and witch-doctors often worked themselves into high emotional states including frenzies or trances prior to attempting any paranormal feats. Usually, the sceptics claim that this is mere showmanship – playing to the gallery. I do not need to say that this is probably total nonsense and that the shamans and witches may have understood the true nature of psi-powers better than we do today. The corollary is that low emotional states – i.e. where we deliberately relax the subjects and provide them with unimportant material to transmit – could well produce lacklustre results in psi experiments. If a person who has been selected as a 'transmitter' in an experiment is shown cards of anodyne symbols, or pictures of sheep and TVs and motor cars, if they are also given a nice warm room and a relaxing chair and then bathed in a gentle red light; is it any wonder that whatever signal they might be able to send is weak? When will someone try an experiment where the receiver and transmitter are place in very uncomfortable conditions, under severe stress. For example, in which the transmitter is asked to send pictures of what they are told might be the cause imminent deaths?

The mind has incredible powers which lie well outside the purely biological boundaries of the brain but it certainly appears as though – at least in the present state of human consciousness – ESP may depend primarily on working the person up into a highly emotional, stressed state or perhaps attempting to anticipate future supercharged events. The approach followed by Dr Daryl Bem that we discussed earlier, illustrated the issues very effectively. Mundane photos were far less effective at stimulating psi-effects than emotionally charged semi-pornographic ones.

The experimental conundrum facing parapsychologists and other scientists is not simply about the clash between the scientific method and empiricism, not solely about the structure of samples and the randomisation of stimuli, but is one that strikes at the very foundations of the experiments themselves – at the need to use the right subjects in the right ways. Should we now alter our approach to use new techniques that put them under high stress to attempt to emulate the most powerful of the apparently potent psychic forces? Some of the most convincing of para-psychological experiments ask subjects to say what a result will be *before* a computer even decides what picture to show. They are testing the ability to see into the future. Might an experiment be designed that asks a range of subjects to 'explore' the future and predict traumatic events?

Psi powers are most definitely real in the sense that humans display and use them. That simple fact makes it impossible for us to avoid the vital issue of where psi powers reside. We have blithely discussed the universe and consciousness – making strong connections between the two concepts. The crucial issue though is: What is the universe and does it even exist in a material sense?

The Universe That Should Not Be

If the reader is anything at all like the author, they will not have questioned anything much about the way the universe is presented to us. It is what it is, and we are happy to accept that it is unimaginably huge, very old, and is expanding in some way that only the scientists can even try to understand. Yet the reality, one that scientists are only now beginning to come to terms with, is that it is a miracle that it exists at all in a way that supports life.

One of the most amazing things about the universe is how incredibly finely balanced it is for both matter and life. We have all imbibed the Big Bang theory and, even if we don't really understand it, we have a vague idea that everything started with an unbelievably miniscule point of somethingness located somewhere in an ocean of nothingness. Then some sort of explosion happened which resulted in all the matter we now see around us – planets, moons, star systems, galaxies, and the universe. We understand explosions, so the story makes sense - sort of. If we ignore the question: 'where did all this matter come from in all that nothingness?', an explosion followed by the birth of suns and star systems and galaxies is well within our (probably misdirected) intellectual grasp. Where we part company with this relatively comfortable picture is when we are told – and this is a recent idea – that the big bang was nothing like an explosion. It actually occurred everywhere at once – which seems to contradict the current notion of it being ever-expanding and that the oldest stars are at the edges. Why should that be if everything came into existence at one moment? Nowadays it is accepted that the expansion of the universe will go on forever. There will be no slowing down as would happen in a normal explosion. That bit does not make sense and when a few people start talking about how the universe really should never have happened in the first place we switch off and go back to a good crime novel.

The universe, it turns out, is actually an extremely finely tuned phenomenon which is *precisely* balanced to permit complex interactions and life. The level of impossibility of our universe is stunning – truly, mind-blowingly unbelievable. The current universe is not a 'one in a thousand outcome, nor even a 'one in a million' chance. The chances of a universe forming with *precisely* the right conditions for galaxies to form (and remain) and life to exist are trillions and trillions and trillions to one. A trillion is 10^{12} (a one with twelve zeros behind it) but the odds *against* the universe emerging as it has are about 10^{119} - one chance in one with one hundred and nineteen zeros behind it!

Those odds are as close to impossible as you'd care to get. To all extents and purposes the universe we live in is an impossibility.

I won't go into them in any detail here but the tiniest difference in what are called 'universal constants' (which include the Lambda Constant, the Fine Structure Constant and even the speed of light) would be enough for the universe never to have existed or to have collapsed very quickly after the Big Bang[11]. Scientists and philosophers are locked in battle over the implications of these freakish findings. And they do seem extraordinary – almost paranormal. In order for life to exist, the Big Bang which created the universe had to fall out to an incredibly accurate balance and all the constants had to be in harmony with each other. Everything had to be as close to perfect as statistics would allow.

Odds of being struck by lightning in the US are about one in 10^4

Odds of the universe being formed as we see it: one in 10^{119}

Those of you with a religious bent will immediately say that you knew this all along. When your deity or deities made the universe he, she, it, or they would obviously have got it absolutely right. The accuracy of the constants, you would say, *proves* divine intervention. In truth this is an entirely valid conclusion. The balance of the universe is so breathtakingly precise that the odds of it occurring by chance are impossibly small. A controlling deity, or a bunch of them, could indeed have made it happen. But we are ignoring the fact that the universe itself could be the conscious force behind everything. The universe is perfect because it made itself perfect.

These are certainly the days to be a physicist – preferably a very open-minded one with metaphysical leanings. Whole mountains of questions are becoming apparent with every passing year but a large proportion of them also involve rubbing shoulders with the paranormal. Witches and shamans have always believed in the 'Force', mediums have always believed in 'the other side', telepaths have always wondered through what medium people can communicate over long distances without electronic means. On one side the hosts of the paranormal who have always known that it is real, on the other the increasingly-uncertain scientists, left high and dry on the shores of the paranormal by weirder and weirder discoveries.

CHAPTER 14
TIME &
CONSCIOUSNESS

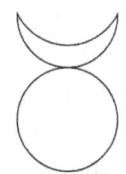

> *If you can look into the seeds of time*
> *And say which grains will grow and which will not.*
>
> — WILLIAM SHAKESPEARE, MACBETH

The Fourth Musketeer

There is also a quite humongous elephant in the room. It's called Time and we now need to speak of that tortured subject. As things stand, we regard time as a fourth dimension – height, width, depth, and time – a four-dimensional universe in which time is the magic ingredient. Time is the fairy-dust that allows us to live. Without time we would be frozen and lifeless, trapped motionless and unchanging in 3D space forever. More to the point this is what might happen if time stopped for any reason. If time had never existed then neither would we. It is time that allows you to press the channel button on your smart TV, time that enables you to take the next step in your morning jog, time that makes it possible for you to revel in that smile on the face of one of your loved ones. The other three dimensions permit you to adopt form but without time that form cannot live.

There may also be other dimensions in addition to the four we believe exist. The late Dr D Scott Rogo argued that the sheer complexity of the paranormal subject points persuasively to there being several interconnected realities. The scientists who study M-Theory have identified up to eleven dimensions but whether and how they affect four-dimensional beings and whether time is actually a dimension at all, are yet to be seen. Time may not be an arrow pointing in one direction, it might be a scrunched-up ball in which all time exists at the same point. This would not only mean that it would be theoretically possible to cross between strands of the compressed ball of time to visit the past or the future but – much more importantly – that the future already exists and that we may live in a deterministic universe in which everything is pre-ordained.

Time is actually the odd-man out in this materialist universe but it has been under our noses all this ... well ... time. Time is the fourth – paranormal - musketeer. The other three are totally normal, material, physical and touchable. The fourth musketeer is insubstantial and, most importantly, does not fit well with our current theories of how the universe works. It's a bit of a rogue. That old Newtonian metronome which ticked steadily away at the back of everything was relegated by Albert Einstein. It was replaced by some weird things based on relativity (everything is relative). Einstein's calculations demand that 'time' is perceived different depending on where you watch an event. He also says that the faster you travel, the slower time flies (this has been tested and verified by placing highly accurate atomic clocks on fast jet aircraft), and that it moves more slowly the higher the gravity field in which you try to measure it. For example time will travel at normal speed on Earth, while close to the event horizon of a black hole it will move like a glacier – well, actually much, much slower. Everything we know about time – which is not very much – tells us that it can easily fit into all sorts of strange theoretical frameworks. The baffling thing is that it does, however, appear to be linked to something called entropy. The famous Second Law of

Thermodynamics states that entropy constantly and irreversibly grows in any closed system. Entropy is a measure of disorder in any system so, if the universe is a closed system, it is gradually becoming more and more disordered and will eventually collapse back into its component parts. In order for this to happen it is clearly a requirement that time continues to pass in a straight line from present to future. Other calculations conclude that the universe will continue to expand forever – that is into infinity – so, how does that tie into entropy?

Even these basics are mind-blowing, but modern science is encountering even stranger possibilities. Which bits are going to turn out to be 'true' we have no idea, but what we do know is that science has partially caught up with what the witches and the shamans have been saying for thousands of years and what those who have been studying psi powers have suspected for many decades. Few laypeople understand the arcane math behind M-Theory but essentially the formulae say that, at the most fundamental level, the universe is made up of tiny, vibrating strings of energy. It also introduces the very strong likelihood that our 'reality' is part of up to perhaps eleven separate but linked dimensions.

Those theories resonate with parallel theories that time is actually a series of points and that time may simply be an illusion. In the beautiful land of quantum physics, a bunch of incredibly intelligent people have developed a possibility known as 'quantum loop gravity'[1]. In a similar way to the strings of M-Theory, quantum loop gravity proposes that a quantum loop is the smallest unit of space/matter and the smallest unit of time. Under this view of the world, time becomes a set of points which are perceived by us as passing in sequence.

Theory after theory about time but very little ... no, nothing at all ... in the way of a convincing consensus even among scientists. Some scientists and philosophers now agree that time is just an illusion – an artifact of consciousness. This approach carries a number of profound connotations not the least of which is that everything that has ever happened and everything that has yet to occur, is here and now and all around us. The scientists who are prepared to get into the mudbath of consciousness and time play with some interesting concepts. The Homewood Professor of Natural Philosophy at Johns Hopkins University is a chap called Sean Carroll. In one of his blogs he discussed the problem of whether time is fundamental or emergent – that is, does it derive directly from the basic laws of the universe or is it dependent on another phenomenon or process? His views in an interview with the great Lawrence Kuhn were that quantum time and Einsteinian time are basically just different manifestations of the same thing and that the 'arrow of time' is perhaps the most persuasive theory of how it all works[2]. But not everyone agrees.

Whether based on strings or on something else, a small but growing number of scientists now accept that consciousness is probably much more fundamental than matter and that it pervades and governs the entire universe. Science, in other words, is tantalisingly close to accepting that the universe is conscious, that it depends on the vibrations of tiny strings or loops of energy, and that whatever 'force' exists may connect a number of different dimensions within and possibly outside what we call our universe.

When, in the early Star Wars films, Obi-Wan Kenobi encouraged Luke Skywalker to accept and utilise the Force, the effect was pretty much the same as we might envisage any modern human accepting and using the psi-powers which may be part and parcel of universal consciousness. We must not lose sight of the fact that a conscious universe would have to control everything – four and possibly eleven dimensions, the quantum realm, dark energy, gravity and – of course – time.

The modern western world is all about 'control', a philosophy that has now infected the whole planet bar a few small, isolated communities and some very special belief systems. Western materialism rests on the scientific method which in turn relies on the concept of reductionism (the notion that studying parts of a whole will enable one to understand the whole). Dr Steve Taylor, who teaches psychology at Leeds Beckett University in England, is someone who believes that scientists can be extremely slow to adjust and adapt to new ideas and new realities. He blames the scientific method and its materialist, reductionist approach. Our belief that the whole universe can be explained in terms of rigid, provable rules about the ways in which atoms and other particles behave, is, Taylor argues, at the base of the problem. Scientists use the reductionist method to experiment on parts of the whole and gradually build up a picture of how they believe the whole works. The belief that the whole is merely the sum of its parts has been a successful materialist approach for the past few hundred years, but Taylor thinks that its value is diminishing. And so do I. What makes up a human is just a few chemicals and minerals plus some water – but humans are far more than the sum of those parts. The reductionist worldview has been questioned by psychics and parapsychologists for a century or more, but few took any notice of them. Today, however, the discoveries of quantum physics and the increasing body of scientific research into psychic abilities demand that we pay fresh attention to the possibility that psi powers may be real[3] and that what we innocently call 'reality' – the material world including its links to time – may actually turn out to be insubstantial and subsidiary.

Taylor argues that the materialist mind-set causes us to see only physical links between things. This leads us to believe that we are conscious only because the neurons of our brains are connected by electrical activity – in the same way as a radio can only function when its innards are enlivened by flowing electricity. Intangible things like happiness, fear, and even insanity are, to materialists, simply different aspects of brain activity. Electricity causes chemistry (or vice versa) to work in different ways and cause different bits of the brain to be more enlivened than others. The materialist framework also leads us to see humans as 'genetic machines' with the physical constituents of our cells – including strands of DNA – being responsible for everything we are. Dr Rupert Sheldrake, as we have seen, has a few things to say about that particular belief.

All of this may, or may not, be the case, but Taylor is definitely right that our worldview is hamstrung by the belief that *everything* has a physical or materialist cause. The automatic corollary is that psi concepts like telepathy and precognition cannot possibly exist because there is no explanation which fits within our materialist framework. Telepathy is impossible because there is no scientifically understood means by which two brains can communicate without physical (which includes electromagnetic) means. Precognition is impossible for the same reasons but also because it overturns our traditional understanding of time. Most physicists are like Sean Carroll – they are honest enough to admit that they do not understand time. In their formulae, time can run in either direction and the numbers can even cope with time being all in one place. So, humanity currently has a number of existential problems:

1. What is gravity?
2. What is time?
3. What is dark energy?
4. How does the quantum realm link up to the material one?
5. What is consciousness?

They might all be answered by the scientific method but we've shown repeatedly throughout this book that that is highly unlikely. Science is struggling to meet challenges that it never foresaw – challenges from proofs that have been shown to be impossible, challenges from studies which show that the statistical likelihood of psi-powers makes them a virtual certainty (and one which lies well outside any scientific method you might dream up), and challenges from a universe which gets stranger every day. The majority of scientists cling to the idea that all will eventually be answered through their method but, more and more, they seem to be swimming against the stream. They are absolutely correct in their assertions that there is no scientific proof for much of what we've been discussing in the preceding chapters, but the $64,000 Question is: Are there genuine phenomena that the scientific method simply cannot handle?

Applying scientific logic means that we must dismiss the forebodings of Lady Duff Gordon about her trip on the Titanic, the vision of a future airfield witnessed by Air Marshall Victor Goddard, the dreams of an air-crash that so afflicted David Booth of Cincinnati, and the way Victor Amole predicted his winning lottery numbers – among hundreds of other solid examples. They cannot have happened because, if they did, we would have to accept not only that psi-phenomena exist but the possibility of a deterministic universe, the incredible possibility that everything has already happened, or that somehow a non-deterministic event can communicate itself back through time to a human mind – that the act of seeing into the future can actually change it. We appear to be dealing with a reality in which a terrible event can be 'felt' in the past by people who can then avoid it and save their own lives. Lady Duff Gordon 'knew' that there would be an accident of some sort to the Titanic but she was able to ensure that she, her husband, and her secretary did not die in it. A few people are known to have had warnings but did not react to them and lost their lives. Were those deaths therefore inevitable – already determined by the future and, if so, why were the warnings necessary? And if someone dreams of a man crashing onto a shingle beach and dying in the process, what does it mean if the person does not die?

So, there are limits to the effectiveness, and even the applicability, of the scientific method. Reductionism may not be the only tool we should be using and we may need to develop a new metaphysical science – a single, overarching combination of empirical science and metaphysics which will enable us to explore the material universe simultaneously with its paranormal elements.

Filters & Flickers

Throughout this book consciousness has been mentioned in connection with a wide variety of paranormal phenomena. It is an extremely strange concept – one of those that we instinctively think we understand but which, as soon as we actually focus on it, becomes a very complex puzzle.

At the most fundamental level we are human because we are

conscious. That is, we are aware of our surroundings, we have a sense of self and of others, and we can amend our environment in many ways all of which in theory are planned and organised. We are sentient in the sense that we think deeply about the meaning of it all and construct theories and hypotheses about what appears to be the reality around us.

There are quite a few people – some of them eminent scientists – who also believe that we live in a *false* reality; one that has been constructed by ourselves to protect us from the real universe. They argue that our real world is a fake, no more than a comfortable illusion that shields us from possibly unpalatable truths, or that enables us to live out a role in a sort of vast computer simulation. It's a fascinating theory. Could the world actually be a consensus simulation with things existing and happening purely because we, as humans, will it to be so? Whether that is true or not, consciousness is what makes us different. Being alive is not enough. A bacterium is alive but as far as we know it is not conscious in the way we have defined it above. So, life, as such, is not the most important consideration – consciousness is what matters. Are animals conscious? Many of them certainly have a sense of self – an identity – but is that sufficient to say they are conscious? Scholars entertain a wide range of theories as to what consciousness might be, ranging from it being limited only to humans, to a theory that everything from the tiniest pebble to the universe itself is conscious.

We have two traditional ways of imagining where consciousness goes when we die. Either everything disappears with death, the whole shebang ends and goes black like a light being switched off, or we somehow have our consciousness reintegrated with the mass of wider consciousness (or the various equivalent beliefs of religions). An iota of consciousness that represents a person is inserted into a human being and it remains with the physical body until that body dies, after which the consciousness represented by that person returns in some way to reintegrate with the whole.

Those who believe in paranormal activities and powers believe fundamentally that the human mind has the power to do much,

much more than we usually use it for – more accurately, than we *think* we use it for. They believe among other things that our minds can connect with each other (even after death), that minds can move objects and change material things in other ways, that our minds/consciousness can see into the future and across great distances. They believe that the ocean of consciousness surrounds us all and permits conscious beings to do things that are thought to be totally impossible in material terms. Some theorists posit that humanity's links with this vast ocean are shut down or masked in most individuals, perhaps as a deliberate decision, or possibly a subconscious wish. The theory is that some people are either genetically or socially attuned to this wider consciousness and that this permits them to excel in specific areas of the paranormal. Some of us are either incapable of linking up or are deliberately preventing ourselves from doing so.

One of the best scientific books on consciousness in recent years is that by Drs Baruss and Mossbridge called 'Transcendent Mind'. It is a logical and detailed review of all the arguments around how consciousness works[4]. Among many other things they discuss what are known as filter models of consciousness and flicker filters. It all comes down to how you see the role of the human brain: Is it totally responsible for consciousness – i.e. consciousness disappears when the physical brain dies – or is the brain merely somewhere that consciousness resides while you are alive and mentally competent? The production theory argues that the physical brain *produces* consciousness and, by implication, that there is no consciousness without the brain. The filter theory, on the other hand, contends that the brain is a receiver which filters and processes whatever information is necessary to individual human life and survival. It's a theory that has been around for at least a century and a half, but it has been debated more fiercely in recent years partly due to the new evidence on topics like near-death and out-of-body experiences and the emerging mysteries of dark energy and quantum physics. This evidence – as we have seen – is not strictly scientific because there are major problems with replication and falsifiability – but the statistical evidence together with a mass of circumstantial data are extremely convincing and they seem to support the filter approach.

The filter theory proposes that the brain acts as a receiver of consciousness and that, just as the brain filters inputs from our material environment, it also filters what we perceive as a wider consciousness. Think for a moment about how you can almost always filter out background noise to listen to a particular a voice in a crowded room, how some people are able to filter out and listen to a particular instrument at a concert, how your mind filters a particular smell so that you are no longer aware of it, or how you sometimes don't notice a minor pain or injury until you actually focus on it. People often say that they have not noticed they've been cut until you point out the blood on their hand. This is the mind filtering physical events. Doctors and psychologists have been aware of the process for a long time. The Filter Theory of consciousness says that your mind also filters, in fact is *always* filtering, whatever is flowing through you from the wider field of consciousness. It is often explained using the TV analogy in which the television can filter out other stations and just show you a single channel even though hundreds of others are there in the ether and are capable of being shown if selected.

The argument is that we all have this 'filtering' ability but that not many of us can consciously control it. Most of us may deliberately block it. Some people can use their minds to filter out noise and listen to future events, or to dead people, or to living people, or to harness the 'force' to do things such as moving objects without touching them[5]. Most of us may occasionally perceive things (i.e. the filter may open a temporary window in a certain way for a moment) but we are usually unaware of how we did it and often ignore whatever it is we see or feel. In some cases, the argument goes, the emotional strength of an event can be strong enough to break through an individual's mental blocks. There are forceful arguments that children go through a stage of learning to block the things they may perceive. Perhaps parents tell them that what they think they are seeing is nonsense – much like some parents whose children tell them that they are reincarnated from an earlier person.

Without realising it, do we teach our children to filter?

A progression from the basic Filter Theory is the Flicker Theory which adds the vital ingredient of time. A number of physicists see time as a series of discrete points – what some call 'now moments'. Each moment in time, each 'now', no matter how continuous it seems to us, is actually a separate and distinct point in time. We live through billions of them every day. Again, it is a bit like a TV picture or a film. TV programmes and films are transmitted to our eyes via a very fast presentation of what are effectively static images. Film and video cameras effectively capture a very rapid burst of still pictures – discrete points in time. Even digital movie films are a set of still images captured at between fifty and eighty frames per second. Look at a single frame of a film and you have a frozen picture – there is no action, no time. But when the single images are presented fast enough, our brains string them together to perceive them as a moving picture. The process is so effective that we fully accept it as normal, lifelike movement. A film, therefore, is just a series of discrete 'points in time' presented fast enough for our eyes not to notice and for our brains to perceive it as a 'real' set of events. The 'flicker theory' is based on the premise that time itself consists of individual and discrete points which we perceive as a flow. It goes further, however, in arguing that this structure of time permits us to see chunks of time that are not 'now'. A bit like being able to rewind the film and see a totally different set of points in the time-stream[6].

The British physicist Julian Barbour believes that time is not real. He argues that change is real – i.e. that we nod our heads – but he regards time as just the way we perceive that nodding motion. He points out that the theories of time that make up our scientific understanding of the universe do not demand that time is an arrow or a river flowing only in a single direction. All the math works just as well with time going in any direction. Barbour says that the 'now moments' are held together not by time but by consciousness. The way we perceive time and events therefore would, under this theory, be dependent on a shared perception or a shared way of accessing consciousness.

Slowly but surely, we appear to be developing an understanding of consciousness which includes as much pure science as possible but which, at a basic level, has to depend upon the paranormal – the idea of a consciousness which transcends the material world and which actually governs it by permitting us to perceive it in certain ways. Thousands of pieces of anecdotal testimony can be brought forward to support this idea. Almost all of it is dismissed as nonsense by many scientists but when you look at the list of things that scientists have, at one time or another dismissed as nonsense, I think we can safely take what they say with a large pinch of salt.

The Earth from Apollo 17. This is the famous 'blue marble' photo and it powerfully suggests Lovelock's Gaia – a living, conscious organism. Wikimedia Commons; NASA/Apollo 17 crew; taken by either Harrison Schmitt or Ron Evans See also https://www.nasa.gov/multimedia/imagegallery/image_feature_329.html; Public Domain, https://commons.wikimedia.org/w/index.php?curid=43894484

The brilliant biologist James Lovelock originated the Gaia principle many years ago. He argued that the Earth is a self-regulating mechanism. We all understand self-regulating mechanisms. Steam engines regulated themselves back in the early nineteenth century and many modern machines do the same. But what Lovelock meant was that the Earth is conscious of its state and that it takes actions to solve problems. Naturally, his theory was regarded as hokum by mainstream scientists but it is now taken much more seriously. One of its possible implications is that the Earth may seek to purge itself of harmful organisms and any activities which seriously unbalance the whole. Some believe that the Earth might, therefore, through a range of different actions, purge itself of humans.

Philosophers and scientists are coming to the belief that the universe is a phenomenon of which matter is not the core. We humans are matter and we believe we live in a material world, but scientists know that matter is just five percent of the universe and that the rest is made up of an unknown force called dark energy. They are becoming convinced that matter is actually a *result* of consciousness and not, as we have believed for centuries, that consciousness is an outcome of a material human brain which dies with the body.

What all this boils down to is that science is now struggling to explain what is going on. Isaac Newton began a scientific revolution which has resulted is us believing whole-heartedly in the 'mechanical universe'. Our utter conviction that the mechanical universe is what everything is all about was not even shaken (initially, anyway) by the relativistic revolution begun by Einstein. But we now know for sure that we do not know a great deal. Even the big bang theory has become more and more mysterious as our physicists have unearthed stranger and stranger questions.

The key to the huge amount of the universe that we have not even begun to understand is going to be something that will change the world so profoundly that humans will never be the same again. It could mean that future humans will look back on the period from the seventeenth to the twenty-first centuries in much the same way we see the Dark Ages – as centuries of ignorance and misinterpretation.

Science had to shift its paradigms several times during the twentieth century. What will it look like in the year 2124? It gets even weirder when you understand that the basis of the universe could lie in harmonies and vibrations rather than in particles. M-Theory is getting closer to revealing some fundamental truths around vibrations and harmonies all around us, linked to 'strings'. The theory is that our love affair with particles is a simplistic attempt to visualise the universe in terms with which we are familiar – sub-atomic particles circling the nucleus like miniscule planets. M-Theory throws much of this into the trash-bin. The universe, say its adherents, is made up of vibrating strings of energy.

One might wonder whether the human love of music is nothing more than an instinctive link with these vibrations and harmonies. Music can take our minds to another level. Is it totally impossible that it provides a first-level entrance to the paranormal? And the opposite question is whether our love affair with the material universe, our total absorption in science and technology, may have diminished our psi abilities and made us less sensitive to the conscious universe. An interesting side issue is the way in which modern dance music emphasises a repetitive and continuous trance-like beat and rhythm very similar to the drums and rhythms of ancient times – those which helped shamans to achieve ecstatic trances and enter into paranormal realms. Why do humans instinctively love that sort of music?

From my reading of the literature, and as a person who would have discounted even the possibility of such things a few decades ago, the phenomena that constitute Out of Body Experiences, Near Death Experiences, and End of Life Experiences are credible to a high order of magnitude. Detailed empirical studies over at least a century have shown the very high probability that the phenomena are real and are often verifiable. As time goes by, we become more and more certain that science – in its reductionist and materialist silo – is ignoring a major truth about the universe and humanity: that consciousness is what really matters and is where everything resides. We could be talking about another dimension, or even a reality which lies beneath even the M-Theory ideas about eleven dimensions. The most important thing is that serious scientists now suspect that consciousness is a far more important consideration and some are even prepared to take on board the possibility that the material universe is secondary to the immaterial one. This idea – that consciousness is the core of the universe and that matter and energy are mere adjuncts – is called 'biocentrism'. One of its leading proponents today is an American medical doctor called Robert Lanza[7]. He is a leading scientist in the field of stem cells and their uses in regenerating organs. We are taught that the universe was created in the Big Bang, that it is a material thing, and that life is something that is so rare that it may even be limited to just the tiny, insignificant planet that we call Earth. This is probably nonsense even in a purely materialist sense, but Lanza's latest book asks ...

> *What if life isn't just a part of the universe... what if it determines the very structure of the universe itself?*[8]

In other words what if consciousness makes the universe tick rather than the material universe making it possible for consciousness to exist? Which came first – the material universe which eventually produced some conscious lifeforms on a single planet, or a conscious universe which willed the rest of everything into existence? In his book Lanza points to some of the more inconvenient facts that cannot be explained by science – such as why some of the most fundamental forces of the universe – the universal constants that we visited briefly in an earlier section – just happen to be set at levels that are ideal for life to exist.

> *On an everyday level, hundreds of physical constants such as the strength of gravity and the electromagnetic force called 'alpha' that governs the electrical bonds in every atom are identical throughout the universe and 'set in stone' at precisely the values that allow life to exist. This could merely be an astounding coincidence. But the simplest explanation is that the laws and conditions of the universe allow for the observer because the observer generates them. Duh!*

Lanza is not alone in believing that consciousness is at the heart of everything. It's a simple yet revolutionary viewpoint that requires us to reconsider everything that we once thought of as impossible – such as telepathy, magic, ghosts, telekinesis, communication with the dead, weird cryptids from other dimensions, and reincarnation. If humans are part of a conscious universe there is no reason why any of those phenomena are impossible. There is also a further consideration that I have not seen discussed anywhere else. If consciousness creates and drives the universe, it must also create and drive human destiny. The massive question waiting in the wings, therefore, is: *Can we actually change our destiny by willing a different future into existence?*

There has been a distinct and apparently accelerating trend over the past century for humans to be pessimistic about their future. Today we are bombarded with negative, pessimistic vibes, with visions of a violent, apocalyptic future, with images of a decaying world, decadent society, and a hard-pressed humanity descending slowly into chaos and primitive violence. *But, if the consciousness theory is correct, we could change all that tomorrow by en-masse simply willing and envisioning a better world.*

If we *believe* that the world will descend into anarchy and violence, if we dream of Armageddon and dystopian futures, are we as a species actually *causing* them to come about? If, on the other hand, humanity were to start to imagine and wish for a better world, if our books and films were to somehow become optimistic and utopian, could that make a healthier, more peaceful world happen? Witches would answer in the affirmative because the very concept of willpower – the ability to change things on the basis of one's will – is a paranormal ability that they regard as perfectly normal. I guess the question must be: Is humanity willing to take the risk that I am wrong?

∼

But how can we prove that there is such a thing as consciousness? The very concept means it can never be proved by the scientific method, which means that people either have to discard it as nonsense or to simply accept it – to believe in it. But our whole modern western society is based on 'seeing is believing'. Show me the proof and I will believe. If you cannot show me a miracle I cannot be expected to believe in a deity.

It's a 'Catch 22' situation. People will never believe without proof and no proof can be put forward without people believing. Religions have this problem too. Adherents simply believe, and that's that. The deal is that you either have faith and believe or you do not. If you fall into the latter camp there's no place for you in that particular religion. Similarly, belief in the paranormal, in psi-powers, and perhaps even in UFOs/UAP and aliens is self-fulfilling. If people believe, they exist.

But aren't humans entitled to expect that there should be a reliable return on their paranormal belief-investment? For example, if we say that a person's mind can influence the course of an illness or even cure them of a disease, shouldn't we be able to teach them how to achieve this and then show evidence on a consistent basis that the approach works? If there is no proof – only belief – the human race is being given a very difficult choice. Science can show that its predictions hold fast. It can prove a theorem and demonstrate that it applies in every relevant situation and produces exactly the same result. Science can do this whether you believe in it or not. Paranorm 2.0 cannot do this, but is that issue alone sufficient reason to discount it?

CHAPTER 15
THE BOTTOM LINE

> *In other words, there are (at least) two levels of reality: One consists of the rules and regularities of the physical world, which science can access and measure. But the other level, the ultimate source of those rules and regulations, science can never even access, much less come to know.*
>
> — DR ROBERT LAWRENCE KUHN; 2016

The Secret Bookshelves

The shelves of books in the paranormal section of any good bookshop can display volumes on witchcraft, wizardry, shamanism, telepathy, fortune telling, scrying, natural healing, telekinesis, alchemy, pagan religions, remote viewing, satanism, UFOs, aliens, and much else. They never carry volumes about the established religions, but they should. After all, what is the difference between a Christian who believes that there is a single deity whose angels and saints control and influence everything on the planet (except the followers of Satan presumably), and the adherents of Australian aboriginal beliefs who live in a world in which an overarching spirit controls everything through a number of gods and spirits, or the pantheists who believe that whatever controls the universe and everything in it is all around us all the time, or those who believe that there is a universal consciousness at the base of everything?

Perhaps more importantly, booksellers have, for many decades, been throwing anything non-standard onto the shelves in that unmentionable section and trying desperately to forget them. If anyone should be unwise enough to ask for books on witchcraft or telepathy or UAP they will receive a knowing raising of the eyebrows, a quick check, up and down to make sure that the enquirer is not wearing a foil hat or an all-encompassing raincoat before advising the customer that they might, or might not, find what they are looking for on the shelves on the extreme right at the farthest side from the lifts on the top floor. The fragmentation of the subject of the paranormal has been exacerbated by authors and publishers – most of whom seem to see the topic as a set of very distinct subjects none of which have anything at all to do with the others.

But the paranormal is a single subject. It may be approached in myriad ways and from many different standpoints, but it is actually a single study of everything that lies beyond what we call 'normal'. Only by treating the topic in this way will we be able to see the connections and similarities and be able to move the whole topic forward.

One Paranormal to Rule them All

In this brief examination of Paranorm 1.0 and 2.0 they have been distinguished in a very simple but extremely important way. The multitude of phenomena of Paranorm 1.0 are always examined and discussed as distinct subjects. Witches, mediums, ghosts, clairvoyance, telekinesis, and all the rest are each investigated by specialised sets of scholars and enthusiasts in slightly different ways. The results are retained in segmented silos which are almost never allowed to overlap. This paradigm is, to me, just a little crazy.

In this book I've discussed a very wide range of paranormal phenomena, including:

- Witchcraft
- Mind-over-matter
- Telekinesis
- Telepathy
- OBE/NDE/ELE
- Reincarnation
- Precognition
- Retrocognition
- Ghosts
- Consciousness

The common denominator of every single one is the human mind – our consciousness, and it seems to me to be illogical and self-defeating to ignore that critical link. There are, of course, aspects of some of these phenomena that could be independent of the human mind. Ghosts, UFOs, and cryptids *might* be things that would appear even when humans are not around to witness them, but there is strong reason to suspect that human psi abilities and predispositions are at the core of those manifestations, too.

Consciousness is what we are and what the universe is. Precisely how it all works has yet to be explained but there are many extremely competent scientists and philosophers who believe it exists and there are still enough unknowns in the universe for us to suspect that it may have a lot to do with dark energy and the quantum domain. We simply do not yet have the data or, indeed, the philosophical basis to make definitive statements about it all.

I am confident however that, if we can accept the oneness of the paranormal and begin exploring it as a single subject, we may then be able to make progress on how exactly humans, currently steeped in the mechanical paradigm and divided by antagonistic religions, can be persuaded that other realities are possible. The social and psychological leaps that will be necessary are immense. How else can humanity be dragged kicking and screaming from its almost total reliance on proof by scientific replicability and falsification to a profound acceptance of the power of consciousness. It requires mass acceptance of something closely akin to religious faith. But where religions demand that adherents accept a very specific story about how we were created, who it is that is ultimately in charge, and how we must lead our lives to achieve entrance to the good places after we die, the idea of a wider consciousness requires only that we attempt to get closer to it and to personally use whatever powers of which we are capable. It is not inconsistent with religions, just more all-encompassing.

The only certain thing in our lives is consciousness. We do not know what it is and we have only the flimsiest of ideas as to how it works and how it relates to the universe but the bottom line is that consciousness is all. As a species we are able to send people to the Moon, build super-skyscrapers, move people around in high-speed trains and comfortable aircraft, and kill each other in ever-scarier ways, but our pride in building things and inventing new technologies is almost certainly blinding us to what might be the genuinely important things – i.e. the universe, us, and our consciousness. Those who wish to study consciousness and the paranormal must, from now on, step up to Paranorm 2.0.

NOTES

1. Rationality Fails

1. Colm Kelleher; The Hunt for the Skinwalker.
2. https://en.wikipedia.org/wiki/Ghost - cite_note-50
3. The original 'Day of the Dead' celebrations in Mexico, for example, before they were commercialised and turned into a tourist festival by the James Bond movie.
4. 2014 YouGov Poll for The Sun newspaper
5. Which may be possible because in Taiwan, for example, around 90% of people say they have actually seen a ghost.

2. The First Ghost Hunter

1. Price, Harry; *Fifty Years of Psychical Research*; Longmans & Green; 1939
2. See Alan Gauld and A D Cornell – Poltergeists, 1979
3. http://dowsing-research.net/ - the site contains some very interesting articles and blogs on the topic of dowsing. The articles are dated between the early twentieth century and up to around 2016 so there is plenty of engrossing material from dowsing experts, academics, and sceptics.
4. https://www.darkhistories.com/harry-price-the-seance-of-rosalie/
5. Stella C seems to have possessed powerful psi-powers. On one occasion she completely destroyed a table and on another correctly predicted a newspaper advertisement 37 days before it was printed. See Price, op cit, and https://www.mysteriouspeople.com/psychic_medium.htm
6. The reasons Price preferred the LSA to the SPR – even though he was a full member of the latter – are somewhat obscure but probably came down to the fact that his background was lower middle class.
7. Sir William was a brilliant chemist and physicist who invented one of the earliest vacuum tubes and is credited with discovering at least one element (thallium) and successfully isolating helium for the first time.
8. Doyle, Sir Arthur Conan. *The History of Spiritualism*; G.H. Doran, Co.; New York, Vols 1 & 2 1926 Volume 2: 1926.
9. Behind the scenes, of course, the owners of the property – the Church of England – would have been appalled at the publicity and particularly the fuss created by the Rev Smith and his wife. Moving that pair away from the centre of attention was a good move.
10. Price, Harry; 'The Most Haunted House in England'; 1940 (republished 2020)
11. I rarely counsel against reading a book and, if you can find a copy, you are welcome to examine 'Mayerling's' arguments but I would suggest making some

12. Underwood, Peter & Tabori, Paul; The Ghosts of Borley: Illustrated Edition; David & Charles, 1973. Peter Underwood was perhaps the best known and most effective ghost hunter and fraud buster since Harry Price – whom he knew. One of Underwood's best known investigations was, in fact, into Price and his claims about Borley Rectory. His knowledge of the case was legendary. He indexed and reviewed both of Price's main books on the matter – the 1940 *The Most Haunted House in England* and his review of the case in 1946 called *The End of Borley Rectory*. Underwood's masterly index of the two was called *No Common Task* (Harrap, 1983). The overall conclusion was that some – but not all – of the things that happened at Borley Rectory were genuine.

3. Paranormal Places

1. https://www.building.co.uk/news/the-ghost-of-bircham-newton/3118367.article
2. https://www.youtube.com/watch?v=TLHXNIEfBTg
3. https://www.bedfordshirelive.co.uk/news/history/raf-thurleigh-haunted-world-war-5443280
4. Harry Price was a famous British debunker of mediums who is discussed at much greater length later in this Volume.
5. https://www.youtube.com/watch?v=9IBiBaPrD5U

4. Photographs 1

1. https://ghostsnghouls.com/100-ghost-photos/
2. Marryat was a fascinating character whose illustrious Royal Navy career was centred on the Napoleonic War and the 1814 war with the United States. He was a friend of Charles Dickens and – in that same year of 1836 – published his most famous novel 'Mr Midshipman Easy'. He also wrote 'The Children of the New Forest' the famous children's novel about the English Civil War which was made into a TV series in the 1970s and a feature film in the 1990s.
3. https://www.rmg.co.uk/queens-house/attractions/tulip-stairs
4. https://www.creativespirits.net/portfolio/tulip-staircase-ghost/
   https://www.theblackvault.com/casefiles/tulip-staircase-ghost/
5. https://www.gettyimages.co.uk/detail/news-photo/mabel-chinnery-behind-the-camera-taking-the-picture-of-his-news-photo/1165538166
6. https://combermereabbey.co.uk/stories/ghost-combermere-abbey/
7. https://en.wikipedia.org/wiki/Wellington_Stapleton-Cotton,_2nd_Viscount_Combermere#Lord_Combermere's_ghost_photo
8. To tie up loose ends - Lady Constance's baby boy, Richard, went on to become a World War 1 hero – several times wounded and winner of the Military Cross – only to die (like many other young British and American men returning from the war) of the Spanish Flu within two weeks of the end of the war. Sybell went on to marry a chap called Edward Blackett.

9. https://combermereabbey.co.uk/stories/ghost-combermere-abbey/

5. Photographs 2

1. One such example would be the story of the events on https://www.theghostbook.co.uk/famous-ghost-photos/
2. The college was the world's first air academy and today flies an incredibly wide variety of aircraft from the heritage Spitfire and Lancaster to the latest Typhoons (Eurofighters) and F-35s.
3. Sir Robert Victor Goddard KCB, CBE, (1975) - Flight Towards Reality
4. A wise decision. The R-101 was the world's largest flying craft for a few years but crashed in 1930 killing 48 of its crew and passengers. It was one of a string of airship disasters including such famous names as the French *Dixmude* (1923), the American *Akron* in 1933, and the German *Hindenberg* (1937). The disaster that befell the R-101 was also the centre of another highly credible set of paranormal events which are described later in this book.
5. https://www.skeptic.com/author/blake-smith/

6. Ghosts in Flight

1. https://en.wikipedia.org/wiki/Stinson_Detroiter
2. Fuller, John G; *The Airmen Who Would Not Die*; Putman's; 1979. A very good book which lays out the detail in a balanced way for these aviation incidents.
3. Eileen J. Garrett was one of the co-founders of the Parapsychology Foundation. Today, they offer a $2,000 scholarship each year – the Eileen J. Garrett Scholarship, Parapsychology Foundation Inc – for US students only.
4. Fuller, John G; The Airmen Who Would Not Die; op cit.
5. Although the engines were heavier diesel was considered to be much safer than petrol – especially for trips to tropical destinations.
6. Fuller, John G. *The Airmen Who Would Not Die*; op cit.
7. The Akron was not a hydrogen airship. It used helium. But in spite of this, US airships suffered multiple explosions – especially during storms.
8. John G. Fuller; The Ghost of Flight 401, Souvenir Press; 1978
9. Although modern, the fire station is built partly on the site of an ancient Temple of the Knights Templar.
10. Most US operators use Jet A, the most common type worldwide is Jet A1 but there is also a cold weather variant called Jet B. All are versions of kerosene specially adapted for high performance jet and turbine aviation engines.

7. A Very Varied Phenomenon

1. The Fleet Air Arm was and is the flying branch of the Royal Navy.

8. Reincarnation

1. The Wikipedia articles illustrates the knots that theologians can create and the unnecessarily complex words that they invent to form the basis of their arguments. https://en.wikipedia.org/wiki/Nestorianism
2. Abydos is one of Egypt's oldest and greatest cities. It lies to the west of the Nile in Upper Egypt about 100 river-miles north of Luxor. The temple and burial remains at Abydos are spectacular. The Temple of Seti contains the famous 'helicopter' hieroglyphs which seem to show 'modern' machines and are 'explained' by Egyptologists as being the result of a layer of plaster which had been placed over an original stone carving. There is considerable debate, however, as to the real age of many of the remains at Abydos with compelling arguments that they may be a great deal older than the dates ascribed to them by Egyptologists.
3. An excellent summary is given by E W Kelly who collected some of his best material in the book *Science, the Self, and Survival after Death: Selected Writings of Ian Stevenson*; Rowman & Littlefield Publisher; 2012
4. Stevenson, Dr Ian; *Reincarnation and Biology*; two Vols; 1997
5. See: Tucker, Professor Jim; *Life Before Life: A Scientific Investigation of Children's Memories of Previous Lives* and *Return to Life: Extraordinary Cases of Children Who Remember Their Past Live*.,
6. https://nautil.us/issue/47/consciousness/roger-penrose-on-why-consciousness-does-not-compute
7. The Search for Bridey Murphy was made into a film in 1956
8. This is absolutely correct and powerful propellor aircraft such as the Vought Corsair were particularly prone to this issue.
9. Leninger, Bruce and Andrea, with Ken Gross, *Soul Survivor: The Reincarnation of a World War II Fighter Pilot*. (Grand Central Publishing, 2010) also available on Amazon Kindle.
10. https://www.honorstates.org/index.php?id=359263
11. Natoma Bay (CVE-62) was an escort carrier. In 1945 she had taken part in the assaults on Luzon and Subic Bay before being assigned to the Iwo Jima invasion. From February her planes flew 123 sorties to assault the island prior to the landings of huge numbers of US Marines.
12. Kean, Leslie; *Surviving Death*; Three Rivers Press; 2017 (which contains a chapter written by Dr Jim Tucker)
13. Kean, Leslie. Surviving Death; Three Rivers Press; 2017. Op Cit..
14. Stevenson, Dr Ian; 'Birthmarks and Birth Defects Corresponding to Wounds on Deceased Persons,' Journal of Scientific Exploration; 1993
    https://med.virginia.edu/perceptual-studies/wp-content/uploads/sites/360/

2016/12/STE39stevenson-1.pdf

9. Death – The Final Frontier?

1. Parnia, S, et al, (2014), AWARE—AWAreness during REsuscitation—A prospective study. Resuscitation, 85: 1799-1805.
2. Greyson, Dr Bruce; *After: A Doctor Explores What Near-Death Experiences Reveal About Life and Beyond*. Macmillan/Penguin; 2021
3. Greyson, Dr Bruce; *Claims of Past Life Memories in Near Death Experiences*; Edge Magazine #46; June 2021
4. Bruce Greyson, op cit.
5. Bruce Greyson, op cit.
6. The study was published in The Lancet in December 2001.
7. Barrett, Sir William; *Deathbed Visions*; 1926
8. Fenwick, Dr Peter; *Past Lives: An Investigation into Reincarnation Memories*; Berkley, 2001
9. Kean, Leslie. *Surviving Death;* op cit.

11. Dreams

1. One example is the New York Tribune of April 20th 1912.
2. A modern westbound voyage on the Cunard liner Queen Mary 2 would cost between £850 and £1,200 for the most basic inside cabin, and ca £35,000 for the best suite on the ship. This vessel does, however, have a monopoly on the route.
3. And that, in itself is a very strange circumstance. One of the least talked-about circumstances in the Titanic incident was that the largest, newest, most prestigious, most comfortable liner in the world (which was heavily promoted as 'unsinkable') sailed with far less than a full complement of passengers on its maiden voyage while other liners were completely full. A number of people who sailed on the Titanic mentioned that they simply could not book a berth on other liners. To this day no-one has really explained why this was the case.
4. McEneaney, Bonnie; *Messages: Signs, Visits, and Premonitions from Loved Ones Lost on 9/11*; William Morrow; 2010. Her husband was one of those who had a very bad feeling but who nevertheless went to work that day and lost his life.
5. **Dossey, Dr Larry; The Power of Premonitions: How Knowing the Future Can Shape Our Lives; Dutton Adult; 2009**
6. Ryback, David, Dr.; *'Dreams That Came True'*; New York: Bantam Doubleday; Dell Publishing Group; 1988

12. The Power of the Mind

1. Shown to work on about half of patients. Why only half? No-one knows.
2. As a side issue (and with suitable ethics warnings) one does wonder whether placebos might be more effective on serious conditions if we had not talked them up as being so life-threatening and serious. People read all the time that cancer is virtually incurable so why would anybody believe that a simple pill might cure it.
3. Kaptchuk, Ted J; Chinese Medicine: The Web That Has No Weaver; 2000 and Kaptchuk, Ted J, Croucher, Michael; The Healing Arts; Summit Books; 1987
4. https://www.theguardian.com/commentisfree/andrewbrown/2009/sep/06/religion-health; Patrick Wall developed the famous 'gate theory' of pain which led to the successful TENS therapy.
5. Radin, Dean; *Real Magic*; Harmony Books; 2018
6. Stephen E. Braude is – at the time of writing - Emeritus Professor of Philosophy at the University of Maryland Baltimore County. He is Editor-in-Chief of the *Journal of Scientific Exploration*.
7. Kean, Leslie. *Surviving Death*; Crown/Archetype.
8. The Society for Psychical Research was established in 1882 to carry out scientific research into paranormal phenomena. Its emphasis is scientific. Sir Arthur Conan Doyle was a long serving member who eventually fell out with the SPR over what he regarded as an insufficiently broad approach to the study of the paranormal.
9. Targ, Russell; *The Reality of ESP*; Quest Books; 2012
10. Bem, Daryl J. and Honorton, Charles; *Does Psi Exist? Replicable Evidence for an Anomalous Process of Information Transfer;* Psychological Bulletin; American Psychological Association; 1994
11. President of the American Statistical Association in 2016.
12. Radin, Dean; Real Magic; Harmony Books; 2018

13. Impossible Experiments

1. Dr Edgar Mitchell was the founder of the Institute of Noetic Sciences. https://noetic.org/
2. David Livingstone Smith; article in The Freud Encyclopedia (Routledge 2001, edited by Edward Erwin).
3. https://www.theguardian.com/uk/2001/sep/30/robinmckie.theobserver
4. https://blogs.scientificamerican.com/cross-check/brilliant-scientists-are-open-minded-about-paranormal-stuff-so-why-not-you/
5. A Dyson Sphere is what Dyson hypothesised an advanced civilisation would do once it had exhausted or exceeded the power potential of its own planet. They might, he suggested, create a massive sphere of power collectors around their star to capture most of its energy. Dyson Trees are his idea for providing a

sustainable habitat in outer space. These would be genetically-modified plants which could grow inside comets and asteroids. Dyson's Eternal Intelligence is a fascinating concept by which an advanced intelligence could continue to think and exist in subjective time even after the universe had completely cooled (known as heat-death).
6. https://www.sheldrake.org/
7. Sheldrake, Dr Rupert; *A New Science of Life*; Icon Books, 2009
8. Sheldrake, Dr Rupert; *The Science Delusion;* Hodder & Stoughton; 2012
9. The callers were selected at random, and the subjects made their guesses before answering the call. These positive results were replicated independently at the universities of Amsterdam, Holland, and Freiburg, Germany.
10. Sheldrake, Dr Rupert: Telepathy in Connection with Telephone Calls, Text Messages and Emails Journal of International Society of Life Information Science (2014), 32 No. 1
11. A term that was invented by the late 1940s by the brilliant but controversial British astronomer Sir Fred Hoyle. At the time scientists criticised him forcefully for using it – they thought it was pejorative – yet now they revel in it.

14. Time & Consciousness

1. Rovelli, C.; *Loop quantum gravity*. Living Reviews in Relativity, 1; 1998
2. Carroll, Sean. *Is time real?* (2013, October 18). https://www.preposterousuniverse.com/blog/2013/10/18/is-time-real/
3. Dr Steve Taylor; Blog: *Open-Minded Science* – Psychology Today. https://www.psychologytoday.com/us/blog/out-the-darkness/201901/open-minded-science
4. Baruss, Dr Imants, Mossbridge. Dr Julia; *Transcendent Mind: Re-thinking the Science of Consciousness*; American Psychological Association; 2017
5. I know this sounds very strange but quite a few serious psychiatrists and psychologists (including the Rhine Research Center) have put some of the activity down to what they call 'Recurrent Spontaneous Psychokinesis' (RSPK) – effectively uncontrolled and often unknowing telekinesis. The usual suspects are adolescents or young people.
6. See also Barbour, Julian; *The Janus Point: A New Theory of Time*; Basic Books; 2020 and Dr Barbour's other highly stimulating books.
7. 'Time' magazine has Robert Lanza listed among the 100 most-influential people in the world today.
8. Lanza, Dr Robert, and *Pavšič, Matej with Bob Berman; The Grand Biocentric Design, BenBella Books, 2020*

GLOSSARY

Alchemy: one of the ancient precursors of modern science. It was part philosophy and part observation and experimentation. It grew up in China, India, Arabia, and Europe and was at its peak in the Middle-Ages up to about the seventeenth century.

A priori: 'from the former'; a deduction based on reasoning rather than empirical evidence. It is, in fact, something known from logic without having to assemble facts. A priori reasoning is used a great deal where the paranormal is concerned.

Astrology: the foundation of astronomy – from which it differs only in that astrologers believe that human affairs and the universe are tightly linked – a not unreasonable idea.

BC/AD: Before Christ and Anno Domini – the dating system based on Christian beliefs which, assumes that the prophet was born either in the year 1 BCE or 1 CE.

BCE/CE: Before Common Era and Common Era. This is the non-religious version of the BC/AD system. It is based on year one of the Gregorian (i.e. Christian) calendar but – because it does not carry direct connections to the Christian faith can be accepted by the many other religions in the world.

Belief: An acceptance that something exists or is true, especially one without scientific proof.

BP: before present (in years – e.g. 5,400 BP is equivalent to roughly 3,400 BCE).

Creationism: the theory that modern humans – homo sapiens– are not the result of evolution (see Darwinism) but of creation by a divine force. Most of the world's religions are based on a creation story.

Darwinism: the scientific theory that living things evolve over long periods of time and that this process is responsible for the evolution of homo sapiens over millions of years from early hominids to our own species. It remains controversial and in some ways scientifically unproven.

Denisovans: a sub-species of modern humans who existed between about 500,000 and 30,000 years ago mainly in south-east and central Asia. They were cousins of the Neanderthals and of homo-sapiens. Their demise as a species is still not understood or explained.

Empirical: Based on or verifiable by observation or experience rather than theory or pure logic.

ESP: Extra-Sensory Perception

Faith: Strong belief in the doctrines of a religion, based on spiritual conviction rather than proof. Strong belief in another doctrine or practice. Even strong belief in groups of fellow humans, e.g. medical doctors.

Ghost: usually interpreted as the spirit of a dead person which manifests itself in various visible and audible ways. The phenomenon is however much more complex.

Homo-sapiens: a sub-species of hominid that seems to have emerged as a modern species between 300,000 and 200,000 years ago. For a while they co-existed with Neanderthals and Denisovans.

Hypothetical: Supposed but not necessarily real or true. Usually stated as a way of introducing an idea or proposition.

Irrational: Not logical or reasoned. But irrational does not necessarily mean wrong.

Magic: The power of influencing events by using mysterious or supernatural forces. Logically it can encompass religions of all kinds as well as witchcraft and wizardry.

Medium: a person who is able to act as an intermediary between the physical world and a non-physical realm. The term includes equivalent roles such as shamans and witch-doctors.

Metaphysical: Based on abstract reasoning. Transcending physical matter or the laws of nature. Many things can only be discussed or argued in a metaphysical context. Good and evil, for example.

Miracle: An extraordinary event, not explicable by natural or scientific laws. Usually attributed to divine agency. Logically, indistinguishable from magic.

Neanderthals: a sub-species of humans mainly located in north-central Asia and northern Europe. They existed – along with their cousins the Denisovans – between about 500,000 and 30,000 years ago. The reasons for their disappearance are still not understood.

Normal: means 'as expected'. A normal situation or condition is one which effectively meets expectations. But these are based on experience, conventional teaching, and current science. Normal is, therefore, a relative concept not an absolute.

Normality (Normalcy in US English): The condition of being normal; the state of being usual, typical, or expected.

Para: means beside or beyond.

Paranormal: anything that is beside or beyond what is considered to be normal or expected. In the modern world this includes a wide variety of phenomena ranging from UFOs/UAP to ghosts, and from psi powers to witchcraft. It is a relative concept.

Paranorm 1.0: The western interpretation of paranormal phenomena prior to about the late-twentieth century. Under this interpretation, paranormal events and beliefs were not only separately defined but were regarded as distinct subjects with few or no connections between them.

Paranorm 2.0: A concept originated by James T Abbott which argues that all paranormal topics are part of a single, overarching phenomenon; that each and every topic that is separately named and described under Paranorm 1.0 is an integral part of the universal whole – the single underlying consciousness in which we exist. These topics may continue to be discussed as separate subjects but they are simply different aspects of the whole.

Placebo: a medical treatment which should not work but which does (to varying degrees) - a harmless and medically useless treatment. For reasons that medics do not understand, placebos can have the same effect as a scientifically-developed drug.

Poltergeist: this is usually interpreted as a noisy or malicious ghost but could equally be a manifestation caused by human mental powers (telekinesis).

Precognition: the ability to see or feel future events. Scientists generally regard it as impossible, but some scientists have shown that precognition is a statistically significant probability and there is a huge amount of empirical evidence for it.

Proof: Evidence or argument establishing a fact or the truth of a statement. Proof is not a fixed quantity or quality. For example, proof of the Higgs Boson required evidence at a level of accuracy of one chance in a million that the findings were not based on chance – this is called Five Sigma Proof. In another context proof might be simply the word of three independent witnesses that they saw a person break into a house that was not their own.

Pseudoscience: anything that cannot be proven using scientific method and that is scientifically unverifiable. The unstated assumption is that the scientific method is the only way of establishing what is possible and what is not. This is not necessarily the case.

Psi: the term used to denote psychic or mind powers such as telekinesis, telepathy, precognition, retrocognition, etc.

Rational: Based on, or in accordance with, reason or logic. Logical reasoning.

Reality: The state of things as they appear to exist, as opposed to an idealistic or notional idea of them. The state or quality of having existence or substance. This definition relies on the acceptance that things can have substance and be 'objective' and 'absolute' – all of which attributes are increasingly coming under question.

Reductionism: the sometimes necessary 'reduction' of complex issues to one of their simpler components. Scientists very often take this approach in order to make things easier and sometimes clearer. If one understands how a brain neuron works that might (or might not) explain how the brain as a whole operates. It is a dangerous concept even though it has resulted in many valuable scientific discoveries.

Reincarnation: the principle that a 'soul' or personal essence (whatever that may be) can be transferred after death from the old body to a new body.

Religion: The belief in and worship of a supernatural controlling power, especially a personal god or gods. There are hundreds of religions across the world ranging from the beliefs of indigenous peoples to the highly organised mass religions of Christianity, Hinduism, Buddhism, and Islam. Within most religions there are separate doctrines, sects, and distinct practices.

Retrocognition: the ability to see or feel past events (see Precognition)

Science: The systematic study of the structure and behaviour of the physical and natural world through observation and experiment.

Scientific method: the rigorously applied process by which proof requires replication and falsification via identical results.

Shaman: a commonly accepted generic term for the witch-doctor, priest, witch, or warlock of an indigenous tribe or people.

Sumer: the earliest civilisation known at present (with the possible exception of whatever emerges from studies of Anatolia's 12,000 year old sites). The Sumerian civilisation grew up in modern-day Iraq around 7,000 BP but its language is not related to any known language and its origins are not clear.

Supernatural: attributed to some force beyond scientific understanding or the laws of nature; e.g. ghosts.

Superstition: A widely held but usually irrational belief in supernatural influences, especially as leading to good or bad luck, or a practice based on such a belief. A superstition is not, however, necessarily wrong simply because it is irrational.

Synchronicity: things or events that seem to be meaningfully related yet lack a causal connection in the normal sense. Carl Jung was convinced that such a phenomenon exists.

Telekinesis: the movement or physical change of objects solely through the power of one's mind.

Telepathy: the linking of two or more minds by non-technological forces as yet not understood.

Theoretical: Based on or calculated through theory and logic rather than experience or practice.

Therianthrope: a half human, half animal hybrid creature

UAP: Unidentified Aerial Phenomenon. The US Pentagon's preferred modern term for what we all know as UFOs.

UFO: Unidentified Flying Object

Wicca: a modern witchcraft movement prevalent mainly in the UK and USA. It has equivalents in other European nations.

Witchcraft: a skillset developed by its practitioners down the ages to cause things to happen by using the powers of human will, possibly linked to or supported by supernatural forces and specified practices, spells, or word-forms.

Xenoglossy: the circumstance in which a person is able to speak or write a language they could not have acquired by the usual means.

Symbols

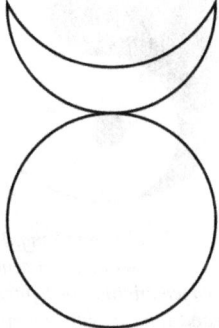

The Horned God symbol has been used by many cultures but especially by witches and modern Wiccans. It has been called Cernunnos from Celtic times but has antecedents and echoes in almost every belief system well before the Celts.

The Khemetian/Egyptian Ankh symbol represents life and is often called the Key of Life. It was one of the three most powerful symbols of ancient Egypt and is as old as that civilisation – arguably at least 6,000 years BP. It carried additional connotations of 'life after death'.

The ancient Asian symbol for Yin and Yang. The representation of opposite but interconnected and interdependent forces. Yin, the dark segment, is Earth and femininity. The lighter segment is yang – male and active. Yin and Yang are different but they are part of the Great Ultimate and cannot be separated.

BIBLIOGRAPHY

Abbott, James T.; *The Outsider's Guide to UAP: Volume 1: Mystery and Science*; (Second Edition) Keatley Publishing; 2023

Abbott, James T; *The Outsider's Guide to UAP Volume 2: What are they?*; Keatley Publishing; 2019

Adams, Paul, Brazil, Eddie, Underwood, Peter; *The Borley Rectory Companion*; History Press 2009

Agrippa; *De occulta philosophia libri tres (Three Books on Occult Philosophy)*; 1531.

Alexander, John; *Ghosts! Washington Revisited: Washington Revisited - The Ghostlore of the Nation's Capitol*; Schiffer; 1998

Baigent Michael, Leigh Richard, Lincoln Henry; *The Holy Blood and the Holy Grail*; Jonathan Cape; 1982

Bainton, Roy; *The Mammoth Book of Unexplained Phenomena*

Barrett, Sir William; *Deathbed Visions*; 1926

Baruss, Dr Imants & Mossbridge. Dr Julia; *Transcendent Mind: Re-thinking the Science of Consciousness*; American Psychological Association; 2017

Becker, Ernest; *The Denial of Death*, Souvenir Press, 2011.

Beischel, J, Boccuzzi, M, Biuso, M, Rock, A. J. *Anomalous information reception by research mediums under blinded conditions*; EXPLORE: The Journal of Science & Healing; 2015

Bem, Daryl J., Honorton, Charles; *Does Psi Exist? Replicable Evidence for an Anomalous Process of Information Transfer*; Psychological Bulletin; American Psychological Association; 1994

Borman, Tracy; *Witches: A Tale of Sorcery, Scandal and Seduction;* Jonathan Cape 2013

Briggs, Katharine M.; *Encyclopedia of Fairies: Hobgoblins, Brownies, Bogies, & Other Supernatural Creatures*; Pantheon; 1976

Broderick, Damien; *Outside the Gates of Science*; 2005

Carroll, Sean. *Is time real?* (2013, October 18). https://www.preposterousuniverse.com/blog/2013/10/18/is-time-real/

Carson Smith, Christopher; Laham, Darrell; Moddel, Garret; *Stock Market Prediction Using Associative Remote Viewing With Untrained Viewers*; University of Colorado; 2010

Cham, Jorge & Whiteson, Daniel; *We have no idea: A guide to the unknown Universe*

Cirkovic, Milan M; *The Great Silence: Science and Philosophy of Fermi's Paradox*

Cott, Jonathan & El Zeini, Hanny; *The Search for Omm Sety: A Story of Eternal Love*; Doubleday & Company; 1987

Cunliffe, Dr Barry; *Druids: A Very Short Introduction*; Oxford University Press, 2010.

Daniken, Erich von; *The End of the Silence*

DK; *A History of Magic, Witchcraft, and the Occult*; Dorling Kindersley Ltd.

Dee, Dr John; *De Heptarchia Mystica (On the Mystical Rule of the Seven Planets)*; 1582

Dee, Dr John; *Quinti Libri Mysteriorum (Five Books of Mystery)*; 1583

Delorme, A, Beischel. J, Michel, L, Boccuzzi, M, Radin, D, Mills, P. J. *Electrocortical activity associated with subjective communication with the deceased*; Frontiers in Psychology, 4: 2013

Dossey, Dr Larry; *The Power of Premonitions: How Knowing the Future Can Shape Our Lives*; Dutton Adult; 2009

Doyle, Arthur Conan; *The History of Spiritualism*; G.H. Doran, Co.; New Vols 1 & 2 1926

Fenwick, Dr Peter; *Past Lives: An Investigation into Reincarnation Memories*; Berkley, 2001

Flamel, Nicolas; *Philosophical Summary*, 1561

Flamel, Nicolas; *Exposition of the Hieroglyphical Figures;* 1612

Foerster, Brien; *Aftershock*

Fortune, Dion; *The Mystical Qabalah';* Aziloth Books, 2002

Fowler, Raymond E; *The Andreasson Affair: The Documented Investigation of a Woman's Abduction Aboard a UFO*; New Page Books; 2014

Friedman, Stanton T; *Captured! The Betty and Barney Hill UFO Experience*; New Page Books; 2007

Fuller, John G; *The Interrupted Journey*; Dell; 1966

Fuller, John G.; *The Ghost of Flight 401*; Souvenir Press; 1978

Fuller, John G; *The Airmen Who Would Not Die*; Putman's; 1979

Garrett, Eileen; *Adventures in the Supernormal;* 1949

Garrett, Eileen; (Unpublished); *Precognition of an Airship*

Gauld, Alan & Cornell A D; *Poltergeists*, 1979

Goddard, Sir R Victor; *Flight Towards Reality*; Turnstone; 1975

Godfrey, Linda S; *I Know What I Saw: Modern-Day Encounters with Monsters of New Urban Legend and Ancient Lore*; J P Tarcher, 2019

Gosden, Chris; *The History of Magic*; Penguin; 2021

Greyson, Dr Bruce; *After: A Doctor Explores What Near-Death Experiences Reveal About Life and Beyond*; Macmillan/Penguin; 2021

Greyson, Dr Bruce; *Claims of Past Life Memories in Near Death Experiences;* Edge Magazine; #46; June 2021

Grosso, Michael; *The New Story: UAP, Psychical Research, and Religion*; Edge #46, June 2021

Guiley, Rosemary; *"The Encyclopaedia of Ghosts and Spirits"*

Hernandez, Rey; Klimo, Jon; Schild, Rudy; *Beyond UAP: The Science of Consciousness and Contact with Non-Human Intelligence*; The Edgar Mitchell Foundation for Research into Extraterrestrial and Extraordinary Experience; 2018

Hinchliffe, Emilie; *The Return of Captain Hinchliffe*; Psychic Press; 1930

Honorton, Charles; *Meta-analysis of psi ganzfeld research: A response to Hyman*; Journal of Parapsychology, 49; 1985
Horsley, Sir Peter; *Sounds from Another Room*; 1997
Hunter, Dr Jack; *Manifesting Spirits: An Anthropological Study of Mediumship and the Paranormal*; 2020
Hunter, Dr Jack; *Spirits, Gods and Magic*; 2020
Hunter, Dr Jack; *Talking with the Spirits*; 2014
Hynek, Dr Alan; *Night Siege: The Hudson Valley UAP Sightings*; Llewellyn Publishing; 1998
Hynek, J Allen & Vallée, Jacques: *The Edge of Reality*; 1975
Johnson, Obed; *The Study of Chinese Alchemy*; Shanghai 1928
Jung, C.G.; *Synchronicity: An Acausal Connecting Principle*; Princeton University Press; 1969
Kaku, Michio; *The Physics of the Impossible;* Doubleday; 2008
Kaku, Michio; *The Physics of the Future*
Kaptchuk, Ted J; *Chinese Medicine: The Web That Has No Weaver*; 2000
Kaptchuk, Ted J, Croucher, Michael; *The Healing Arts*; Summit Books; 1987
Kean, Leslie; *Surviving Death*; Three Rivers Press; 2017
Keel, John; *The Mothman Prophecies;* 1975
Kelleher, Colm A; *Hunt for the Skinwalker;* Paraview; 2006
Kelly, E W; *Science, the Self, and Survival after Death: Selected Writings of Ian Stevenson*; Rowman & Littlefield Publisher; 2012
Kerven, Rosalind; *English Fairy Tales*
Knight, Christopher & Butler, Alan; *Civilisation One;* Watkins; 2010
Lanza, Dr Robert, Pavšič, Matej & Berman, Bob; *The Grand Biocentric Design*, BenBella Books, 2020
Lavater, Ludwig; *De Spectris*; Zurich 1570
Leasor, James; *The Millionth Chance.*
Leggett, D M A; *The Implications of the Paranormal*; 1977
Leninger, Bruce and Andrea & Gross, Ken: *Soul Survivor: The Reincarnation of a World War II Fighter Pilot.*; Grand Central Publishing; 2010
Lindbergh, Charles A.; *The Spirit of St Louis*; Scribner Book; 1953.
Lodge, Sir Oliver; *Raymond's Life and Death;* 1916
Lodge, Sir Oliver; *Ether & Reality;* 1925
Mack, Dr John E; *Abduction: Human Encounters with Aliens*; Scribner; 2007
Mack, Dr John E; *Passport to the Cosmos: Human Transformation and Alien Encounters*; White Crow Books; 2010
Macmillan, Norman; *Sefton Brancker*; 1935
McEneaney, Bonnie; *Messages: Signs, Visits, and Premonitions from Loved Ones Lost on 9/11*; William Morrow; 2010.
Mitford, Mary Russell; *Our Village*; 1824-1832
Osis, Karlis; *At the Hour of Death;* Avon; 1977

Parry, Richard Lloyd; *Ghosts of the Tsunami*: Vintage Books; 2017

Pollan, Michael; *The Botany of Desire: A Plant's-Eye View of the World;* Bloomsbury; 2003

Price, Harry; *Confessions of a Ghost Hunter;* 1936

Price, Harry; *Fifty Years of Psychical Research – A Critical Survey;* Longman & Green; 1939

Price, Harry; *The Most Haunted House in England;* 1940 (republished 2020)

Price, Harry; *The R101 Disaster;* Article in Nash's Magazine; Jan 1931 & Cosmopolitan, 1931

Price, Harry; *Leaves from a Psychist's Case-Book;* Victor Gollancz Ltd.;1933 (Ch 6 deals with the Oct. 7th 1930 séance with Eileen Garrett

Radin, Dean L; *Real Magic*

Rhine, Dr J B.; *Research on Spirit Survival Re-examined;* Journal of Parapsychology; June 1959

Rhine, Louisa E.; *Hidden Channels of the Mind;* W. Sloane Associates; 1961

Rhine, Louisa E.; *ESP in life and lab: Tracing Hidden Channels,* Macmillan; 1967

Rhine, Louisa E.; *Mind Over Matter: Psychokinesis.* Macmillan; 1970

Rhine, Louisa E.; *Something Hidden.* McFarland; 1983

Rice T. W.; *Believe it or not: Religious and other paranormal beliefs in the United States;* Journal for the Scientific Study of Religion; 2003

Ring, Kenneth; *Mind sight: Near-Death and Out-of-Body Experiences in the Blind;* iUniverse, 2008.

Ring, Kenneth; *The Omega Project: Near-Death Experiences, UAP Encounters, and Mind at Large;* Morrow, 1992.

Ripley, Sir George; *The Compound of Alchemy or, the Twelve Gates leading to the Discovery of the Philosopher's Stone (Liber Duodecim Portarum);* 1471

River, Charles (Eds); *Ghost Tales of the United Kingdom: Historic Hauntings and Supernatural Stories from the UK;* 2018

Ryback, Dr David; *'Dreams That Came True';* New York: Bantam Doubleday; Dell Publishing Group; 1988

Scully, Frank; *Behind the Flying Saucers;* 1950

Sheldrake, Dr Rupert; *A New Science of Life;* Icon Books, 2009

Sheldrake, Dr Rupert; *The Science Delusion;* Hodder & Stoughton; 2012

Sikes, Wirt; *British Goblins*

Simpson, Jacqueline & Westwood, Jennifer; *The Penguin Book of Ghosts: Haunted England*

Sinclair, Paul; *Truth Proof.*

Sinclair, Upton; *Mental Radio;* 1930

Spanner, R F; *About Airships;* 1929

Spanner, R F; *The Tragedy of the R101;* 1931

Stevenson, Dr Ian; *Reincarnation and Biology;* two Vols; 1997

Stith, Geraldine; *The Kelly Green Men: Alien Legacy Revisited;* Authorhouse; 2015

Strieber, Whitley; *Communion: A True Story*; Souvenir Press; 2016
Targ, Russell; *The Reality of ESP*; Quest Books; 2012
Tucker, Professor James; *Life Before Life: A Scientific Investigation of Children's Memories of Previous Lives*
Tucker, Professor James; *Return to Life: Extraordinary Cases of Children Who Remember Their Past Lives*.
Underwood, Peter & Tabori, Paul; *The Ghosts of Borley: Illustrated Edition*; David & Charles, 1973
Underwood, Peter; *Gazetteer of British Ghosts*; 1971
Underwood, Peter; *A Ghost Hunters Handbook*; 1980
Underwood, Peter; *The Ghost Hunter's Guide*; 1986
Underwood, Peter; *No Common Task: Autobiography of a Ghost Hunter*; 1983
Underwood, Peter; *A-Z of British Ghosts*; 1992
Underwood, Peter; *The Borley Rectory Companion*; 2008
Underwood, Peter; *Ghost Hunting with Peter Underwood*; 2014
Vallée, Jacques; *Passport to Magonia – From Folklore to Flying Saucers*; Daily Grail Publishing Edition; 2015
Walton, Travis; *Fire in the Sky: The Walton Experience*; Parragon Press; 1996
Westwood, Jennifer and Simpson, Jacqueline; *The Penguin Book of Ghosts*; Penguin Books Ltd.; 2006.
Wilson, Colin; *The Occult: A History*; 1971
Wilson, Colin; *Enigmas and Mysteries*; 1978
Wilson, Colin; *Afterlife*; 1985
Wilson, Colin; *The Laurel and Hardy Theory of Consciousness*; 1986
Wilson, Colin; *From Atlantis to the Sphinx*; 1996
Wilson, Colin; *Alien Dawn*; 1998
Wilson, Colin; *The Atlantis Blueprint*; 2000
Wilson, Colin; *Super Consciousness*; 2007

INDEX

abductive reasoning: 126
Abraham Lincoln: 103, 168, 188
Abydos: 128, 129
Achy: 94, 95
Active spirits of the dead: 11
acupuncture: 198
Air Marshal Sir Hugh Trenchard: 67
Air Marshall Sir Robert Victor Goddard: 64, 68, 76, 114, 169, 187, 243
Air Vice Marshall Sir Sefton Brancker: 95
airships: 14, 65, 67, 69. 89, 98
Alan Hynek: 103, 116, 217
Alan Turing: 227, 230
Albert Einstein: 219, 226, 238, 249
alchemy: viii, 255
Amelia Earhart: 85
anomalous anticipatory event: 168, 187
Archerfield: 39
arrow of time: 240
Arundel: 107
astrology: viii, 120

Athenodorus: 9, 13
Atlantic: 83, 88, 178, 180, 183
Australasian: 117
Avro Lancaster: 40
Avro Lincoln: 40
AWARE: 149, 152

Barra: 135
Barrett Naylor: 184
Bassano's: 69, 75, 78, 81
Battle of Nechtansmere: 166
BBC: 21, 31, 36, 42, 54, 100
Beatrice Earl: 87
Beauvais: 93
believers: 25, 203
Big Bang: 234, 249, 251
birthmarks: 134, 145
Blue Book: 25
Bob Loft: 99
Bobby Capel: 63, 66, 70, 74, 76, 80, 169, 174
Borley Rectory: 20, 24, 26, 45, 161
Bridey Murphy: 137
British Museum: 8, 128
Brown Lady: 49, 61, 82
Bruce Greyson: 152
Buddhist: 8, 121, 124, 145, 193, 219
'Building' magazine: 33

Cameron Macaulay: 135
Captain Hubert C. Provand: 49
Captain W G R Hinchliffe, DFC: 14, 21, 84, 94, 98, 102
Captain W H Gregson: 26
cardiac arrests: 150, 155
Cardington: 93
Carl Jung: 227, 230

Catherine Bystock: 38, 102
Central Intelligence Agency: 205
Chaeronea: 9
Charles Dickens: 2, 8
Charles Honorton: 194, 210
Chicago: 101, 180, 185
China: 120
Christian: 123, 132, 219, 255
Christopher Carson Smith: 192
circumstantial evidence: 51, 62, 114, 125, 154, 232
clairvoyance: 192, 213
coherence: 218
Coleen Buterbaugh: 165
Colonel Henderson: 88, 98, 102
Combermere: 56, 82
consciousness: 69, 114, 134, 136, 148, 156, 188, 199, 218, 220, 230, 233, 237, 239, 242, 256
consciousness theory: 252
Consol: 44
Constance Cummings: 141
Construction Industry Training Board: 32
Country Life magazine: 49, 51
Cranwell Maintenance Group Photo, 1919: 68
cryptids: 116, 252, 257

Daedalus: 65, 72
Daily Mirror: 23
Dakota Crash: 171
Daniel Danielsen Gronnestad: 179
Daniel Douglas Home: 16
Darrell Laham: 192
David Booth: 243
David McCourt: 185
David Ryback: 190
dead-reckoning: 173

Deborah Hatswell: 167
de-icing: 173
DNA: 200, 202, 204, 241
Don Repo: 99
Doppelganger: 31, 101
Dorothy Eady: 127
Dorothy Stella Cranshaw: 19
double exposure: 47, 55, 59, 71
dowsers: 16
Dr Barrie G Colvin: 207
Dr D Scott Rogo: 238
Dr Daryl Bem: 211, 233
Dr James (Jim) Tucker: 133
Dr John Mack: 161
Dr Larry Dossey: 189
Dr Louisa E Rhine: 189, 230
Dr Peter Fenwick: 157
Dr Pim van Lommel: 155, 221
Dr Rupert Sheldrake: 211, 228, 241
Dr Sam Parnia: 149
Dr Ted Kaptchuk: 197
dreams: 5, 84, 106, 128, 148, 157, 162, 168, 171, 176, 177, 186, 190, 203, 209, 225, 242, 252
Drem: 114, 169, 187

E F Smith: 166
Earth: 125, 202, 218, 238, 248, 251
Edinburgh: 169
Egyptians: 2, 8, 118, 120, 127, 167
Eileen Garrett: 14, 19, 86, 94, 98
electromagnetic: 4, 156, 242, 251
Elsie MacKay: 85, 88
Emilie Hinchliffe: 14, 87, 89
Emily Wright: 33

Emotion: 12, 83, 88, 99, 102, 114, 133, 140, 148, 165, 167, 183, 187, 207, 215, 224, 227, 230, 246
end of life experiences: 2, 114, 147, 156, 158, 250
entanglement: 202, 218
entropy: 238
Eugene Wigner: 221
Experiential evidence: 125
experimental conundrum: 215, 222, 233
Extra-Sensory Perception (ESP): 190, 193, 209, 211

falsifiability: 227, 229, 245
father: 22, 27, 78, 85, 104, 135, 138, 140
Federal Aviation Administration (FAA): 186
Fetches: 11, 101
filter theory: 245
flicker filters: 245
Flicker Theory: 247
footsteps: 7, 11, 22, 35, 107, 115
Franck Adelman: 180, 183
Freddie Jackson: 66, 70, 75, 78, 81, 169
Freeman Dyson: 227

Gaia: 248
Ganzfeld experiment: 210
Garret Moddel: 192
George Raft: 141, 143
ghost photos: 3, 45, 48, 63, 66, 72, 74, 79, 82
ghosts: viii, 1–16, 18, 21, 25, 31, 38, 41, 45, 47, 52, 56, 59, 62, 79, 83, 87, 96, 98, 103, 106, 108, 113, 120, 157, 161, 165, 167, 169, 185, 190, 207, 213, 231, 252
Goddard: 64, 68, 76, 114, 169, 176, 187, 192, 243
Greeks: 118, 219
Guy Smith: 22, 28
Guy William Lambert: 191
Gwyn Richards: 43

Hampton Court Palace: 47
happiness: 96, 154, 201, 204, 241
Harold Puthoff: 214
Harry Price: 13–28, 38, 41, 87, 92, 94
haunted castles: 2
Haunted Cottage: 107
Hawker Hart: 169
Healing: 118, 193, 213, 219, 255
Henry Bull: 22, 28
Hinchliffe: 14, 21, 84, 94, 98, 102
Hindenburg: 98
Hindu: 118, 121, 124, 131, 145, 219, 271
HMS Daedalus: 65
Holly Winter: 184
Hollywood: 141
Homer: 8
Honourable Elsie MacKay: 85, 88
Hynek: 103, 116, 217

Ian Stevenson: 123, 130, 136, 144, 147, 152
impossible: vii, 6, 51, 63, 121, 148, 188, 209, 213, 217, 224, 233, 235, 242, 245, 250, 252
Indra Shira: 49, 51
inductive reasoning: 126
Irish Linen Girls: 47
Isaac Newton: 219, 249
Ivan Spenceley: 41
Iwo Jima: 138

J B Rhine: 167, 189, 227, 230
J K Rowling: 2
J. W. Dunne: 188
Jack De Manio: 36
Jacob Marley: 8
James Leininger: 137, 139, 143

James Lovelock: 248
Jaques Vallée: 116, 217
John Bell: 221
John Roberts: 76, 80
Julian Barbour: 247

Kaku, Professor Michio: vii, 63
karma: 8, 125, 145
Katie King: 20
Kevin Garry: 35
King Brude mac Beli: 166
King Ecgfrith: 166
Kuhn, Robert Lawrence: 240, 255

Levant: 110
levitations: 206
Lieutenant Kevin Hammons: 139, 143
Lights, mists and orbs: 11
Lionel Foyster: 24, 27
Locked Book: 25
Lockheed L-1011 Tristar: 99
London Spiritualist Alliance: 19
Lord Inchcape: 85, 89
Lord Thompson: 92
Louisa Rhine: 189, 230
Lt (JG) James Huston: 138
Lucy Christiana, Lady Duff-Gordon: 180
Lynn News & Advertiser: 35

Mabel's mother: 54, 82
Mae West: 141
magic: viii, 14, 252
Maintenance Group: 65, 76
Major Oliver G G Villiers, DSO: 14, 95
Marryat: 50, 62

Mary, Queen of Scots: 103
materialism: 219, 221, 240
materialist: 6, 202, 221, 238, 241, 250
Max Plank: 136
Migaloo: 8
Migraines: 198, 203
mind over matter: 193, 225
Mitchell, Dr Edgar: 218
monocausality: 10
Morphic Fields: 228
morphine: 199
Mr. and Mrs. Edward W. Bill: 179
mRNA: 200, 204
Mrs Chinnery: 54, 56, 82
Mrs Crandon: 18
M–Theory: 239, 250
music–induced analgesia: 197

Navy News: 76
near death experiences: 2, 149, 152, 154, 157
Nebraska Wesleyan University: 165
Night after Night: 141
nocebo effect: 194
non–local consciousness: 156, 158
non–locality: 218
Norman Carlyle Craig: 183

Okinawa: 39
Omm Seti: 129
optimism: 204, 215
Ouija board: 87
out–of–body experiences: ix, 147, 149, 152, 161, 245, 250

pain: 194, 197, 201, 203, 231, 246
pantry: 109, 114

Paranorm 1.0: viii, 2, 5, 15, 120, 256
Paranorm 2.0: ix, 2, 117, 120, 131, 144, 146, 253, 256, 258
paranormal: vii, 1, 5, 13–25, 28, 31–35, 38–45, 62, 63, 68, 77, 84, 87, 89, 99, 102, 108, 116, 120, 123, 131, 154, 156, 165, 167, 169, 171, 174, 177, 189, 193, 203, 207, 209, 218, 220–229, 232, 235, 238, 243, 245, 248, 250, 252, 255
parapsychologist: 157, 175, 210, 233, 241
Passive spirits of the dead: 10
Pete the Poltergeist: 41
Peter Clark: 35
Peter Fenwick: 157
Peter Underwood: 13, 27
Petit Trianon: 162, 165
Pew Research Center: 9
Pharoah Seti I: 127
physics: vii, 1, 63, 123, 125, 136, 209, 219, 224, 227, 239, 241, 245
placebo effect: 194–200, 205
planet: 202, 218, 251
Plutarch: 9
poltergeist: 11, 15, 41, 207, 231
precognition: ix, 156, 161, 167, 174, 178, 183, 187, 213, 231, 242, 257
precognitive: 168, 171, 175, 177, 180, 188
premonition: 158, 168, 171, 174, 176, 180, 182, 184, 191
priests: 53, 118, 124, 127, 194, 196, 221
production theory: 245
Professor Brian Josephson: 226, 230
Professor Kuhlmann–Wilsdorf: 123
Professor William Barrett: 16, 59, 157
pseudoscience: 6, 193, 213, 222, 228
psi: 161, 169, 184, 190, 192, 212–215, 217, 221, 224, 228, 242, 250, 257
psi power: 168, 223, 225, 239, 242, 253
psychic: 18, 38, 117, 120, 165, 167, 174, 184, 188, 204, 209, 212, 214, 219, 224, 232, 241
psychokinesis: 116, 190, 204, 208
pub: 11, 44, 110, 113, 161

quantum: vii, 84, 135, 201, 219, 221, 226, 239, 245, 257
quantum effects: 134, 136, 202
quantum entanglement: 202, 218
quantum loop gravity: 239
quantum particles: 154, 202
Queen's House: 52, 82

R–100: 92, 98
R–101: 14, 21, 69, 89–95, 97
Radin, Dean: 203, 214
RAF Bircham Newton: 32–35, 37, 42, 44, 82
RAF Cosford: 39–42, 44
RAF Cranwell: 65–70, 77, 79, 169
RAF Grove: 39
RAF Metheringham: 38, 102
Ray Hyman: 210
Raynham Hall: 49
reason people see ghosts: 4
reborn: 124, 144
Recurrent Spontaneous Psycho-Kinesis: 16, 116
reductionism: 240, 243
reductionist: 241, 250
reincarnation: 118, 121, 123–125, 127–137, 139, 143–146, 148, 152, 231, 252, 257
remote viewing: 17, 156, 192, 213–215, 219, 221, 255
resonance: 17, 218, 228
retrocognition: 116, 162, 165–168, 213, 257
revenants: 11, 98, 109, 185
Reverend Ralph Hardy: 52
Ringcroft Disturbances: 15
RMS Mauretania: 179, 183
Robert Lanza: 251
Roberta ('Bobby') Capel: 63, 66, 70, 74, 76, 80, 169, 174
Roger Penrose: 136, 221
Roman Empire: 2
Romans: 110, 118

Rosalie: 15, 17, 20
Royal Flying Corps: 32, 65
Royal Naval Air Service (RNAS): 64, 67
Royal Navy: 50, 66, 92
RSPK: 16, 116
Rupert Sheldrake: 211, 228, 241
Russell Targ: 209, 214
Ryan Hammons: 139, 143

Sado: 173
Samhain: 9
Samsara: 124
science: vii, 1, 5, 48, 63, 73, 82, 103, 123, 133, 136, 152, 195, 200, 204, 214, 217–222, 225, 227–231, 239, 242, 248–251, 253, 255
scientific method, the: 205, 220–222, 225, 227, 230, 240–243
scientific-evidence: 125
Scrooge: 8
Sean Carroll: 240, 242
Second Council of Constantinople: 124
shamans: 102, 118, 193, 232, 236, 239, 250
Shanghai: 171
Sigma: 126
Sigmund Freud: 226, 230
Sir Arthur Conon Doyle: 87
Sir Cosmo Duff Gordon: 181
Sir E A Wallis Budge: 128
Sir Roger Penrose: 136, 221
Sir William Barrett: 16, 59, 157, 184
Sir William Crookes: 20
Skinwalker Ranch: 5, 31, 45, 156
Society for Psychical Research (SPR): 14, 16, 23, 87, 167, 191, 208
spells: 117, 193
squash courts: 32, 34–38
Stargate Program: 214
Stella C: 19–21

Stephen Braude: 206
Stephen Hawking: 136
Sting: 31
Stinson Detroiter: 85
Stockwell Ghost: 15, 16
Strength of Case Scale: 134
Stuart Hameroff: 136
Sumer: 7
Sumerians: 8, 117
Sybell Corbet: 57–62

Taylor, Dr Steve: 240
telekinesis: 121, 136, 190, 193, 204, 206, 209, 213, 219, 252, 255–257
telepathy: 121, 136, 146, 159, 193, 209, 211–213, 219, 221, 223–226, 230, 242, 252, 255–257
Temple Back: 100
Terry Pratchett: 147
The Night My Number Came Up: 174
Time: 237
time slip: 7, 112–114, 116, 162
Time Window: 110
Titanic: 102, 139, 177–180, 182, 183, 188, 232, 242
traumatic death: 102, 133, 140, 145, 146, 160, 231

UFO: 117, 120, 156, 174, 203, 208, 213, 217, 223, 253, 255, 257
unconscious premonition: 185
universal consciousness: 114–116, 220, 256
universal constants: 235, 251
universe: viii, 10, 103, 120, 125, 134, 136, 146, 177, 188, 193, 202, 206, 218–221, 233–244, 247, 249–252, 256–258
Uri Geller: 204, 205
US National Research Council: 225, 226
USS Akron: 98
USS Hornet: 39
USS Natoma Bay: 138

Utts, Professor Jessica: 214
Uvani: 87–89, 94, 96

Vallée, Jacques: 116, 217
van Lommel: 155, 158, 221
veridical out of body experiences: 148
Versailles: 162, 164
Vicki Noratuk: 148
Victor Amole: 187, 192, 243
Victorians: 15, 123
Villiers: 14, 95–98
Virginia Tighe: 137
Vought Corsair: 138

waking dream: 4, 106
White Star Line: 177, 179
Wikipedia: 6, 59, 213, 222, 228, 230
Winning the Lottery: 187
witchcraft: 118, 120, 187, 209, 255–257
witches: viii, 102, 117–120, 167, 193, 232, 236, 239, 252, 256
World Trade Centre: 184

YouGov: 10

www.ingramcontent.com/pod-product-compliance
Lightning Source LLC
Chambersburg PA
CBHW070138100426
42743CB00013B/2744